BATTLE OF
THE ATLANTIC

BATTLE OF
THE ATLANTIC

by
Bernard Ireland

LEO COOPER

First published in Great Britain in 2003 by
LEO COOPER
an imprint of Pen & Sword Books
47 Church Street,
Barnsley,
South Yorkshire,
S70 2AS

ISBN 0 84415 001 1

A catalogue record for this book
is available from the British Library

Typeset in 11/13pt Sabon by
Phoenix Typesetting, Burley-in-Wharfedale, West Yorkshire

Printed in England by CPI UK

Contents

Introduction

During the First World War German submarines destroyed 11.1 million gross registered tons of Allied and neutral merchant shipping. A quarter-century later they returned to sink a further 14.7 million tons. By far the greater proportion of these totals represent British ships, most of them lost in Atlantic waters.

It has been remarked – probably far too often – that a nation heedless of its history is doomed to repeat it. Nonetheless, if proof were ever needed of the underlying truth of this assertion, the Battle of the Atlantic provides it.

Peacetime democracies, by their very nature, prefer to devote ever-scarce financial resources to the direct benefit of the public rather than to pay the stiff premium demanded by an adequate defence. Like the imprudent householder who neglects necessary insurance, however, that public is very exposed when the roof is blown off.

Governments are notoriously short-termist, rarely looking beyond the next election, but there is, or certainly was in this case, little excuse for the professional armed forces compounding failure through poor strategic planning.

The First World War had already demonstrated the benefit of air cover for convoys yet maritime cooperation, a highly special-ized aviation skill, was lumped in with all other aspects of flying as part of the remit for the new unified air force. The results, of naval laissez-faire as much as air force ambition, were inadequate numbers of the wrong aircraft, inadequately trained and deploying inadequate weapons.

When the United States entered the war in 1917, their representatives had found the British Admiralty despairing of its chances of beating the U-boat menace.

The urgent need, they discovered, was not of capital ships, but for huge numbers of flotilla vessels. Yet, came the peace, these same craft were among the first to be discarded. Big guns retained their glamour, offering the surest path to professional success. Between the wars, neither of the major fleets conducted the regular and realistic exercises that would have highlighted the continuing need for adequate numbers of ocean-going, specialist anti-submarine escorts.

In 1939, therefore, history repeated itself as the slaughter of helpless shipping began again. In 1914 there had been some excuse, for the success of the U-boat as commerce destroyer had proved as much a surprise to the Germans as it had to the British. Twenty-five years later there could be no such excuse. Ships protect, protocols do not.

Until mid-1943 the Admiralty again radiated an overwhelming sense of crisis, that again the nation might go under for loss of its merchant marine. Statistics show, however, that the Royal Navy's little ships were performing so effectively that by Admiral Dönitz' own yardstick – tonnage sunk per U-boat per day – his force's success was already in decline by the latter half of 1941, its rate of sinking inadequate to destroy British-controlled shipping within his prescribed timescale.

That this trend was brutally reversed during 1942, after the United States became a belligerent, only served to illuminate similar deficiencies on the other side of the pond.

The sense of crisis long persisted, yet building rates for replacement Allied shipping quite quickly outstripped losses, and by an ever-increasing margin. Doubtless the still-lengthening toll of merchantmen engendered a degree of genuine pessimism in Britain, but the statistics suggest that there was also a degree of politicking involved, to impress upon the United States the need to bolster the British war effort. It is hoped that this narrative gives a balanced view.

Bernard Ireland
Fareham 2002

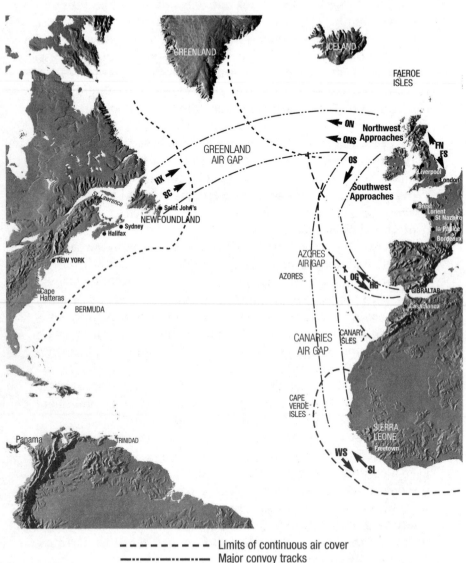

- - - - - - - - Limits of continuous air cover
- · - · · - · · - · Major convoy tracks

Chapter One

The Background

As, in the late sixteenth century, Spanish adventurers opened up Central and South America to conquest and colonization, their nation was locked in dispute with England. Religious differences were responsible for a continuous state of quasi-war, hostilities financed and sustained through the wealth that flowed back in the holds of the periodic *flota* and the individual great ships coming up from the Isthmus.

Elizabeth I of England was resourceful, but presided over an impoverished Treasury. To prey on Spanish trade offered the chance of both striking at Spain's ability to fight and the prospect of national (and personal) enrichment.

Of the fighting ships with which the Queen faced the enemy, less than twenty per cent were the property of the Crown. The remainder were owned and equipped by merchant adventurers, patriotic but with an eye to profitable return. Their inducement was the Letter of Marque, issued by the Crown to its captains to legitimize their activities. As they sailed private ships, they became known as 'privateers'.

Letters of Marque were no new device, having been issued as far back as 1243 'for the annoyance of the King's enemies'. Ships taken by privateers had, by international law, to be taken to the nearest port at which they could be condemned by a Prize Court, valued and sold off. The income would be split in agreed proportion between Crown and privateer captain, the welfare of crew and passengers of the prize having been observed.

In reality, unfortunately, it was risky and time-consuming to bring a prize to port. Far simpler for her to 'disappear' with all hands. In short, there was always incentive for privateering to degenerate into something akin to common piracy, being frequently rewarded accordingly and summarily at the end of a convenient yardarm.

Usually profitable, occasionally hugely so, privateering was exceedingly widespread. Even as Elizabeth issued her own licences, for instance, others of her honest seafarers were being persecuted in the near seas by men of like persuasion from the provinces of Holland and Zeeland, under the pretext that English merchants 'were assisting Dunkerque, Spain and Antwerp'.

As west-European maritime powers founded and extended their empires, trade increased and, with it, rivalries that led often to war. To the detriment of recruitment to the regular services – English, French or Dutch – the best and most enterprising seamen were immediately drawn by the undoubted glamour and potential of privateering.

By the eighteenth century, the Royal Navy operated scores of minor warships in an effort to counter the activities of privateers. Sloops, brigs, cutters and, later, schooners, they offered superb experience for their commanders and lieutenants-in-command. While many enjoyed individual success however, their overall activities were not well directed.

In the course of the unnecessary 'War of 1812' British trade endured some very enterprising American privateering. Over five hundred American Letters of Marque were authorized, these taking some 1,300 British merchantmen. This effort would not, of itself, have won a war against a major maritime power, but each capture aided the enemy and racked up insurance rates a further notch.

The so-called Crimean War was terminated by plenipotentiaries who, gathering in Paris in 1856, also made a declaration outlawing the practice of privateering. Powers including Great Britain, France, Russia, Austria and Prussia, later joined by others, agreed the following fundamental points:

1. That privateering was abolished.

2. That a neutral flag protects an enemy's goods, excepting contraband.

3. That an enemy flag protects a neutral's goods, again excepting contraband.

4. That blockades, to be legal, must be effective.

Probably the last gasp of privateering on any scale was from the United States where, during the Civil War, some eighty licenced Confederates took a similar number of Union vessels. Following the 1856 agreement, however, most neutral ports were now closed to prizes and, with the near-disappearance of the profit element, private operators turned to blockade running. From now on, war against trade would be conducted by regular navies, either with warships or auxiliary cruisers, operating under naval control and ensign.

The nineteenth century had been a period of great upheaval for the major fleets, not least the Royal Navy. Technological advance had seen lines of battle, little-changed in centuries, displaced by steam power, metal hulls and the leap-frogging competition between ever larger guns, their explosive projectiles and the protection with which to withstand them. Varying opinion on how best to combine these elements had resulted in an eclectic force of warships, many with considerable 'presence' but few with appreciable fighting power.

Despite its shortcomings, the Victorian navy was still the standard against which others were measured. With the passing of the Naval Defence Act of 1889 and the adoption of the Two Power Standard the Royal Navy began to receive coherent classes of modern warship in something like predictable numbers.

The rising costs of Britain's armed forces depended for funding much upon popular support, but the government's more radical wing was already challenging expenditure through the un-doubted need to invest in improved social programmes. Britain's naval rivals were experiencing much the same problem, that of providing a credible response to overwhelming strength with only a limited budget.

Predictably, it was the French who arrived at what appeared to be the answer, in the philosophy of the Navy Minister, Admiral Théophile Aube.

Whitehead's self-propelled torpedo had been used successfully during 1878–80 by both the Russians and the Peruvians. Known, from the youth of its followers, as the *Jeune École*, Aube's beliefs included using large numbers of inexpensive 'torpedo boats' to render armoured 'battleships' (as they were becoming known) impotent. While an enemy's fleet was thus contained, cruisers – large, fast and unarmoured – would prey on his commerce. Aube saw that the key to success was ruthlessness, writing 'War is the negation of law . . . the recourse to force . . . Everything is therefore not only permissible but legitimate against the enemy.'

British response to Aube was predictable, maintaining numerical superiority in capital ships and cruisers while outbuilding the French in torpedo boats. Countermeasures, such as rapid-firing medium-calibre guns, electric searchlights and torpedo nets, disproved the supposition that the day of the battleship was over. Torpedo gunboats admittedly had proved too slow for their intended role but, by 1893, the first torpedo boat destroyer had appeared.

Although large, coal-hungry 'commerce destroyers' continued to be built by major navies, Aube's theories were looking discredited. In 1885, however, the Swedish innovator Nordenfelt had successfully married the Whitehead torpedo with a practical submersible. This combination was promptly adopted by the French as a substitute for the obsolescent torpedo boat concept. By the turn of the century, they were the acknowledged leaders in this new technology and, at a time when battleships practiced gunnery at 4,000 yards, the torpedo could already reach 3,000 and was being rapidly improved.

As with all new developments, the Royal Navy's attitude to submarines was to keep an unobtrusive watch while taking no action that would unnecessarily make any part of its own armoury obsolete. This policy had been expressed nicely by the First Lord, St Vincent when, long before, the Prime Minister, Pitt, had shown interest in Fulton's experiments: 'Pitt was the greatest fool that ever existed, to encourage a mode of war which they who commanded the seas did not want and which, if successful, would deprive them of it.'

Only when the Admiralty learned that the French had approved funds sufficient to build 150 torpedo boats and submarines did it start its own programme. In 1901 Vickers began building to the American Holland's design.

The French vote had been part of the Fleet Law of 1900, a plan for general naval expansion which began to produce results just as the nation finally reached rapprochement with Great Britain. With the Entente of 1904 the two states agreed to solve conclusively all the petty differences that had, so often in the past, led to hostilities. Both now needed to recognize the fact that Germany posed the greatest common threat.

Following unification, Germany maintained a small fleet headed, significantly, by the army. It was viewed as a force to be used to safeguard the military's seaward flank or as a means to project military power onto a foreign shore. Coastal defence was a major role and Aube's theories accorded well with general plans.

In 1888, however, the young Wilhelm II acceded as emperor. Ambitious, he was steeped in the ideas, not of Aube, but of Mahan. He wanted a battle fleet the equivalent of the Prussian army. With it, he would gain for Germany some of the world stature enjoyed by his grandmother, Queen Victoria.

It was, nonetheless, 1897 before Wilhelm appointed Rear Admiral Alfred Tirpitz to head the Navy Office. Although a torpedo specialist, Tirpitz was another Mahanian disciple. Entrusted by his patron with the creation of a battle fleet, he proved to be both single-minded and a consummate politician, persuading a reluctant Reichstag that Germany's future 'place in the sun' depended upon credible maritime strength. The result was the successful passage of the 1898 Navy Bill.

Tirpitz did not stop here. Exploiting a wave of popular anti-British sentiment over the Boer War, he returned to parliament and had it pass a second bill, that of 1900. This effectively doubled the capital ship element to thirty-four hulls, with an agreed automatic replacement following twenty-five years of service.

Nothing deflected Tirpitz' plans, and those espousing Aube's ideas on cruiser or submarine/torpedo boat warfare received short shrift. His strategy was based on so-called 'risk theory', the battle fleet not being numerically superior to that of the 'greatest sea power' but, being concentrated in the North Sea, would be too powerful to be brought to decisive action except at the price of unacceptable loss. Wilhelm's fleet would be both threat and deterrent.

Only in April 1904 was Tirpitz finally moved to order a first U-boat. In light of later events, his tardiness was much criticized but he defended himself as '[refusing] to throw away money on submarines so long as they could only cruise in home waters . . . as soon as sea-going boats were built, however . . . I went as far as the limits of our technical production would permit'.

Six months after Tirpitz placed the fateful order that launched the German submarine service, Admiral Sir John ('Jacky') Fisher was appointed First Sea Lord, a post that he was to hold for sixty-three months. A small, volatile man of prodigious energies, Fisher was a dedicated reformer. To him, war with Germany was inevitable and his response was decisive and controversial. He formed and chaired an expert committee that would inaugurate the 'Dreadnought revolution'. He reorganized the dockyards and scrapped 154 obsolete warships. Alliances formed with France and Japan allowed considerable naval strength to be withdrawn from the Mediterranean and the Far East. By also revising or closing distant foreign stations, Fisher moved even more ships into home waters, going far to offset Tirpitz' ambitions.

Importantly, Fisher appreciated the potential of the submarine. During his tenure as C.-in-C. Portsmouth, his responsibilities included the Navy's submarine base and he could learn at first hand. At a time when service opinion was still sharply divided, Fisher was enthused, believing that submarines and aircraft would eventually revolutionize war at sea.

The Navy's major tasks were to prevent invasion and to protect trade. For deep sea operations, Fisher envisaged a battle fleet headed by fast, heavily-armed but lightly armoured battle cruisers. Against invasion, the narrow seas would be made untenable for big ships by swarms of submarines and torpedo boats, organized in every port in what was termed 'flotilla defence'.

While Tirpitz saw the submarine's future in the defence of the German coast, Fisher looked further at its potential in commerce warfare. Conferences in the Hague (1907) and London (1909) considered the tightening of international maritime law, including that governing *guerre de course*. Depressingly for the British, who saw in it a return to privateering, all other delegates were in favour of the legalization of arming merchantmen to act as naval auxiliaries. Submarines were, apparently, still too primitive to be considered in this role.

In 1912, however, Fisher (by then officially retired, but still a member of the Committee for Imperial Defence) presented to the Cabinet a prescient memorandum on the use of the submarine against commerce. Repeating the warning in 1914, he pointed out that a submarine could not capture a merchant ship, and had no spare hands to sail her as a prize to a neutral port. She had no space to take survivors aboard and her invisibility was her major asset. In short, 'there is nothing a submarine can do except sink her capture'. This would be even more likely should the merchantman be defensively armed.

Fisher went on to ask the unthinkable: 'What if the Germans were to use submarines against commerce without restriction?' Churchill, First Lord and political head of the Navy, considered it inconceivable that 'this would ever be done by a civilised power'. Senior opinion in the Service held it to be 'impossible and unthinkable'.

A paper, read in 1914, pointed out optimistically that, during the Russo-Japanese war of 1904–5, only about 5.5 per cent of torpedoes actually hit their targets. The author neglected to mention that, in the intervening decade, extreme ranges had doubled to 11,000 yards, speed at effective range increased to 45 knots and size increased from fourteen to twenty-one inches diameter.

Once the diesel engine had been developed sufficiently to displace petrol and paraffin units, submarine design on both sides advanced rapidly. By 1914, 'state-of-the-art' classes had leading particulars as shown in the table on page 8.

At the outbreak of war, Germany still had only twenty-nine commissioned boats to Britain's seventy-seven, although many of the latter were early craft with little fighting value.

Submarines of both sides had demonstrated pre-war an ability to operate off the other's coasts but it came as an unpleasant surprise to discover just how easily major warships, not yet

Great Britain: Later 'E' Class

Displacement:	surfaced 667 tons
	submerged 807 tons
Length overall	181.0 ft (55.14 m)
Breadth	22.7 ft (6.91 m)
Designed speed:	surfaced 15.25 knots
	submerged 10.25 knots
Endurance:	surfaced 2000 miles at 15 knots
	submerged 65 miles at 5 knots
Torpedo tubes	2 forward, 2 amidships, 1 aft
Torpedoes	10 of 18-inch diameter
Crew	3 Officers 27 men

Germany: U.23–26

Displacement:	surfaced 669 tons
	submerged 864 tons
Length overall	212.4 ft (64.7 m)
Breadth	20.7 ft (6.3 m)
Designed speed:	surfaced 16.7 knots
	submerged 10.3 knots
Endurance:	surfaced 7620 miles at 8 knots
	submerged 85 miles at 5 knots
Torpedo tubes	2 forward, none amidships, 2 aft
Torpedoes	6 of 19.7-inch (50 cm) diameter
Crew	4 Officers 31 men

'submarine-wise' could be sunk. Within the first ten weeks, five British cruisers were lost, three with great loss of life.

Senior officers of both navies voiced disappointment at the lack of all-out attacking policies. Claims by Germany that an alternative submarine war against commerce was never planned seemed confirmed by the few available U-boats and their small torpedo capacities.

The German cruiser war against commerce was proving to be unprofitable, however, and a different offensive strategy was required. It was claimed that British minelaying and the institution of blockade were illegal, the latter because tightened definitions of what constituted 'contraband' affected both military and civil population indiscriminately.

British ships were already being sunk, mostly in accordance with the prize rules, but there was now an irresistible clamour for a retaliatory submarine blockade. With the Kaiser's assent, the waters around the British Isles were, on 4 February 1915, declared a war zone. All shipping encountered within was liable to destruction. U-boat skippers were given the safety of their own boats and crews as paramount, and they would not surface to attack. Neutral ships were thus liable not to be identified, while the safety of their crews and passengers could not be guaranteed. Thus, after just six months of war, the 'unthinkable' was a reality.

Germany had a first whiff of trouble ahead when a concerned American government stated that it would hold the Germans 'strictly accountable' in the event of American lives or ships being lost. Nonetheless, while U-boat skippers were counselled to caution, the campaign went ahead.

It was fortunate for the British that there were not only so few operational U-boats but also that rapid expansion of their numbers under wartime conditions was proving difficult. To their deep-sea boats the Germans added small coastal (UB) and minelaying (UC) types, some working from Bruges in Belgium.

Following a slow start, the enemy in 1915 commissioned more than one new boat per week and an average of about 139,000 gross registered tonnage of British and neutral shipping was being destroyed monthly.

British countermeasures were ineffective. An 'offensive' strategy involving destroyers and auxiliary craft patrolling sea lanes and hotspots, and responding to calls for assistance, just did not find submarines. Towed explosive sweeps, lance bombs, ramming and gunfire produced less results than passive measures such as mining.

Since the introduction of the submarine to the Royal Navy, the service had been looking at the question of underwater communication. This work had produced, by 1914, a practical hydrophone. Still crude and unreliable, lacking directional discrimination, its possibilities in submarine detection were now being examined by service and civilian scientific staff.

Detection by hydrophone was allied to attack by depth charge, the first of which had been trialled as early as 1911. That it was effective as a weapon was proved through its accounting for two U-boats by 1915. Its utility was, however, dependent upon a reliable means of detecting the enemy.

The few torpedoes carried by U-boats meant that, to conduct a patrol of worthwhile duration, many sinkings would need to be made by deck gun. Some warning could thus be claimed to have been given, but the British policy of arming merchantmen, and encouraging masters to attempt to ram a surfaced boat, gave U-boat skippers little scope for niceties.

Large targets required torpedoes, leading to problems of mis-identification, particularly with neutrals. An over-hasty sinking of the British liner *Falaba* in March 1915 led to the deaths of 104 passengers. It preceded the *Lusitania* tragedy, which was hugely damaging to the German cause, the 1,200 dead including over 100 American citizens. A terse threat to sever diplomatic relations resulted in a re-imposition of restrictions on U-boat activities.

More submarines were, however, now in service and their loss rate was low. Sinkings remained high although much tonnage was being replaced by new construction. High freight rates ensured the continuing assistance of neutrals.

With the brakes re-applied to what was seen as a successful campaign, furious argument developed between German naval and diplomatic circles. In September 1915 Tirpitz resigned his post at the Navy Office, although much for his own reasons.

U-boat strength grew only slowly, passing the fifty total only in the spring of 1916. Conversely, the net total of tonnage available to the British was being decreased at a rate too low to be decisive.

Aware of the campaign faltering, Holtzendorff, Chief of Naval Staff, accepted the arguments that armed merchantmen (now the majority) must, by definition, be auxiliary ships of war. He ordered that operations were to be 'sharpened' but that 'mistakes' were to be avoided. During March and April 1916 nearly 360,000 GRT was destroyed, much of it in the Mediterranean where incidents involving American nationals would be less likely. The latter's continued exasperation resulted in a particularly stiff note, delivered in April 1916 after Americans had been lost in the torpedoing of the cross-channel packet *Sussex*.

Ordered to re-apply full prize rules, Vice Admiral Reinhard Scheer, recently-appointed C.-in-C. of High Seas Fleet, called his boats off altogether in protest. Scheer had brought a newly aggressive policy to his command, seeking a confrontation, but on favourable terms. Following several minor clashes, the battle fleets finally collided at Jutland in May 1916. Failing to secure a Trafalgar-style annihilation of the enemy, the British were despondent. German joy at a clear matériel victory was, however, tempered by the realization in high circles that the British Grand Fleet could not be defeated in straight battle. Recognizing the need of a different strategy, Scheer pressed for an all-out U-boat war.

Holtzendorff had been influenced by shipping experts who had calculated that, with the existing submarine force, 630,000 GRT could be destroyed monthly if restrictions were to be lifted. So heavy were Britain's shipping committments that just six months at this level of loss would oblige her to seek a negotiated peace. True, the Americans would probably declare war but, as it would take them more than six months to make a decisive intervention, the objective would have been achieved.

Further 'sharpened', yet still with restrictions, the campaign accounted for about 1.4 million GRT between October 1916 and January 1917, horrifying enough but still only half the required figure. A poor harvest in 1916 made Britain even more dependent upon imports, while war-weariness began to be evident in Germany. A quick decision was vital. With over 100 boats available, backed by an ambitious construction programme, the unrestricted campaign was re-launched, although not without reservations, on 1 February 1917.

As predicted, the United States quickly severed diplomatic relations, and incidents involving their nationals soon followed. Worse, interception of the notorious 'Zimmermann telegram' betrayed Germany's intention of involving Mexico and Japan should President Wilson declare war. This he did in April 1917.

Sinkings, averaging 160,000 GRT monthly, rose in March 1917 to over 350,000 GRT and, in May, to 550,000. Many ships, seriously damaged by torpedo, were recovered but, requiring major repair, clogged facilities better employed on new construction. Fortunately the Germans, short of materials and skilled manpower, were able to commission only seven or eight new U-boats monthly, a figure which scarcely offset their losses of about five per month.

The Admiralty was deeply concerned that its countermeasures remained largely ineffective, the enemy now rarely showing himself. Neutrals, alarmed at losses, remained supportive largely through British coercive measures. Newly-arrived American liaison officers were dismayed to discover the air of resigned despondency. The smell of defeat was definitely abroad.

In planning the defence of trade pre-war, the Admiralty had barely considered the submarine. The enemy would deploy cruisers, regular and auxiliary, which would be a nuisance but, cut off from supplies and dockyard support, would be quickly hunted down. In this, their assessment was sound.

During the sailing era, merchantmen were protected from enemy cruising squadrons by sailing them in convoy, powerfully escorted by the Navy. In the context of 1914, however, such measures were deemed counter-productive. Any advantage, it was reasoned, would be offset by delays to shipping waiting for convoys to be formed and by following fixed routes. Periodic arrivals of convoys would congest ports, causing further delay. Faster ships would be wasted in having to steam at the speed of the slowest. Collisions would occur as masters, unused to manoeuvring in company, failed to cope with low visibility. Modern communications would make it impossible to keep secret the assembly of a convoy while, at sea, its towering smoke cloud would make it unmissable for any enemy cruisers. The arguments against the use of convoy were so extensive, so often repeated, that when the U-boat, rather than the cruiser, emerged as the major threat, the arguments in favour were not reassessed.

It is a deeply-ingrained naval instinct to operate aggressively and, in the absence of surface raiders, it appeared to be good 'offensive' policy to dispatch hunting groups after the U-boats. The results, for a great amount of effort, were woefully inadequate. For far too long, and in vain, they who supported convoys pointed out that submarines wanted to sink merchantmen and, if these were sailed in convoy, then the submarine would have to approach that convoy, and the anti-submarine (AS) escort would have solved its major problem, that of knowing where the submarines were.

Because of the route's proximity to enemy bases, a twice-weekly convoy had, since July 1916, been successfully operated by the Harwich Force between England and the Netherlands.

With much of its coal reserve now in occupied territory, French industry was greatly dependent upon British shipments. The many colliers involved had suffered badly at the hands of the enemy's coastal submarines and, with trade disrupted, the French persuaded the local British authorities to organize a convoy system. Starting in February 1917, this was a major success, which was paralleled on the Shetlands–Norway route.

Renewed calls to extend the principle deep-sea were met by resistance at the very top, both the First Sea Lord and Chief of the War Staff arguing that experienced gained on small-scale, near-sea operations could not be extrapolated to the scale required. They argued, for no sound reason, that escorts would be required at a rate of one, even two, per convoyed ship. They then used the official weekly list of arrivals and departures at British ports to 'prove' the number of escorts inadequate. It was analysis by the Anti-Submarine Division at the Admiralty itself that debunked this, showing that by far the greater proportion of these movements were by passenger ferries and coasters. Those by large and valuable deep-sea cargo vessels were few enough to be covered without undue difficulty.

In April 1917 a horrifying 880,000 GRT was destroyed. The Admiralty's hand was forced, not least by powerful political pressure and, on 10 May 1917, the first experimental deep-sea convoy left Gibraltar for Britain.

AS 'escort' at this time was effectively synonymous with 'destroyer', and as the Grand Fleet alone required over 100, the Royal Navy was stretched and appeals were made to the US Navy to send over as many as possible.

The beginning of the European war in 1914 had heightened the United States' awareness of their own military unpreparedness, enabling the naval hawks to successfully pressure the president for parity with the Royal Navy.

Calls for a fleet 'second-to-none' resulted in the 1916 programme which promised that, by 1921, the US Navy would have twenty-seven battleships, six battle cruisers and 350 lesser vessels. It now, however, found itself in a war where further capital ships were neither required nor capable of being built in time to be of use. What was needed was a maximum number of flotilla craft, for the want of which the war might well be lost.

Following a wasted four months of agonizing, the Americans slowed their capital ship programme to release resources. By August 1917, 266 destroyers were on order, but even these could never have been completed in time. To British relief, the convoy principle in itself proved to be their salvation.

In practice, U-boats had a limited performance and horizon. Convoys might appear enormous but, in the immensity of the ocean, they were insignificant. Routed clear of obvious choke points, they were difficult to find. Even if a boat were fortunate enough to find itself ahead and in a firing position, it would be kept at a distance by the threat of the escort and had just one chance of loosing a salvo before the convoy swept on, un-catchable.

Sinkings dropped reassuringly. The 512,000 GRT of August became 289,000 in November. This remained about average, serious enough but manageable.

During 1914, British yards had launched over 1.5 million GRT. Shortages of materials and manpower had reduced this to 660,000 GRT in 1915 and less in the following year. An important remedial measure was to limit choice to a dozen, no-frills standard designs to derive the benefits of series production. Launchings increased to 1.23 million GRT in 1917 and 1.58 million in 1918. At the armistice, 148 'standards' had been completed, and 289 were under construction to replenish the ranks of war-wasted fleets and to replace requisitioned neutral tonnage.

The contribution of the United States was immense. In 1913 their total output was barely one-eighth that of the British. Approached for new construction, the Americans established in 1916 a Shipping Board, which spawned an Emergency Fleet Corporation to deal with the dynamics of the actual construction programme. In 1918, American yards completed about 3 million GRT, in 1919 4 million.

Their success lay in taking standardization a stage further, introducing the concept of pre-fabrication. Ship sections were built at widely-separated sites, being brought to a launching facility only for assembly. It was industrial experience that would prove even more valuable at a later date.

Formed from the Naval Wing of the Royal Flying Corps (RFC) shortly before hostilities, the Royal Naval Air Service (RNAS) operated a string of air stations down the east coast and along the English Channel. The enemy had successfully developed large rigid airships, known collectively to the British as 'Zeppelins'. The British themselves had shown no great expertise in this field, preferring larger numbers of smaller non-rigids, or 'Blimps'. Loaded with fuel rather than bombs, the Zeppelins could remain aloft for extended periods, being very useful in long-range reconnaissance. The shorter-legged Blimps' greatest service was in the escort of coastwise convoys and valuable individual ships. Marauding U-boats could be spotted more easily from the air and, while none was actually sunk by an airship, they could be marked for a destroyer's attention. It was soon apparent that U-boats rarely attacked in the presence of an airship.

The RNAS was notable in the development of the flying boat, with the Anglo-American combination of Porte and Curtiss producing the Felixstowes and the Large and Small Americas. These tough aircraft had endurances of up to six hours and flew constant, interlocking patrols over the southern North Sea. Their major quarry was the UBs of the German Flanders Flotilla, a great nuisance in coastal waters, but they also had regular scraps with enemy aircraft.

As the Germans had calculated, it took time for the American contribution to be decisive. By the time of the armistice, over a dozen air stations had been established by them in Europe, but full operations had begun only in July 1918.

On 1 April 1918 the RNAS and RFC were amalgamated as a unified Royal Air Force (RAF). Naval cooperation became the responsibility of the RAF's Coastal Area, part of which would become the Fleet Air Arm in 1924.

It was unfortunate that, in an atmosphere of post-war stringencies, and with the new service pursuing its own major strategies, the needs of maritime air operations became neglected, a situation not helped by a dearth of strong voices at the Admiralty. From very promising beginnings, the story for much of the interwar period was to be one of too few and obsolescent aircraft, armed with inadequate weapons.

From May 1918, long-range 'U-cruisers' operated off the American eastern seaboard. Their objective was the large liners being used to transport hundreds of thousands of troops to Europe. In this they failed but, by the end in November, they had sunk thirty-three steamships and a few score small craft. Although this short campaign was a failure, in terms of results for effort expended, destruction so close to home badly upset sections of the American public, while AS counter-measures here had proved no more effective than in European waters.

To summarize, the First World War resulted in the loss of about 12.85 million GRT of Allied and neutral merchant shipping, 7.76 million GRT being British. Of the 419 U-boats that the enemy commissioned, 186 were lost to hostile action.

The belated success of the convoy system may be gauged from the fact that, in the 1,134 ocean convoys that were run, 16,539 ships were escorted. Of these, only 102 were torpedoed and sunk while in convoy, a numerical loss rate of only 0.6 per cent.

For Germany, the terms of the Versailles peace treaty were harsh. Among much else, the size of the surface fleet was greatly limited and submarines banned. Indeed, the British delegation pressed for the submarine's universal abolition, but the Americans were divided on the proposal and the French totally against.

Britain returned to the theme at the landmark Washington Conference on the limitation of naval armaments, held in 1921–22. Again, the French led the outright opposition and no restriction was agreed on submarine construction. Unrestricted submarine warfare was, however, once again condemned.

Germany duly disposed of her U-boats but carefully preserved her design expertise. Foreign enquiries for consultative assistance led to a design bureau being unobtrusively established in the Netherlands. It answered to the German Admiralty via a 'front' company in Berlin.

The purpose of the bureau was to use genuine work for foreign governments as a means of developing standard designs of eventual use to the Germans themselves. Contracts for Spain and Finland thus provided the basis for the 750- and 250-ton designs. Against the day of the rebirth of the submarine arm components, supposedly destroyed by treaty requirement had, in fact, been carefully stored by another front company in Denmark.

Planning to rebuild the German navy began in secret in 1927, and was endorsed by the Chancellor in 1932, before the march of National Socialism. Included was a sixteen-strong submarine force.

By 1935 the nation had rediscovered pride and assertion, contrasting with a war-weakened Britain whose leaders craved peace and pursued economies. Having repudiated the Versailles Treaty, Germany was openly rearming. Faced with inevitability, Britain sought to set some limit on this through negotiation. The much-criticized Anglo-German Naval Agreement was the result. By its terms, Germany would build to no more than 35 per cent of British tonnage in all major classes except, inexplicably, submarines. In these, 45 per cent was agreed, with building to parity 'should Germany deem it necessary'.

It was an open secret that U-boats were already under construction and, just two months later, in September 1935, a first group of nine 250-tonners commissioned as a training flotilla. They were the responsibility of the newly-approved head of the submarine arm, Captain Karl Dönitz.

In November 1936 the treaty nations and Germany signed the London Submarine Agreement, a protocol which yet again made illegal the destruction of commercial shipping except under prize rules.

Learning little from the recent near-catastrophe to commerce and nation, the British government adopted the notorious Ten Year Rule, a rolling assumption that it would be involved in no major war in the ensuing decade. The still-embryonic naval scientific service was cut almost to extinction, while the

17

Anti-Submarine and Trade Divisions of the Admiralty were eliminated on grounds of economy.

Despite this, work continued, much of it in commercial laboratories, to develop a means of locating submerged submarines. These efforts were paralleled in the United States, France and Germany. Improved hydrophones, matched and grouped, could indicate the bearing of a sound source, but not its range. Suitably energized piezoelectric quartz transducers were therefore used to emit pulses of sound energy. Having contacted some solid object, such as a submarine hull, some small fraction of this energy would be reflected. This could be detected by a hydrophone located adjacent to the transmitter.

Such was the basis of what the British called 'Asdic'. Although many in the service assumed this to be the definitive answer to the submarine, the practical difficulties were (and remain) considerable. Signals are very small, and difficult to extract from background noise resulting from water flow, ship motion, nearby machinery and other ships. As, however, the principle also had considerable commercial application in automatic depth sounding, work continued to the point where, by the early thirties, all British destroyers were fitted with Asdic.

Between the wars the Royal Navy made little effort to exercise the protection of slow mercantile convoys. Exercises were directed primarily at fleet operations to pass a convoy in the face of mainly surface opposition. During the Second World War this would be relevant to Malta and, to an extent, Arctic convoys, but not Atlantic.

Stringent cuts to naval budgets meant that development of less-glamorous ships such as AS escorts enjoyed low priority. Despite all First World War experience indicating a likely shortage of destroyers, combined with the type's general lack of suitability for the task, it was generally assumed that destroyers would still be used as convoy escorts. Until 1936, and the growing threat of a new war, the Admiralty's interest in AS craft had been confined to identifying a suitable trawler design and designing a small corvette. Even these had their performance degraded by the need to be 'multi-purpose' and, therefore, cluttered with minesweeping gear.

By 1935, the experience of 1917 had receded to the extent that the Permanent Secretary to the Admiralty was able to announce to the House that the convoy system would not be introduced 'at once' on the outbreak of war. As justification, he then repeated all the standard arguments that experience had already proved spurious.

Admiral Erich Raeder had been appointed Supreme Commander of the German Navy in October 1928. The elderly rump of the Imperial Fleet that he had inherited was already, under Versailles rules, mostly due for replacement. New 'armoured ships' were now limited to 10,000 tons apiece. There was no limitation on gun calibre but maximizing this could only be at the cost of speed or protection.

The accepted combination was of six 28cm (11-inch) and eight 15cm (5.9-inch) guns, armour up to 100mm in thickness and a twenty-six knot speed. The Reichstag approved construction of the first early in 1929.

Dubbed a 'pocket battleship' by the popular press, the ship would have the firepower and protection to deal with any of the 10,000-ton 'treaty' cruisers. Her speed would enable her to decline combat with any heavier capital ship except a battle cruiser. Adoption of diesel machinery gave an unprecedented radius of action. Three were eventually built, their obvious potential in commerce raiding causing considerable disquiet abroad.

Raeder was convinced that old-style battle fleets were outmoded and that maritime war would be conducted by small squadrons of mutually-supportive ships, in short the task group concept. Naval aviation was forbidden but the ban was circumvented by the formation of the *Luftdienst*, a private company that provided aircraft for exercises with the fleet.

On becoming the Reich's Chancellor early in 1933, Adolf Hitler expressed his belief that Germany's defeat in 1918 had stemmed from the influence of joint British and American seapower. To avoid a repetition he would, therefore, be pursuing a 'continental' policy. It was he who instigated discussion that had led to the already-mentioned Anglo-German Naval Agreement of 1935. By this time, Hitler was also President and head of the armed forces, and just three weeks after the signing a construction programme was announced.

Quite legally, this included the two capital ships that would become the Scharnhorsts and twenty-eight submarines (twenty of

250 tons, six of 500 and two of 750). Plans would be progressed for further battleships and an aircraft carrier.

Given no specific naval policy, Raeder's aim was to create a balanced fleet. Hitler's unacceptable activities in continental Europe were, however, bringing about a hardening of British public opinion and, in May 1938, Raeder was warned by his leader of the possibility of war. He was to accelerate completion of the two battleships (the Bismarcks) then under construction and to invoke the parity clause in submarine construction.

Raeder proposed two options. The faster and cheaper was to concentrate on building submarines and pocket battleships for an all-out assault on British trade. Alternatively, the 'balanced fleet' concept could be continued. With the first, the Royal Navy could not be challenged for naval superiority, but achieving the second would take time, during which period war with Britain could not be risked. The fleet option would enable convoys to be attacked by surface groups, including capital ships and a carrier, which would overwhelm the escort before destroying the convoy.

Surprisingly, Hitler opted to continue on the latter path and Raeder went on to produce the so-called 'Z-plan', the grandiose scale of which would occupy Germany's full warship-building capacity for ten years. As a precaution, however, construction of the 'smaller' battleships and submarines should receive priority, for completion by 1943.

The submarine programme comprised about 250 boats of the three main sizes, numbers which would allow Dönitz to put into practice the group attack theories that he had been long proposing. It was something of a blessing to Britain, therefore, that Hitler's 'foreign policy' became so reckless that war was precipitated in 1939, at which point just thirteen submarines were under construction.

In the battle to come, German aircraft would play an important part, diminished more than somewhat by *Reichsmarschall* Göring's insistence on total control, based on his deep suspicion that the navy might be trying to create a private air force. Since 1935 there had been plans to expand maritime cooperation aircraft numbers to about 700, organized in sixty-two squadrons. By 1939 this had been cut back to a target of forty-one squadrons, of which only fifteen were ready for operations.

The planned breakdown had been:

1. Reconnaissance, AS operations, etc., – eighteen squadrons

2. Long–range reconnaissance – nine squadrons

3. Carrier-borne – twelve squadrons

4. Ship-borne catapult aircraft – two squadrons.

For (1) and (2) together, fourteen squadrons were operational. To this could be added one squadron of category (4). Progress on the sole aircraft carrier was intermittent, and construction was eventually discontinued. With her disappeared all category (3) squadrons. This meant that when, in 1942, there was an urgent requirement for auxiliary carrier conversions, no air groups existed for them.

Royal Navy fortunes meanwhile, revived somewhat in July 1937, when the Service regained full control of its Fleet Air Arm. Too late in the day, this terminated an era of friction between the two services over divided areas of responsibility.

In 1936 the RAF's Coastal Area had expanded to the point where it had become a full command. In 1937, the Air Ministry defined its priorities as trade protection, reconnaissance and naval cooperation. From 1941 the Admiralty would assume operational control of the Command's aircraft, although they remained an integral part of the RAF.

At the outset, with no knowledge of the exact form of the coming struggle, the Admiralty could define the Command's priorities only tentatively. Firstly, the North Sea's northern exits were to be patrolled to detect any enemy raider breaking out. Enemy submarines, restricted by protocol to observation of the prize rules, and now detectable by Asdic, were considered a lesser threat. AS operations were thus rated a second priority. Last came cooperation with a new Northern Patrol. To discharge these responsibilities the Command was calculated to require a total of 339 aircraft.

In September 1939 the establishment was a reasonably-near 296 aircraft, but there were trained crews for only half of them. There were eleven general reconnaissance squadrons, five of flying boats and two of torpedo bombers. With no aircraft or crews specialising in AS warfare, the task was subordinated to reconnaissance.

The aircraft themselves left much to be desired. Only one reconnaissance squadron had, so far, re-equipped with the 1,000-mile, American-built Hudson in place of the 500-mile Anson. Flying boat squadrons were due to re-equip with the excellent new Sunderland but, to date, only two had. The sole active torpedo/strike squadron relied on aircraft of such antiquity that it was decided to delegate the tasks to Bomber Command.

Belatedly, it was realized that the huge volume of east coast shipping traffic would require cover. This fell between the responsibilities of Fighter and Coastal Commands, so it was decided to create four Trade Protection squadrons. Equipped with Blenheim fighters, these would be part of Fighter Command. None yet existed, however, as hostilities began.

Should minds in the United Kingdom still have needed concentrating, the Directive No.1 of the German Supreme Command (OKW), and dated 31 August 1939, would have provided the necessary impetus. This stated, unequivocally, that 'the Navy will concentrate on commerce destruction, directed especially against England'.

Chapter Two

The Line-up

Although by 1921 British shipping again totalled 19.3 million GRT, the same as in 1914, it now represented just 32.8 per cent of the world total, rather than the 39.3 per cent of seven years earlier. The long decline had already begun and, by 1939, the figures were 17.9 million GRT or 26.1 per cent.

Much of the problem had begun during the First World War. About one-seventh of Britain's business lay in the entrepôt trade, most of which was lost to Japan and the United States. Traditionally strong in the cross-trades, British companies lost the business to eager neutrals as their ships were withdrawn under central direction. Desperate for tonnage, the British government was pleased to pay Scandinavian neutrals and the Dutch generous charter rates, while employing domestic shipping at compulsory barebone 'Blue Book' rates. With peace, therefore, the foreign flag operators were far better placed to replace and expand. Figures speak for themselves. Between 1921 and 1939, when British tonnage shrank by 7.3 per cent, the Netherlands, Japan and Norway increased theirs by 36.4, 64.7 and 100 per cent respectively.

Non-traditional shipping powers began to operate own-flag tonnage as a matter of national pride, while gathering recession encouraged some governments to indulge in restrictive practices and hidden subsidies, collectively termed 'protection'.

Many British tramp companies who owned just one or two ships, quickly succumbed to plunging freight rates. Smaller multi-ship concerns were bought in considerable numbers by larger groups, retaining their livery and business but losing their independence. British shipping became dominated by perhaps half-a-dozen conglomerates, whose vigour declined as their acquisitions grew.

Access to plentiful and cheap British coal prolonged the popularity of the steam reciprocating engine as competing foreign owners were turning wholesale to motor ships. Diesel engines consumed little over one quarter (by weight) the fuel of a coal burner and, even with the greater cost of diesel oil, worked out some 33 per cent cheaper once higher capital costs had been defrayed.

Engine room staff in motor ships worked in clean, if noisy, conditions but were only 40 per cent the number required in a coal burner, which needed stokers and trimmers. Prime space in a steamer was devoted to gravity-fed bunkers and boiler spaces. Requiring neither, a motor ship gained a space and weight margin, improving her cargo capacity.

Conservatism thus contributed to the decline and many smaller owners, competing with foreign-flagged ships of higher efficiency, cut corners on crew welfare, causing many seafarers to live in truly appalling conditions.

By the 1930s British imports averaged some 56 million tons annually of which 44 per cent arrived in foreign bottoms. Just a few industries accounted for the bulk of the trade: 9.2 million tons of grain, 2.0 million tons of sugar, 3.1 million tons of meat, 1.7 million tons of fruit, 8.7 million tons of steel products and iron ore, 8.0 million tons of oil products, 2.7 million tons of paper and 1.6 million tons of textiles in a typical year. Through food rationing and cutting back to essentials, the British government calculated that the nation could function on an absolute minimum of 26–27 million imported tons. This figure allowed 3 million deadweight tons (dwt) of shipping to be dedicated to service use and a further 3.9 million to be employed primarily in the carriage of military supplies.

British and Dominion shipping comprised some 2,520 dry cargo units and 445 tankers, to count only those exceeding 1,600 GRT. These aggregated some 17.5 million GRT or 23.4 million dwt. On faulty assumptions, the government calculated that there would be a comfortable surplus over requirement.

On 26 August 1939 all British merchant shipping came under

Admiralty control. The Admiralty Trade Division organized the formation, routing and conduct of convoys, establishing Naval Control Staffs in all major ports.

Provision and procurement of shipping, and its manning, was the responsibility of the Ministry of Shipping which, in May 1941, was amalgamated with the Ministry of Transport to form the Ministry of War Transport. Shipping was then operated through that ministry's Sea Transport Department.

First World War experience had shown defensively-armed merchant ships to suffer far fewer casualties from surfaced submarines. Plans had, therefore, already been made for the provision again of the necessary weapons and personnel. Small- and medium-calibre guns had been preserved as warships were scrapped, although they included very few of the modern anti-aircraft weapons that were to be most needed.

To be considered truly 'defensive', a merchant ship's armament was sited to fire only 'abaft the beam'. As the Germans had already claimed, however, that armed merchantmen were auxiliaries, and thus liable to be sunk on sight, there was little to lose in locating weapons for best effect, a policy that applied particularly after the United States became involved.

The task was considerable, initially applying to about 3,000 deep sea ships and 1,500 coasters. Personnel, mainly 'Hostilities Only' (or HO), were drawn from the Royal Navy, emerging after a hasty course as DEMS gunners (from Defensively Equipped Merchant Ship). From February 1940 they were joined by military personnel and formed into the Maritime Royal Artillery. Modern weapons were in such short supply that two-man teams, with a Lewis or Bren gun, would move from ship to ship, and provide defence against air attack while alongside.

A single, medium-calibre gun, usually sited right aft, could be supplemented by stop-gap weapons such as the Holman and Harvey Projectors, the Parachute and Cable (PAC) and Fast Aerial Mine (FAM), both based on rockets and parachutes.

Because British ports were expected to be subjected to severe bombing, it was first assumed that shipping normally handled in ports from the Tyne to Southampton might be diverted to less vulnerable west coast and Scottish ports. Studies showed this to be impracticable, for ports tended to serve the population and

25

industry of their hinterland, and diversion of shipments would involve the rail system in more freight movement than it could bear. Further, ports tended to be equipped for specific types of cargo, examples being iron ore to the Tyne and Tees, sugar and meat to London and Liverpool, and oilseed (some 1.5 million tons of it) to Hull and London.

During the earlier war, shortage of shipping due to losses had been compounded by significant delays while in port. The drafting of experienced dock workers to satisfy the insatiable demands of the army had been largely responsible. Now, however, dock management faced the prospect of transit sheds being destroyed, slowing the process of sorting and dispatching discharged cargo, while preventing further discharge. At any one time, the great storage warehouses along the Thames alone would contain over one million tons of valuable assorted merchandise and it was readily apparent that this, together with the docks and ships alongside, would be an attractive target for aerial bombing.

Following years of recession, considerable tonnage, mostly elderly, remained laid up abroad. Slowly realizing its potential value, Britain purchased a quantity, mainly American- and Panamanian-flagged. A considerable block of American tonnage, offered for sale to the British, was refused because it was equipped with steam turbine propulsion. Astute foreign owners quickly concluded, however, that their ships would be better retained, in the hope of later lucrative time charters.

A huge windfall would come when, in spring 1940, Germany overran the great maritime nations of Norway, Denmark, the Netherlands and France then, later, Greece.

The enemy himself thus acquired 1.4 million GRT but three times that was at sea or in foreign ports. Most of this ultimately came under British control by time charter or requisition. At any time in the coming war, an average figure of about 4 million GRT of foreign shipping sailed under British direction.

An important factor would be the ability of the British ship-building industry to replace losses. In 1930 some 1.5 million GRT had been put in the water, but lack of demand during the 'thirties had greatly shrunk the industry. Surviving yards had neither the capital nor the incentive to modernize. A government scrap-and-build initiative saw owners cheating by retaining their own veteran tonnage and purchasing abroad for demolition.

With the threat of war, demand picked up and, in 1938, British yards built 1 million tons, indicating that, although there were fewer yards, there remained a high potential capacity.

Concentrated on the Tees and the Tyne, the Clyde, the Mersey and at Belfast, the largest yards were in areas most distant from enemy airfields but, if this eventually reduced the bombing to which they were exposed, it was by an unquantifiable degree. Output of new tonnage was as much affected by the great influx of naval work and the need to repair grievously-damaged merchantmen. When, to this, is added shortage of materials and skilled personnel it is, perhaps, not surprising that, even in its best wartime year, the industry produced only 1.5 million tons of new shipping.

Germany would ruthlessly destroy neutrals in order to discourage cooperation with the British, but Swedish ships were usually spared as German industry depended upon Swedish iron ore. Because of this Britain, too, could freely acquire Swedish ore as long as it was transported in Swedish bottoms.

Although, as we have seen, Britain failed in her attempts to get submarine warfare outlawed, no potential enemy at first posed a credible threat. Anti-submarine warfare (ASW) was not, therefore, among the Royal Navy's higher priorities. This changed in 1935, when a re-invigorated Germany virtually forced on Britain the bilateral naval agreement. A U-boat force would again be a reality and the Navy took the quiet view that, despite all protocols, unrestricted submarine warfare would again be a possibility. Convoys would be organized from the outset and the Admiralty prepared a register of suitable retired naval personnel, both to act as convoy commodores and to staff the shore-ends.

There existed too few escorts, inexcusable in light of experience and the belief that more were needed than was, in fact, the case. As the official history would note: 'The comparative neglect of escort vessels in between the wars surely indicates that the lessons of 1914–18 were ignored or misinterpreted.'

Although modern destroyers were needed for the fleet, this left a considerable number of veterans. But destroyers were not satisfactory convoy escorts. Their high-power machinery was not efficient when used extensively at low speed, reducing further an already poor endurance. Their fine forms made them un-comfortable and wet at low speeds in ocean conditions, a situation aggravated by additional personnel and topweight.

To compensate for increasing outfits of depth charges, destroyers sacrificed mainmasts, funnel tops, torpedo tubes and guns. Some had their forward boiler space converted to extra accommodation and bunkerage, still leaving sufficient power for about 25 knots.

The Admiralty had foreseen the requirement for two broad classes of escort. The first, completed to full Admiralty standard, would be suitable for a wide range of missions while simpler types, designed to mercantile standards for series production, would be confined to convoy escort but built in yards unused to naval work.

Both the Hunt-class escort destroyer and the Black Swan-type sloop were built to Admiralty standards. Each had a useful high-angle, anti-aircraft (AA) armament in addition to its anti-submarine (AS) outfit.

Starting mid-1939, the Hunt programme ran to eighty-six ships, but their high speed and low endurance made them more suitable for the English east coast and Mediterranean, and they were little used in the Atlantic.

Dating from a year earlier, the sloops ran to thirty-seven vessels. Larger and more seakindly, they boasted a modest speed but were to prove very effective. They would be employed in support groups rather than as convoy close escorts.

It was the Flower-class corvette that took the brunt of the earlier action. Of a size with a smaller Hunt-type, a Flower was intended also to act as minesweeper and fleet tug, being designed with deep draught aft and a large diameter propeller. Its weak points were a fierce movement in a seaway and an inadequate speed of 16 knots. Escorts were often diverted from their desig-nated station and the Flowers' low speed resulted in their taking considerable time in regaining position. By mid-1942, when the larger frigates were entering service, some 135 Flowers had been completed.

The above programmes were started perilously late, with the first-of-class Black Swan completing in November 1939, the first Hunt in March 1940 and the first Flower in July 1940.

During 1938 and 1939, as the common threat increased, British and French navies discussed cooperation. The British anticipated having to send a considerable proportion of the Mediterranean Fleet to Singapore and were happy to accept the Mediterranean being a largely French responsibility. As far as trade protection was concerned, the main British request was for the cooperation of the two fast French battleships until Armed Merchant Cruisers (AMC) could be fitted out. The emphasis, it will be noted, remained firmly on meeting the threat posed by the enemy's surface raiders rather than his submarines.

Early in 1939 the Admiralty began to bring its Operational Intelligence Centre (OIC) to full readiness. This organization maintained a Surface Ship Plot and an associated Submarine Tracking Room. These were equipped with direct links to a chain of stations whose function was both to intercept enemy radio traffic and to 'fix' its point of origin. The signals were sent on to cryptographers for decoding while the locations of their source were essential to the conduct of the battle against the U-boat.

In the hands of a skilled operator the British Asdic (later termed 'sonar') of 1939 was an efficient device. Its major limitation was that, while reasonably determining range and bearing of a target, it gave no idea of its depth. During the final run-in to attack, transmission and echo were effectively simultaneous and contact was lost. Standard depth charges, released from the after end of an escort, thus had to be placed on a target's estimated position. There followed a further delay as the charges sank to the required depth of up to 500 feet. Because of the uncertainties, it was customary to lay patterns of ten, or even fourteen, charges set for two levels. Three such patterns could exhaust the capacity of a small escort.

Even before 1930, the need for an ahead-throwing weapon, capable of reaching a submerged target while it was still 'fixed' in the Asdic beam, was well recognized and a practical 'bomb-thrower' prototype was tested. Economic stringencies then saw the work abandoned, only to be reinstated in 1939. Such a weapon was of critical importance but its entry into service had been unnecessarily delayed.

As noted above, the Coastal Command of the Royal Air Force was below par in both number and standard of aircraft, and in trained personnel. The London flying boat, dating from 1935, remained in service following the failure of the proposed Lerwick and Stranraer. For patrol and reconnaissance it was supplemented by the twin-engined Anson, a land plane with much the same 700-mile range.

Southern Ireland (Eire) was now neutral territory, so reconnaissance squadrons worked from Cornwall, Northern Ireland and northern Scotland to cover a swathe from the Loire to the Faeroes and the Naze in Norway. Numbers were few, however, and coverage was patchy and intermittent.

Fortunately, Imperial Airways had developed a promising new design of flying boat for its Australian service. Acquired and modified by the government, it was put into production as the Sunderland. There were still only two squadrons operational in September 1939 but the aircraft's 1,000-mile range enabled it to reach Iceland and cover most of the Bay of Biscay.

The Admiralty's first priority for Coastal Command was to watch the North Sea's northern exits against the break-out of surface raiders. Because Scottish-based Ansons had insufficient range to reach Norway, the eastern end of the patrol line had to be maintained by submarines which, with their limited horizon and mobility, were a poor alternative. Meanwhile, every effort was made to speed up deliveries of the American Lockheed Hudson, which had twice the Anson's range.

The need to back up reconnaissance with torpedo-armed strike squadrons was well recognized, but the only available Coastal Command force was a single, Norfolk-based squadron of obsolete Vickers Vildebeest, whose range was insufficient even to reach the Heligoland Bight. A squadron of Bomber Command Hampdens was, therefore, given a subsidiary role in torpedo attack pending the introduction of the Beaufort. From Lincolnshire they could reach Norway and the Baltic exits.

In line with the general lack of interest in ASW, the only available specialist weapons were small bombs, whose erratic fusing made them a greater danger to a low-level attacker than to the submarine attacked.

Hitler's total miscalculation of the likely date of war with the United Kingdom reduced Admiral Raeder's Z-plan to ruin, and left the Luftwaffe far better prepared for hostilities than the German Navy. The war plan stated that shipping in British coastal waters should be attacked by submarine, while ports were to be the responsibility of the Luftwaffe. This offensive would not be isolated but be part of a greater objective of reducing shipping, ports and the rail network to progressively weaken the national economy, and its means and will to wage war.

Of the Luftwaffe's 4,000-odd aircraft only 258 were yet devoted to maritime duties, about half the planned total. There were a score of floatplanes working as catapult flights on major warships, with the remainder split roughly equally between the Baltic and the North Sea.

Long and medium-range reconnaissance and patrol squadrons were equipped with flying boats – the Blohm and Voss Bv138 and Bv222, or the Dornier Do18 – or with Heinkel He115 seaplanes. A formidable force of eighteen squadrons of Heinkel He111 medium bombers were specialist-trained in minelaying and shipping strikes in addition to their more conventional bombing activities. Entering service was the versatile Junkers Ju88 which, with suitable modification, could function as light bomber, torpedo bomber, divebomber or heavy fighter.

Newly introduced as long-range maritime aircraft (LRMA) were the modified civil Junkers Ju290 and the Focke-Wulf FW200, the latter known as the Kondor.

It was Britain's good fortune that relations between Raeder and Göring, the head of the Luftwaffe, remained poor. Raeder considered resignation over the question of maritime aircraft and their control but, as Göring had Hitler's ear, he knew well that his departure would only strengthen the position of the *Reichsmarschall* to the detriment of the navy.

A total of 50,000 magnetic mines had been due to be stockpiled by the spring of 1940. A necessary prelude to a major offensive against ports and shipping, this was a Luftwaffe responsibility, but a dispute with the navy over the mine's design greatly delayed and diluted the offensive. Similarly, the navy considered the torpedo to be the best air-dropped, anti-shipping weapon. Despite this, the air force went its own way, preferring the bomb, only to be proved wrong as the war progressed.

Having superintended the German submarine arm since its

31

renaissance Dönitz, now a commodore, maintained a close, almost paternal, relationship with his skippers. Close bonds developed across the force, resulting in high morale and a powerful sense of competition.

Despite his Führer's pronouncements, Dönitz believed from 1937 that war with Britain was inevitable. He continually impressed upon Raeder the need for rapid expansion of the U-boat force but the C.-in-C. insited upon faithfully complying with Hitler's directives.

Dönitz wanted numbers. As a submarine commander in the earlier war, he knew from first hand how convoys had defeated the U-boats in 1917. He believed that the answer was a simultaneous assault by a maximum concentration of boats. Fully alive to the threat posed by Asdic, he began to train his skippers in the art of surface attack by night. In this mode the U-boat would have a speed advantage over a convoy, be virtually invisible by virtue of its small silhouette, and significantly, be immune to the probing finger of the Asdic. Although published in the open press before the war, Dönitz' ideas do not seem to have made any impact on the British Admiralty.

To qualify, each U-boat commander had to undertake about sixty each submerged and surfaced torpedo attacks, by day and by night respectively. At least one major Baltic exercise against a simulated convoy was considered to have proved the group attack principle to everybody's satisfaction.

Realizing, too, that convoys would be difficult to find in the open ocean, Dönitz proposed to reinforce submarine 'lines of search' with aerial reconnaissance and dedicated intelligence resources.

Bound by the terms of the Anglo-German Naval Agreement, Dönitz' force could not exceed the Royal Navy's 52,700 tons. He vehemently opposed the Naval Staff's proposal for large 'U-cruisers', each of which would absorb the tonnage of two, even three, of the handy-sized boats that he required. Fortunately for him, the two pre-war prototypes, termed Type I, proved to be poor performers.

Of the fifty-seven U-boats operational in September 1939, thirty were small Type IIs. Derived from the clandestine IvS design bureau from the earlier UB and UC types, they had low endurance. Limited mainly to Baltic and North Sea operations, they were nonetheless valuable in training and minelaying.

The backbone of the force would be the medium-sized Type VII and the long-range Type IX, Dönitz requiring three of the former to one of the latter.

The prototype Type VIIs stemmed directly from the earlier UBIII but, while they approached Dönitz' ideal in terms of size and offensive power, they suffered from insufficient range. The deficiency was solved by a small increase in length and the addition of external saddle tanks. This variant, the Type VIIB, enjoyed a 50 per cent longer range at the expense of poorer submerged handling. They could, however, dive in twenty to twenty-five seconds, compared with the Type IX's forty seconds.

Early in 1939 the Type VIIB was modified with improved equipment, particularly sound gear, creating the Type VIIC, which, in several later variants, went on to form the bulk of the force. The larger, long-range Type IX was favoured by Raeder, and Dönitz' insistence on building a great majority of the smaller boats caused friction between the two.

The rationale behind the larger design was logical enough in the requirement to make patrols in the Mediterranean, deep into the Atlantic and along the African coast, none of which supported bases. Adequate bunker space was required along with a good surface speed to minimize transit times. Generous torpedo reload capacity was also necessary to make lengthy patrols viable.

Although 136 U-boats were under construction in September 1939 (the London agreement having been renounced), the operational force comprised six Type II, eighteen Type IIB, six Type IIC, ten Type VII, eight Type VIIB and seven Type IX, together with the near-useless pair of Type Is. Their characteristics may be summarized in the tables on pages 34 and 35.

Torpedoes were of 53.3cm (21-inch) diameter with 280kg (616lb) warheads, compared with those of 160kg (352lb) of the First World War. Their Duplex firing pistol operated either on contact with the target or magnetically, when passing directly under it. In the latter case, the detonation caused the target to whip severely enough to result in structural failure of the hull girder.

On 19 August 1939, Dönitz received the order to dispatch his

Class: **Type II**

Displacement:	surfaced 254 tons
	submerged 303 tons
Length overall	134.3 ft (40.9 m)
Breadth	13.5 ft (4.1 m)
Designed speed:	surfaced 13 knots
	submerged 6.9 knots
Endurance:	surfaced 1050 miles at 12 knots
	submerged 35 miles at 4 knots
Torpedo tubes	3 forward, none aft
Torpedoes carried	6
Guns	One 20mm
Crew	25

Class: **Type IIB**

Displacement:	surfaced 279 tons
	submerged 329 tons
Length overall	140.2 ft (42.7 m)
Breadth	13.5 ft (4.1 m)
Designed speed:	surfaced 13 knots
	submerged 7 knots
Endurance:	surfaced 1800 miles at 12 knots
	submerged 43 miles at 4 knots
Torpedo tubes	3 forward, none aft
Torpedoes carried	6
Guns	One 20mm
Crew	25

Class: **Type IIC**

Displacement:	surfaced 291 tons
	submerged 341 tons
Length overall	144.1 ft (43.9 m)
Breadth	13.5 ft (4.1 m)
Designed speed:	surfaced 12 knots
	submerged 7 knots
Endurance:	surfaced 1900 miles at 12 knots
	submerged 43 miles at 4 knots
Torpedo tubes	3 forward, none aft
Torpedoes carried	6
Guns	One 20mm
Crew	25

Class: **Type VII**

Displacement:	surfaced 626 tons
	submerged 745 tons
Length overall	211.7 ft (64.5 m)
Breadth	19.0 ft (5.8 m)
Designed speed:	surfaced 16 knots
	submerged 8.0 knots
Endurance:	surfaced 4300 miles at 12 knots
	submerged 90 miles at 4 knots
Torpedo tubes	4 forward, 1 aft
Torpedoes carried	11
Guns	One 88mm, one 20mm
Crew	44

Class: **Type VIIB**

Displacement:	surfaced 753 tons
	submerged 857 tons
Length overall	218.3 ft (66.5 m)
Breadth	20.4 ft (6.2 m)
Designed speed:	surfaced 17.2 knots
	submerged 8.0 knots
Endurance:	surfaced 6500 miles at 12 knots
	submerged 90 miles at 4 knots
Torpedo tubes	4 forward, 1 aft
Torpedoes carried	14
Guns	One 88mm, one 20mm
Crew	44

Class: **Type IX**

Displacement:	surfaced 1053 tons
	submerged 1153 tons
Length overall	251.1 ft (76.5 m)
Breadth	21.3 ft (6.5 m)
Designed speed:	surfaced 18.2 knots
	submerged 7.7 knots
Endurance:	surfaced 8100 miles at 12 knots
	submerged 65 miles at 4 knots
Torpedo tubes	4 forward, 2 aft
Torpedoes carried	22
Guns	One 105mm, one 37 mm
Crew	48

operational boats to their war stations. Eighteen boats passed northabout around the British Isles. Unseen, six Type VIIs arrived in the near North-West Approaches, six longer-legged VIIBs in the further South-West Approaches, and five Type IXs to the west of the Gibraltar Strait. A single Type I entered the English Channel from the west to lay mines.

In home waters, eighteen various Type IIs watched off British naval ports and laid mines off British and French commercial ports.

Over 63 per cent of the available U-boat force was thus on station during the initial phase. This would soon reduce to about one-third, with a further one-third in transit and the remainder under repair or refit.

U-boat skippers were under orders to observe the agreed Submarine Protocol, with the following exemptions:

1. 'Merchantmen proceeding under escort of enemy warships or aircraft' (which, by definition, included all ships in convoy);

2. 'Merchantmen which take part in any engagement or which resist when called upon to submit to inspection' (which included all defensively-armed merchantmen who opened fire, which tried to ram or to transmit the 'SSS' distress message, as required by the Admiralty), and

3. 'Transports, which are deemed to be on active service, to belong to the armed forces, and are therefore to be regarded as warships' (difficult to establish).

Correctness was further tempered by the general instructions then emphasizing that 'It goes without saying that effective . . . fighting methods will never fail to be employed merely because some international regulations . . . are opposed to them'.

Chapter Three

Bitter Tide
(September 1939 – December 1941)

It was March 1938 before the Admiralty arrived at the conclusion that 'the institution of a convoy system, wholly or in part, may be necessary from the outbreak of war'. Not surprisingly, therefore, the provision of suitable escorts was disastrously inadequate despite Lord Jellicoe's warning, four years earlier, that 'fast vessels needed for escort against submarine attack cannot be improvised'. Germany's signature on the Submarine Protocol had been justification for further reductions in the naval vote, the Admiralty's response being weak even when faced with the excision of two flotillas of destroyers and nine smaller vessels from the 1938 programme. It is against this abject political failure to learn from even recent history that the early slaughter of merchant shipping should be viewed.

Late on 3 September 1939, the first day of hostilities, the *U-30*, an early Type VII, was patrolling south of Rockall. In the gathering gloom, her skipper, *Kapitänleutnant* Fritz-Julius Lemp, was keeping a close periscope watch on a large vessel that was closing him, blacked-out and zigzagging. Satisfied that she was an Armed Merchant Cruiser (AMC), he fired. Hit by one torpedo, she settled only slowly, enabling Lemp to observe the result of his enthusiasm. For the ship was the 13,600-ton Donaldson liner *Athenia* and, of the 1,100-odd people aboard, over three hundred were American.

Offering no assistance, Lemp crept silently away. As the *Athenia* remained afloat throughout the night, all were rescued except the 118 killed by the initial explosion. These included twenty-eight American citizens.

To cover for Lemp's excess, the German propaganda machine accused the British of engineering the incident in order to bring the United States into the war but Hitler, mindful of consequences, ordered that all 'passenger ships', even in convoy, should remain unmolested.

If the Admiralty reacted with uncharacteristic vigour, it was due to the return to office of Winston Churchill as First Lord, the post he had relinquished twenty-four years earlier.

Ships on passage through the Western Approaches would be convoyed, but only those capable of speeds between 9 and 14.9 knots. Faster or slower vessels, together with neutrals, would still proceed independently. In this early period of hostilities, the convoy system expanded to include the Atlantic, the British east coast and to Scandinavia (until April 1940). Following the capitulation of France in June 1940 it was necessarily extended to include the inshore routes along the English south coast and northabout around Scotland.

Coastal convoys included not only coasters and colliers, vital though they were. Deep-sea ships joined or left convoys usually in Liverpool Bay or the Firth of Clyde, and those bound for the larger south and east coast ports – Southampton, London, the Humber, Tees and Tyne – formed part of the regular, almost daily, coastal convoy cycle. After June 1940 the English south and east coasts faced a continuous, and all too close, occupied enemy shore. Knowing the value of the traffic, the enemy attacked it continually and with every possible means. The routes were very much an extension of those across the Atlantic and many a laden vessel, having survived the deep-sea hazards, was destroyed in sight of a friendly shore.

Beginning on 6 September 1939 the East Coast Convoys were coded 'FN' (northbound) or 'FS' (southbound). They ran roughly every other day between the Thames (Southend) and the Firth of Forth (Methil), collecting and dropping-off ships en route. Their escorts worked mainly out of Rosyth and Harwich.

The western terminal for Atlantic convoys was initially only

Halifax, Nova Scotia. Westbound convoys to Halifax from Southend (until October 1940 only) were coded 'OA', and from Liverpool 'OB'. Eastbound convoys were all 'HX'.

Lack of bases in the Irish Republic aggravated the acute shortage of escorts, so that cover could be given only to meridians 12.5 or 15 degrees W, barely 200 miles west of Scotland. Some fortunate convoys then continued with an anti-surface raider escort, the remainder stayed in company for a day or two before dispersing. Shipping from eastbound convoys, arriving at Liverpool or the Clyde but bound elsewhere, were taken north or southabout by Liverpool or Plymouth-based escort groups. Coastal Command air cover, itself rare enough, extended only to 8 degrees W, equivalent to Tory Island or Cork.

A key element in convoy organization was the Ministry of Transport's Diversion Room where, every morning, users and suppliers of port and transit facilities met together. Acting on Admiralty information on which ships were included in a convoy, details of their cargoes from the Ministry of War Transport, the status of ports from their relevant Port Emergency Committees, and the current situation with respect of inland transport and coastal shipping, decisions were made on which ships should go where.

It is not exactly true to say that the speed of a convoy is that of its slowest ship. At the pre-sailing masters' conference, which soon included neutrals, the speed of the convoy would be agreed. Once at sea, the convoy took its manoeuvring instructions from the commodore. Each noon, with the exact position fixed, the commodore would hoist a flag signal, repeated by every other ship, giving the position of a rendezvous point for the following day. Any ship falling out with machinery problems would thus have the opportunity to steer a direct course to rejoin the convoy, which zigzagged.

Mindful of the need to use shipping efficiently, the government fretted that convoys were delaying faster ships unduly, and planners were beguiled into reducing the upper convoy speed limit from 14.9 to 13 knots. Many better-class ships now became 'independents' and their loss rate tripled. Within three months the old upper limit was reinstated.

It was from among the slow independents, however, those

incapable of making the minimum 9 knots for the convoy, that the U-boats made their easiest kills. Their loss rate could reach one in four.

Limited to an eighteen-day endurance and a maximum surface speed of 13 knots, the Type II U-boats were pretty well confined to North Sea operation. In British coastal waters, stop and search procedure in conformance with protocol was simply too risky, and sinkings were negligible. Farther out, there was plenty of neutral tonnage carrying British cargoes, but the Type IIs lacked both the speed and the deck gun necessary to persuade reluctant skippers to submit.

Initially anxious to avoid upsetting the neutrals and the French, Hitler declared their shipping beyond attack. Under pressure from both Raeder and Dönitz, however, he soon (23 September 1939) relaxed the ban considerably, also permitting passenger ships carrying fewer than 120 passengers to be sunk under prize rules. It took just a dozen neutral sinkings to bring down diplomatic opprobrium sufficient to see the ban re-imposed.

The freedom of movement of the Type IIs was further constricted by the early Anglo-French creation of a Dover Strait mine barrage, the efficacy of which was proved by the loss of the *U-12* and *U-16*, together with the *U-40*, one of the big Type IXs, in the first two months.

For the first wave of eighteen ocean-going U-boats, fortunes were mixed. Experience showed that merchantmen had to be fired upon before they would stop.

Following Admiralty instructions, radio operators would transmit the repeated SSS ('Submarine Attack') signal, some remaining on the key even when brought under deliberate fire. Few at this stage had defensive armament. For their part, U-boat skippers began by observing the rules, assisting wounded survivors and ensuring that lifeboats were provisioned.

Such chivalries existed, of course, only in the absence of AS forces for, where these were braved, retribution could be swift. When the aircraft carrier *Ark Royal* was attacked on 19 September by the *U-27*, the latter's torpedoes 'prematured' due to faulty magnetic pistols. Alerted, the carrier's destroyer escort quickly located the culprit and blew her to the surface. A boarding party attempted to gain entry but the submarine's scuttling charges had already been blown.

In a gross misuse of the Royal Navy's most valuable assets, both the *Ark* and the *Courageous* were being employed in AS operations. The latter had been sunk just two days earlier by another Type VII, the *U-29*. Schuhart, the submarine's skipper, then went on to be an early 'ace', sinking fourteen ships on this patrol alone.

Mines, laid off the east coast by the Type IIs and off Portland Bill by a big Type I, successfully claimed eight large seagoing ships, several of them neutral. Between them, this first wave of deep sea boats had destroyed thirty-nine ships of about 186,000 equivalent GRT, little better than two ships per patrol but a highly encouraging start for Dönitz.

It had been the intention of Admiral Raeder to saturate the vital British coastal shipping routes with magnetic mines before the British discovered an antidote but, as already mentioned above, inter-service disagreements had delayed the production programme and only a few hundred of the available 22,000 mines were magnetic.

Where submarines could plant mines with considerable precision, this was not the case with aircraft. Night navigation and wind drift on the parachute rendered positioning a little hit-and-miss and, at the end of November 1939, the British recovered two examples. This enabled a huge programme of degaussing ships and production of 'Double L' sweeps.

Until April 1940, when many were lost in Norway, German destroyers made nocturnal minelaying forays to the East Coast, supplemented by at least one disguised merchantman. The role of the destroyers was then assumed largely by torpedo boats. The latter (known as S-boats to the enemy, E-boats to the British) operated out of nearby Dutch ports after May 1940 and proved to be a constant menace to coastal convoys.

By March 1940, prominent headlands and the approaches to major British ports had all been fouled by offshore minefields, causing disruption to traffic and the commitment of large, and growing, resources in their clearance. Mine design was already, however, growing more sophisticated and, after submarines and aircraft, the weapon proved the most efficient destroyer of merchant shipping. Convoy routes were regularly swept, and it was again the independents that suffered most from mining, accounting for at least three-quarters of the losses.

Detailed analysis of their First World War submarine offensive had convinced the Germans that it failed because U-boats needed to attack convoys unsupported, the might of their fleet being confined to the North Sea by the British Grand Fleet. Interwar German theorists thus developed a new strategy, whereby submarine action would oblige the British to run convoys, only for these to be attacked by surface forces powerful enough to dispose of both escort and merchantmen.

Such surface forces would have resulted from Raeder's Z-plan but, as we have seen, his Führer's chaotic policies precipitated a naval war five years too soon. The only available heavy warships were thus the trio of 'pocket battleships', the two *Scharnhorsts* and the heavy cruiser *Hipper*.

Two of the pocket battleships had sailed well before hostilities commenced, the *Graf Spee* for the Central Atlantic and the *Deutschland* for the sea area east of Newfoundland. Restraints were placed on their molesting British and French shipping, these being lifted on 25 September and in mid-October respectively. Operational instructions included the following:

1. The disruption and destruction of enemy merchant shipping by all possible means.

2. Merchant warfare *in the beginning* (author's italics) to be waged according to Prize Law.

3. Enemy naval forces, even if inferior, to be engaged only if it furthers the principal task.

4. Operational areas to be changed frequently to create uncertainty.

Although the Admiralty had long anticipated such raider warfare, years of political parsimony and constricting naval agreements had resulted in too few cruisers to undertake the necessary countermeasures. About fifty good-class merchantmen were thus taken for conversion to Armed Merchant Cruisers (AMC). However dedicated their manning, such vessels can never be substitutes for regular warships, and the enemy scored an effort-less success in removing such valuable ships from their proper business.

The instructions given to raider commanders encouraged them to prey on independents. Required withdrawal in the face of even inferior opposition did nothing for offensive spirit while, conversely, it encouraged escorts to resist the harder.

Each raider had one or more supply ships in support, stationed in designated cruising areas. As they were a feature of German surface raider operations, the British employed cruisers specifi-cally in their hunting down.

The two pioneer raiders began cautiously. The *Deutschland* operated between Newfoundland and Bermuda in seas yet to see a convoy and teeming with independents. Nonetheless, she appre-hended only three ships. The third was a still-neutral American, which was released with the crews of the first two.

Her consort, the *Graf Spee*, followed her instructions to the letter, sinking nine ships of about 50,000 GRT over a wide area before being intercepted by Commodore Harwood's cruisers off the River Plate. Fleeing rather than fighting, she arrived, damaged, off Montevideo. With no prospect of ever being able to get back to Germany, she was destroyed by her crew.

A total of eleven merchantmen sunk in no way compensated for the morale-sapping loss of a capital ship. Despite an in-auspicious start, however, the enemy persevered, causing the British to divert significant resources in response.

In 1945, expert opinion, when asked to list the 'outstanding fail-ures, the avoidance of which might have shortened the war', came up with a near-unanimous verdict – the British escort programme.

In September 1939 the Royal Navy had about 180 Asdic-equipped vessels. About 150 of these, however, were destroyers, the bulk of which were required for fleet work. An urgent programme for AS escorts, when it came, was driven by many priorities and the limitations of the many smaller yards that had to be involved. The resulting corvettes were, therefore, too small to be truly effective as ocean convoy escorts. Even so, it took time to start commissioning them in numbers and it was indeed fortunate that, over the same period, the equally ill-prepared Germans were struggling to increase U-boat production.

Despite their obvious shortcomings, the Flowers could be built in numbers, and it was numbers that were so desperately needed.

Canada had never built a warship larger than a minesweeper but, demonstrating much of the 'can-do' attitude of her mighty neighbour, she offered to create facilities and skills sufficient to provide a corvette force to cover the western end of the Atlantic convoy routes. With various programme extensions, Canadian yards eventually built seventy-nine Flowers in addition to large numbers of other types. Equally valuable to the British, who were already experiencing manpower shortages, Canada recruited and trained her own crews, ending the war as a seapower in her own right.

As 1940 progressed, Britain's prospects of survival looked ever bleaker. With the likelihood of democracy in Europe being finally extinguished, the United States became ever more supportive. Winston Churchill, now Prime Minister, established a close personal rapport with President Roosevelt, who was already considerably relaxing the Neutrality Acts. Britain was thus able to procure matériel on a 'cash and carry' basis but, after the disaster of Dunkirk, the President made his momentous offer of all help 'short of war'.

An immediate result was the transfer to the Royal Navy of fifty 'four-stacker' destroyers in return for American basing rights in Newfoundland, Bermuda, British Guiana and five West Indian islands. The latter part of the agreement assured local defence while enabling the United States to establish an outer perimeter. The destroyers were in variable condition, being of First World War vintage, and not ideal for North Atlantic operations. With reduced armament and some boiler space converted for extra fuel tanks and accommodation, however, they gave valuable service at a time of great escort shortage. Some were manned by Canadian and Norwegian crews while, later, some were transferred to the Soviet navy.

During the earlier war AMCs, backed by the authority of the nearby Grand Fleet, had maintained the Northern Patrol in the successful blockade of enemy trade. Now with their ancient armament and rudimentary fire-control, they were given the impossible task of escorting ocean convoys to deter attack by powerful enemy raiders.

While still First Lord, Churchill described them as a 'care and anxiety' but was assured by the Naval Staff that they were 'indispensable auxiliaries at the present time'. Their low deterrent value, however, was matched by their large crews and maintenance requirements while, as the war progressed, their value as troopships became far greater.

The unfolding British strategy may be seen in the allocation, by February 1940, of four AMCs to the Halifax Escort Force, ten to the Freetown (Sierra Leone) Escort Force which covered convoys of traffic to and from the Cape, twenty to a re-established but now highly vulnerable Northern Patrol, and a dozen or so spread between maritime theatres yet uninvolved in hostilities. Following a necessary re-disposition after the German invasion of Norway in April 1940, the AMC force at Halifax grew to eleven.

That the AMC had its uses had been demonstrated in the previous November, when the fast battleships *Scharnhorst* and *Gneisenau* evaded British patrol lines between the Shetlands and Norway. Still south-east of Iceland and short of the open ocean, they encountered the AMC *Rawalpindi*, late of the P & O. In a hopeless action during the brief winter afternoon, the armed liner fought to the end. Even as the *Scharnhorst* rescued her survivors, however, the next ship in the patrol arrived in response to her raider warning. This vessel was the light cruiser *Newcastle*, which represented a threat sufficient to make the enemy abandon their activities and make off into the murky north-east. In the conditions the Germans could maintain the higher speed and, knowing that he had been reported, their admiral aborted their intended cruise and, blessed by heavy overcast weather, returned safely home.

Observance of the prize rules was progressively abandoned by the Germans. From 23 September 1939 they warned that any ship using its radio could be sunk. All rules were abandoned for the North Sea from the 30th, and to the meridian of 1.5 degrees west four days later. On 19 October permission was given to sink any darkened ship out to 20 degrees west. From mid-November even passenger liners 'clearly identified as hostile' could be sunk without warning.

With their neutrality regulations still in place the Americans banned their shipping from entering a declared War Zone which bounded the British Isles at 20 degrees west and extended between the latitudes of Spanish territorial waters and the Shetlands. Germany then warned all other neutrals within this zone to avoid any defensive precautions, such as darkening ship or zigzagging, on pain of being sunk without warning.

In October 1939 Dönitz first tried out 'wolf pack' tactics. Only six boats could be mustered, with three Type VIIBs and two Type IXs being dispatched northabout. The sixth, a further Type IX, *U-40*, was delayed and ordered to take a short cut through the English Channel. Running foul of the new mine barrier, she was sunk in barely 100 feet of water, becoming one of many to yield useful intelligence via the navy's specialist divers.

First in action was another of the Type IXs. Encountering the dispersed Ropner ship *Stonepool*, the *U-42* surfaced and attacked with her deck gun. The freighter was not only armed but defended herself vigorously while continuously transmitting a submarine warning. Two destroyers, detached from a nearby convoy, arrived promptly enough to fire on the U-boat, which promptly submerged. Her position known, she was quickly brought to the surface with depth charges. Only sixteen of her crew escaped before she slid under for good.

His control still shaky, Dönitz assumed that, by now, all six boats were concentrated as a group. He did not know that two had been lost and a third, the designated leader *U-37*, had lost touch in pursuing and sinking two neutrals.

The German *B-dienst* was intercepting all British radio traffic and, at this time, decoding much of it. It forecast the imminent arrival of the virtually-unescorted fast convoy KJF.3 on a short-lived route from Kingston, Jamaica. Dönitz directed his pack to intercept but, by now, only a pair of Type VIIBs, *U-45* and *U-48*, could respond. The latter picked off the large (14,120 GRT) French tanker *Emile Miguet* and a passing British straggler, the 5,200-ton *Heronspool*, another Ropner ship. On the following day she added the 6,900-ton French ship *Louisiane*.

For her part, the *U-45* disposed of the new Royal Mail liner *Lochavon* (9,200 GRT) and the 10,100-ton French passenger liner *Bretagne*. The latter, a well-known CGT ship, was carrying passengers but, being blacked-out and in convoy, was considered fair game. The *U-45* was then believed to be lining up an attack on the 10,530-ton British refrigerated ship *Karamea* when she was located by three British destroyers that had arrived in response to several distress calls. From the *U-45* there were no survivors.

Where the final Type VIIB, *U-46*, failed to locate the convoy, the erstwhile pack leader, *U-37*, turned up in time to catch a straggler, the 5,190-ton French ship *Vermont*, another CGT ship.

Reporting in by radio, the surviving U-boat skippers over-estimated their successes, a common failing. It took time for Dönitz to discover that the attack had not been coordinated and that three boats had been lost in exchange for some 35,500 GRT of shipping destroyed. This was alleviated only by the *U-47* continuing her patrol to add five more ships, including the Bibby liner *Yorkshire*, for a further 24,300 GRT.

As a qualified success, the attack was carefully analysed. This resulted in the instruction that the first boat to detect a convoy should not attack immediately but home-in the remainder of her group for a coordinated assault.

With the approach of war the Director of Naval Intelligence, Rear Admiral J.H. Godfrey, appointed Rear Admiral J.W. ('Jock') Clayton from retirement to head the Admiralty's Operational Intelligence Centre (OIC). Within the OIC the Submarine Tracking Room was placed in the care of a career-barrister and RNVR Commander, Rodger Winn. Clayton and Winn were to be of pivotal importance in the developing intelligence war against the U-boat.

An essential feature of this silent struggle was a chain of radio intercept stations, eventually numbering fifty-one and effectively ringing the North Atlantic. Continuously upgraded equipment in these had the twin objectives of intercepting the actual coded text of a U-boat transmission and obtaining a precise fix on its point of origin. Despite the vagaries of atmospheric conditions it was eventually possible to place a boat to within fifty miles, anywhere in the North Atlantic.

Messages, first encrypted in so-called Naval Enigma, were sent in a burst transmission that required so little time that the Germans felt it impossible that it could be intercepted with precision sufficient to record it accurately.

At the Government Code and Cypher School, Bletchley Park, a war-long struggle was maintained to break, and to continue breaking, the various *Wehrmacht* Enigma codes. The naval version was, nontheless, not broken 'on demand' until August 1941, and the continual changes made by the enemy required regular captures of material by the Royal Navy to maintain the priceless flow of information termed 'Ultra'.

In addition to Direction Finding ('D/F-ing') and decryption, signal interception was used in two other modes. In Traffic Analysis, the length, regularity, pattern, call signs and all other discernable characteristics were analysed and changes noted. Radio Fingerprinting attempted to identify specific operators and transmitters, to associate them with their boats.

Following seven months of a so-called 'Phoney War' Hitler, accepting that France and Great Britain would not seek a negotiated peace, unleashed a series of campaigns in the west. First Norway and Denmark were overrun, then the Low Countries and France herself. In three months it was all over and, by the end of June 1940, continental Europe, less the uneasy neutrals, was subjugated.

In summing up his force's accomplishments to date, Dönitz must have had mixed feelings. To the end of March 1940, operating under restrictions, his skippers had destroyed 222 merchantmen of about 763,000 GRT compared with only sixteen of 63,000 GRT by surface raiders. Allied countermeasures had been much as expected, eighteen U-boats having been sunk. New submarine construction was slow, and his total strength had actually fallen, to fifty-two boats.

Although still operating for the most part in the near Atlantic, U-boat skippers had shown themselves to be resourceful, and 'aces' were already emerging. Once their initial defects had been rectified, the Type VIIs proved excellent. Necessary for more distant operations, the larger and less agile Type IXs were not universally popular. Boats had, so far, been deployed in 'waves' and dockyard facilities had found themselves stretched to meet peaks of demand for repairs on their return.

A worrying trend was the growing clamour of complaints about malfunctioning torpedoes. As other navies would discover, the Duplex magnetic contact firing pistol was unreliable, but a peculiarly German problem was running deeper than set. Rectifying the problems took time and Dönitz' personal routine of chatting to all returning skippers and, often, their crews, was vital in the restoration of shaken confidence.

During April 1940 most operational U-boats were re-deployed to support the surface fleet's risky move against Norway. As a result, only twenty ships, aggregating some 88,000 GRT, were sunk by submarine attack in April and May.

In early May, as his panzers tore the French army asunder, Hitler believed that a French defeat would oblige Britain to seek terms. With the front moving inexorably westward it was apparent to the German High Command that traffic must temporarily increase between French Atlantic ports and Britain. Dönitz duly deployed what boats were available but their fortunes were mixed. One, however, the *U-37* under a replacement skipper, destroyed ten ships, totalling over 41,000 GRT in a short, twenty-six day patrol, a near record to date. Analysis of the score is interesting in that all of the *U-37*'s victims were independents, and only two were British. Three were French, two Greek and one each Swedish, Finnish and Argentinian. Five were sunk by gunfire, four by torpedo, one by gunfire and torpedo, and just one, the Argentinian ship *Uruguay*, by scuttling charges.

Hard on the heels of the retreating Allies, Dönitz' advance parties moved westward with equipment and orders to select suitable U-boat bases on the French Atlantic coast. They worked quickly and, on 6 July 1940, the first boat, *U-30*, entered Lorient. Other bases followed at Brest, St Nazaire, la Pallice (near la Rochelle) and Bordeaux.

From French bases, transit times to and from the U-boat's Atlantic operational areas were greatly reduced, extending the time that each could remain on station. Hazardous passages northabout around the British Isles were no longer necessary, while even the little Type IIs were now able to operate in the south-western approaches. French facilities could also undertake the normal run of maintenance and refits, although major repairs still needed to be carried out in home yards.

Keeping pace with the situation, Dönitz moved his operational headquarters from Wilhelmshaven to Paris in August 1940 and then, in the November, to Kerneval, near Lorient.

For the British, the balance of naval power shifted drastically at the end of June 1940, with the French Navy no longer an ally and the Italian added as a foe. The Norwegian campaign and the evacuation of France had cost the Royal Navy a dozen destroyers and minor warships, with damage to many more. Invasion of Britain was expected at any time.

Norway had also been expensive for the German Navy but repairs to Dönitz' force were complete by June, enabling him to dispatch a further 'wave' of eighteen boats to join the three patrolling west of the British Isles. Within a few days they destroyed over 160,000 GRT.

Already lionized as the 'Bull of Scapa Flow' for his sinking of the British battleship *Royal Oak*, Prien in the *U-47* accounted for seven ships of about 35,000 GRT. With one torpedo remaining, Prien made for home but, soon after midnight on 2 July, he encountered a large, darkened ship north-west of Ireland. Obviously a passenger liner, she was armed and zigzagging. Under German rules of engagement, she was fair game and Prien's last torpedo slammed into her.

The ship was the 15,500-ton *Arandora Star*, well-known pre-war as a cruise ship but now carrying about 1,300 German and Italian prisoners of war and internees to Canada. As the ship took an hour to founder many got away and a Sunderland flying boat was able to direct the Canadian destroyer *St. Laurent* to the scene. She was able to rescue about 850, but a like number perished, 700 of them aliens.

Tonnage lost at this time was increased through the sinking of several passenger liners acting as AMCs, including Cunard's *Andania* and *Carinthia*, and the Anchor liner *Caledonia*. To these was added the French MM liner *Champlain*.

The general westerly movement of U-boats, once their French bases were operable, obliged the Admiralty to reorganize its assets to escort convoys as far as 17 degrees west. Beyond this limit the westbound OB convoys remained in company for a day or so before slowly dispersing. Their late Western Approaches escort would, meanwhile, have taken over an eastbound HX convoy on its final leg.

Beginning in July 1940, Western Approaches Command also assumed responsibility for the northern section of the new OG and HG convoy routes, to and from Gibraltar, and the SL route from Freetown, Sierra Leone.

With HX convoys working on a four-day cycle, Halifax was becoming congested, so ships joining from ports south of New York were now assembled at Bermuda before sailing as a supplementary BHX convoy to join an HX movement at sea. Slow (SC) convoys were now sailing from Sydney, Cape Breton.

Delayed further by evasive routing and winter weather, Atlantic convoys could take fifteen or more days to cross and it was possible to have over ten convoys at sea in the theatre at any one time. Westbound legs, against the grain of the weather, took longer than eastbound and a delay could mean missing a rendezvous with the escort, whose priorities were driven strictly by their timetable. This outcome could have serious consequences.

To pre-empt any enemy move, British and Canadian troops began in May 1940 to establish bases in Iceland and the Faeroes, at that time both dependencies of newly-occupied Denmark. Use of Icelandic airfields and anchorages would assist in the shrinking of the yawning mid-Atlantic gap where there yet existed no escort cover. A fleet base slowly grew at Hvalfjord, an inhospitable wind-lashed bay north of Reykjavik. For the moment, Coastal Command's priority was anti-invasion patrols over the North Sea and it would be April 1941 before it had resources sufficient to mount reconnaissance and AS patrols from Iceland.

To the Germans, their new Italian ally ran the gamut from mixed blessing to downright liability. Requested to tie down the British in North Africa, Mussolini dissipated his strength in invading Albania, insisted on sending squadrons to assist the Luftwaffe's assault on Britain and, to Dönitz' endless frustration, dispatched a considerable submarine force to operate in the Atlantic.

In the first instance, three Italian boats were sent to the

Canaries/Madeira area in June 1940. These were followed by three more to the Azores. Having completed their patrols, all returned to a new base in Bordeaux, where they came under Dönitz. The latter saw them initially as eager to help but not very competent, and was content to 'allow them to find out their own shortcomings and gradually gain from experience'.

By early November 1940, half a dozen (more than the Germans could themselves muster), were deployed in the North-West Approaches, beyond 14 degrees west and the then limit of British escort cover. Dönitz expected few sinkings by them but saw them as valuable in reconnaissance. By December, he was in despair about them. They sighted convoys but were unable either to maintain contact or to return useful reports. Even charged with the simple but important task of reporting the weather they returned such garbled data that the Germans did it themselves.

'Inadequately disciplined' and '[unable] to remain calm in the face of the enemy', Dönitz concluded that they were prejudicing his own operations and banished them to the southern periphery of German operations and no longer a part of them.

Up to their capitulation in 1943 the Italians operated about thirty boats from Bordeaux. They were responsible for a useful number of sinkings but their overall influence on the campaign was slight.

The Italians certainly operated differently. The record of the *Malaspina* shows her on the surface on 12 August 1940 at 38N, 23W (east of the Azores) when she sighted the tanker *British Fame*. At the time, 'the officer of the watch and lookouts were on the bridge and the captain was dozing in a deckchair below'. Hit by one, possibly two, torpedoes the tanker returned fire to such good effect that the *Malaspina* was taken down to fifty metres. Torpedoed again, the tanker was stopped, but refused to sink. All officers in turn viewed through the periscope 'this extraordinary sight' of the British crew lowering their boats. Two hours and two more torpedoes later, the tanker was finally sent down, whereupon the Italians chivalrously spent the better part of twenty-four hours towing the lifeboats to a point safely off the Azores.

Between June and October 1940 the U-boats enjoyed their first 'happy time'. Before this, sinkings had been overwhelmingly in the western approaches to the British Isles but, with the availability of French bases, there was a shift westward into a zone of still easy pickings. In Atlantic and British waters, June witnessed the destruction of 130 ships of about 505,000 GRT, a toll maintained for about five months until British countermeasures began to take effect.

These were the halcyon days of the U-boat 'aces'. Postwar analysis showed that just twenty skippers accounted for about 23 per cent of all tonnage destroyed. Kretschmer, Schepke, Prien, Topp and many others were eulogized by the enemy propaganda machine. They benefited through operating at a time when countermeasures were weakest but, for the most part, the careers of the boldest were brutally short.

Many had graduated from the ranks of the merchant marine. This was, perhaps, appropriate in that many of the opposing escort commanders were of the naval reserves, the so-called 'Wavy Navy', while convoy commodores were frequently former naval flag officers, called from retirement.

Once Dönitz managed to mount an attack on group principles, it could be horrifyingly effective, depressing the spirits of both the merchant navy crews and those whose task it was to protect them. Inevitably, dissident voices claimed immediately that the convoy system would ultimately prove disastrous. At times, it must have been difficult to disregard them, with even the Prime Minister admitting to deep concern.

Like any system, convoy could never be made perfect but, nonetheless, statistics spoke more coolly than heated opinion. During 1940, 662 ocean convoys were run, the great majority in the North Atlantic. In total, these included 17,882 ships. Of these, the enemy sank 126, of which U-boats claimed 101. The overall loss rate was, therefore, just 0.7 per cent.

The major problem was that twice this amount was simultaneously being lost from the great number of independents. Some of these went alone because of their speed, some were neutrals who were prepared to take the risk, others were stragglers or rompers from convoys. All provided the easiest pickings for marauding enemy submarines.

Since their passage times were longer, slow convoys had a higher loss rate. If located well out in the Atlantic, they could come under heavy attack as the enemy had time to marshal his resources.

A typical example of the latter was SC.7, a 7.5-knot convoy which sailed with thirty-four ships from Sydney, CB on 5 October 1940. On the 16th it was entering the danger zone of the outer North-West Approaches. At this point, its AS escort comprised just one sloop, but was expecting to be joined by a Western Approaches group of two further sloops and two corvettes.

On this day the straggling Hain freighter *Trevisa* was picked off by the *U-124* but the convoy remained unreported until sighted the following day by *U-48*. It was then well to the north-east of the *Trevisa*'s location and the *U-48*, instead of tracking and reporting, attacked immediately, sinking the large British tanker *Langedoc* and the Ropner ship *Scoresby*, totalling about 13,300 GRT.

Dönitz directed five boats onto the convoy's projected course but the *U-48*, which should have been holding contact, broke away to pursue an independent. Westbound and in ballast, she was the Whitby tramp *Sandsend* and, in adding her 3,600 GRT to his score, Bleichrodt of the *U-48* lost the convoy.

Now heading south-eastward, and only a few hundred miles from safety, it was SC.7's misfortune to be located again soon after midnight on 17–18th by the *U-38*. By that evening, six submarines were in contact, four of them commanded by ace skippers. On a night of brilliant moonlight there ensued ten hours of mayhem. In all, seventeen ships were lost and, in the confusion, it cannot be stated with certainly which sank what.

In working around to the head of the convoy, Kretschmer's surfaced *U-99* encountered two colleagues before he submerged to unsuccessfully attack an isolated cargo vessel. The now-reinforced escort, sensing trouble, was firing star shell which, Kretschmer noted, was of little use in the moonlight. Nonetheless, a hurried bow shot, taken again on the surface, missed. He swung the boat, loosing his stern tube at a '6,500-tonner'. Struck, the ship sank in about twenty seconds. From the description, she was probably the *Empire Miniver*, fully laden with nearly 11,000 tons of steel products. She was an old, 1918-vintage American-built freighter and, in the circumstances, it was something of a miracle that only three of the crew were lost.

With the convoy now in some disarray, Kretschmer headed straight into it, remaining on the surface. He missed with another bow shot as a merchant ship spotted him, altering course to ram. It was now 23.30 and, still on the convoy's right flank, he aimed at one ship and hit another. Twenty minutes later another torpedo found a vessel which 'burned with a green flame'; probably the sulphur-laden Greek ship *Niritos*.

Pursued by escorts, Kretschmer retired temporarily to reload, to the sound of other boat's torpedoes 'constantly . . . exploding'. His pursuers had to return to their charges, leaving *U-99* free to again work ahead of the convoy. Within a quarter of an hour, he destroyed two more ships at ranges of under 1,000 metres. Both laden with heavy cargoes of steel, copper and lead, they were the *Empire Brigade* and the Greek ship *Thalia*.

Probably himself wearied by the night's activity, Kretschmer went for a specific large ship, which he eventually managed only to damage. At about 04.00, with his last two torpedoes, he again only damaged a 'rather small, unladen ship' which appeared not to belong to the convoy. As he closed her with the intention of finishing her with gunfire, a colleague, Moehle in the *U-123*, did the same thing from her other side, his 'overs' landing close to Kretschmer, who withdrew 'quickly'. This final victim was the 3,100-ton North Shields tramp *Clintonia*.

As the mauled SC.7, half its ships sunk, gratefully entered the sanctuary of the North Channel, those boats with any torpedoes remaining were redirected by Dönitz onto a further convoy, the inward-bound HX.79. This had been located by Prien in the *U-47*, and four others were successfully vectored in. During the night of 19–20 October 1940, the carnage was repeated with ten ships being destroyed out of forty-nine, representing a further 55,000 GRT.

Dönitz was understandably ecstatic at this double success vindicating his policies. Awards were plentiful, with the *Ritterkreuz* (Knight's Cross) going to those skippers credited with a total of 100,000 GRT and a special new award of the Cross with Oak Leaves to Prien, whose tally had passed 200,000 GRT. Although their claims were considerably inflated,this small group of skippers inflicted grievous damage, in this case at the trivial cost of two U-boats damaged.

Although the enemy, himself, was surprised at the success which attended this form of attack, it is well to keep matters in perspective by remembering that, in the preceding seventy-eight 'HX' convoys, only fourteen had lost any ships at all, and those that did averaged only 2.5 ships.

Loss of life was reduced by the introduction of Convoy Rescue Ships. Small passenger ships, of a size well suited to pulling survivors from the water, these kept to the rear of the convoy. The thirty that were eventually commissioned saved, between them, over 4,000 personnel, although six of their own number were lost.

The Navy sought every means to overcome the dearth of escorts. By November 1940 the receding risk of invasion enabled destroyers to be re-allocated. Others, damaged in Norway and at Dunkirk were re-entering service after repair. Those ex-American 'four-stackers' that had required dockyard attention were also coming forward.

More significantly, new escorts were coming from the yards. Since the summer, each had had to undergo a month's intensive AS training at Tobermory, where presided Commodore Gilbert O. Stephenson, a lately-retired vice admiral with very definite views about working-up to full efficiency.

Initial training complete, escorts would then be attached to groups working from the Clyde, the Mersey or from Londonderry. These trained as a tactical unit and every effort was made to keep them together. Usually of eight ships, a group was often an eclectic bunch, which proved to be less of a handicap than might have been supposed.

Dönitz' centralized control system also began to be used again. Its reliance on the sighting U-boat transmitting regular tracking reports meant that it could be D/F-ed from shore stations and targeted to ensure that it lost contact. Urgent research was also aimed at the production of a shipborne D/F unit to enable an escort to get a bearing on a transmitting submarine, but it would be July 1941 before a practical set went to sea.

Despite the enemy having used the tactic of attacking with surfaced submarines during the earlier war, it appears not to have been anticipated in 1940. When re-introduced it rendered Asdic useless and triggered yet more high-priority work, this time for a suitable radar. Tests of prototypes began early in 1941 in both escorts and aircraft, while interim improvements included the Snowflake high-intensity flare illuminant and more efficient radio telephony to enable escorts to communicate clearly, the better to coordinate a convoy's defence.

In February 1941 Western Approaches Command moved its headquarters from Plymouth to Liverpool for convenient access to the shipping control organization, masters' conferences, escort groups and the headquarters of 15 Group, Coastal Command. From the April, the Command's operational control was passed to the Admiralty.

Western Approaches Command's new flag officer, Admiral Percy Noble, also had at Liverpool a duplicate Trade Plot and a direct link to the Admiralty's Submarine Tracking Room, which was now directing convoys further north to put them beyond the attentions of the enemy's Kondors.

It was at about this time that Prime Minister Churchill labelled the still-intensifying struggle officially as the 'Battle of the Atlantic'.

Beyond the surface activity lay the shadowy world of intelligence and the ongoing effort to break Naval Enigma. The fall of France in June 1940 brought an influx of Polish and French expertise, specialists who had been involved since before the war. The Poles had succeeded in building a replica service Enigma machine but this only pointed up the necessity of accessing knowledge of the actual wiring details, or settings, being used at any specific time. This wiring was embodied in a series of rotors, which not only worked in cascade but which could simply be re-keyed to change their rotational relationship, one with the next, to give the possibility of millions of combinations.

An early success, in February 1940, was the recovery of some rotors from the sunken minelayer *U-33* in the Firth of Clyde. As Enigma machines were apparently carried by all German warships and auxiliaries, the hunt was on to recover them wherever possible. The associated problem was to prevent the enemy knowing of a capture and suspecting the compromise of his codes.

Activities of German trawlers during the Norwegian operations in April 1940 marked them as probably auxiliaries. One, the *Polares*, was targeted and, sure enough, yielded documentation that enable Bletchley Park cryptographers for the first time to decipher a Naval Enigma signal, albeit one a fortnight old. Then, in March 1941, during the raid on the Lofotens, the trawler *Krebs* yielded both rotors and current documentation. The latter, though ephemeral, enabled Bletchley Park to further advance its techniques.

In April 1941 Dönitz noted 'it seems that the British ships are getting around the locations selected for attacks. This leads one to suspect that our ambush points are known'. Success with Enigma had not yet advanced sufficiently to have been the cause, credit being due to the evasive routing of convoys as recommended by the Submarine Tracking Room, whose conclusions were deduced from a mass of often contradictory inputs.

Luftwaffe operations in particular required accurate weather forecasting. This depended greatly on weather reports from German trawlers stationed in the deep Atlantic. As their reports were encoded, they too suddenly became of great interest to the Royal Navy which, in May 1941, snatched the *München*. Although her crew had jettisoned all classified gear, sufficient documentation was recovered to permit the Enigma codebreakers to read current signal traffic during the month of June, but for one month only.

On 9 May 1941 the westbound OB.318 was attacked by two U-boats, *U-110* and *U-201*. The former was commanded by Fritz-Julius Lemp, who had infamously sunk the passenger liner *Athenia* on the first day of hostilities. It was about midday when Lemp made a first, submerged attack, his salvo sinking two ships. One was the 5,000-ton *Esmond*, coincidentally owned by the Glasgow firm of Donaldson, owners also of the *Athenia*.

The convoy was screened by the Iceland-based Escort Group 3 (EG3), one of whose ships, the corvette *Aubretia*, located Lemp and brought him to the surface with two well-placed patterns of depth charges. Under orders to board submarines wherever possible, two more of EG3's ships closed, spraying the wallowing *U-110* with machine-gun fire to panic the crew. This measure appeared to succeed, the destroyer *Bulldog* getting a party aboard by whaler. The boat was deserted but settling slowly from leaks that could not be stopped. Working quickly, the boarders removed an Enigma machine and full current documentation, together with a mass of booty that included Lemp's *Ritterkreuz*. Lemp and fourteen of his crew had died and the *U-110* herself sank under tow but the ransacking was successfully kept secret from the survivors.

Inadequate numbers of escorts were still not exacting any great toll of the enemy's U-boat strength when, in March 1941, they sank five in the North Atlantic. Of these, three were commanded by 'ace' skippers.

Early in the month the westbound OB.293, of thirty-seven ships, was located by Prien, whose signals brought in four other boats. The convoy had four escorts, two veteran 'V&Ws', *Wolverine* and *Verity*, and the new corvettes *Arbutus* and *Camellia*.

In the course of the first attack, the *U-70* was badly damaged when spotted by a Dutch tanker and overrun at periscope depth. The contact was followed up by the corvettes which, with great persistence, expended fifty-four depth charges in her destruction.

At the same time, however, Prien in *U-47* and Kretschmer in *U-99* were active, the latter adding 27,200 GRT to his score with the destruction of the Norwegian whale factory ship *Terje Viken* and the British tanker *Athelbeach*. Prien made no score and, indeed, was not heard of again. The two destroyers had depth charged various contacts but had quickly to move on. One such attack had accounted for the much-vaunted Bull of Scapa.

Barely a week later, on 17 March 1941, HX.112 was brought under attack in very thick weather. Among the several boats involved were Kretschmer's *U-99* and Schepke's *U-100*. With his accustomed boldness, the former ran surfaced to the centre of the convoy and, pumping out his last eight torpedoes, hit six different ships, of which five sank. Spotted by the old destroyer *Walker*, leader of EG5, Kretschmer submerged but was promptly brought up again by six depth charges. Brought under fire by *Walker* and *Vanoc*, *U-99* was scuttled, her skipper spending the remainder of the war a prisoner.

The *Walker* also located Schepke but, called away, left him to the *Vanoc*. With several small patterns, this destroyer sent the *U-100* down to an unprecedented depth of 230 metres. Out of control, Schepke managed to bring his boat to the surface, only to be betrayed by the *Vanoc*'s primitive radar. Without hesitation, the destroyer rammed, killing Schepke on his own bridge. Only six of his crew survived.

Between them, Kretschmer, Prien and Schepke had destroyed 112 ships, aggregating over 605,000 GRT and their removal put great heart into the escort forces.

With their poor performance, the surviving four British 'R'-class battleships could not be considered front-line units. In addition, the *Malaya* and *Barham* had never received the full moderniz-ation of the other three Queen Elizabeths. Less the *Barham*, active in the Mediterranean, this pool of elderly heavyweights found useful employment in supporting special operations and in accompanying ocean convoys. In the latter role their presence deterred any enemy raider, none of which could risk damage.

During March 1941, for instance, the *Scharnhorst* and *Gneisenau* closed the fifty-four-ship SL.67, northbound off West Africa. Two U-boats were in support but, although these destroyed five merchantmen, they were unable to get at the battle-ship *Malaya*, obliging the German capital ships to change their plans.

Concern at shipping losses led Churchill to give the war against the U-boat the highest priority. In his 'Battle of the Atlantic' direc-tive of 6 March 1941 he ordered an offensive against 'the U-boat and the Focke-Wulf . . . at sea . . . in the building yard or in dock . . . in the air and in their nests'. This implied Bomber Command's diversion of considerable resources from its main task of striking at the enemy's industrial capacity. Involvement in the war at sea was, understandably, seen as a secondary role by the RAF and resisted.

Knowing well that the British would not underestimate the value of French bases to his efforts, Dönitz took measures to protect both boats and crews. As, between patrols, U-boats underwent intensive repair and maintenance, their officers and crews relaxed in considerable luxury, remote from the bases.

With its limitless resources of enforced labour, the *Todt Organisation* began the construction of enormous bomb-proof pens at each base. Within, U-boats could be berthed in cells, docked or afloat, refitting secure from any bomb. An early type of such a facility had been erected at Bruges during the earlier war and, with hindsight, repetition could have been anticipated. Preliminaries involved huge excavations and foundation-laying behind watertight caissons. For months, therefore, the work was highly vulnerable to bombing yet, although aerial reconnaissance laid bare the enemy's purpose, the opportunity was allowed to pass. The Air Ministry was pre-occupied with Germany and the Admiralty with a powerful enemy surface squadron at Brest. Over 1,000 sorties were directed at the latter, ten times the effort aimed at the U-boat bases. The Admiralty had definitely got its priorities wrong: within eighteen months the massive roofs were in place and the monoliths virtually impregnable. Until the very end of the war, bombing of U-boat construction facilities was also singularly unproductive.

Churchill's 'Focke-Wulf', the FW200 Kondor, had much the same effect on the Royal Navy as had the Zeppelin in the earlier war. Covering a swathe from Bordeaux to Stavanger, its main task was to locate convoys, with the diversion of picking-off any straggler or independent. Its presence was loathed and feared, generating an active response.

For Dönitz, however, the aircraft were always in short supply, despite the transfer to his command in January 1941 of the specialist maritime reconnaissance unit KG40. Its FW200s were intended as a stopgap pending the arrival of the more suitable Heinkel He177. This, however, was regarded as a failure and the menace of the Kondor had faded by the end of the year.

In practice, the aircraft's availability was low and, even if carrying no bomb load, its endurance rarely allowed it to dally around a located convoy. Submarines often, therefore, had to seek a convoy on the basis of a single sighting report. As, following a protracted over-sea flight, navigational errors of eighty miles were not uncommon and a convoy, observing a 'snooper', might make a radical change of course, it is not surprising that many an intended interception failed to connect.

The threat of the Kondor did, however, have the far-reaching consequence of the urgent development of the auxiliary aircraft carrier. The prime minister ordered 'extreme priority' be given to the fitting-out of ships capable of catapulting or otherwise launching defensive fighter aircraft.

The first such stopgap was the Catapult Aircraft Merchant

(CAM) Ships, of which thirty-five were converted and thirteen sunk. All retained their cargo capacity but were fitted with a catapult, usually paralleling the port side of No.1 hatch and extending over the forecastle. On the catapult, an early mark of Hurricane or Fulmar fighter sat on its launching trolley in all weathers until 'scrambled' to pursue a snooper. Following an engagement the fighter rarely had fuel sufficient to reach an airfield ashore, being obliged to 'ditch' alongside a friendly ship. The procedure closely paralleled that of the First World War.

Only a handful of kills were credited to CAM pilots but their deterrent value was considerable. The first CAM ship entered service in May 1941, the Red Ensign units being supplemented by four naval-manned Fighter Catapult Ships, which were primarily auxiliary anti-aircraft ships.

The real need, of course, was for ships with flight decks. Pre-war plans existed for the conversion of diesel-driven passenger liners to carriers, but these proved to be too elaborate and the ships were required equally urgently as troop carriers.

In March 1940, off the coast of the Dominican Republic, the Hamburg-Amerika ship *Hannover* was captured by the British cruiser *Dunedin* and Canadian destroyer *Assiniboine*. Heavily fire-damaged, the ship had the distinction of being the first to be reconstructed as an auxiliary carrier, for which role she was completed in July 1941 as HMS *Audacity*. In parallel, the British ordered six roughly similar conversions from American yards. Where the *Audacity* had no hangar, the American ships could strike their aircraft below. The first of them, HMS *Archer*, commissioned in November 1941. Apparently independently, a programme of these 'escort carriers' had been commenced for the US Navy also.

A variation on the escort carrier was the Merchant Aircraft Carrier, or MAC. These differed in retaining their mercantile status and ability to load the better part of a full cargo of grain or oil, both of which bulk commodities could be handled by hose. Six grain and thirteen oil carriers were thus converted but the first did not enter service until April 1943. The former incorporated a small hangar while the latter, several of which wore the Dutch flag, had none.

The *Audacity*'s career was to be short but she would prove

beyond doubt the value of the escort carrier. She carried only six aircraft, either all fighters (American-built Wildcats, known as Martlets in British service) or four fighters and two AS Swordfish.

On 20 September 1941, she was accompanying her first convoy, the Gibraltar-bound OG.74, when two U-boats made contact. These sank two ships during the night and, with daylight, Kondors arrived, one sinking a ship engaged in rescuing survivors. *Audacity*'s fighters shot down one Kondor and strafed a trailing U-boat, causing it to dive.

Three more ships were torpedoed and sunk during the next night but, again with the dawn, carrier fighters cooperated with the AS escorts to keep U-boats at a safe distance.

A few weeks later the *Audacity* was part of the escort covering the northbound HG.76, whose AS ships were those of the redoubtable Commander F.J. Walker's EG.36. Again the carrier's aircraft made the enemy continually dive, losing contact with the convoy, although actual sinkings were left to Walker's ships which, in fine form, destroyed three. The *Audacity* lost one Martlet in a strafing run but others disposed of two Kondors.

Although the new Snowflake illuminant improved the escorts' chances of seeing a surfaced U-boat in a convoy, it also silhouetted potential targets for the attackers. The *U-571* was thus given a clear shot at the *Audacity*, hitting her with three torpedoes. Without the effective sub-division of a regular warship, she sank rapidly. In searching for the culprit, Walker exacted a high price in return, for he destroyed not the *U-571* but the *U-567*, whose skipper was Endrass. Credited with a score of 138,000 GRT Endrass had been one of a diminishing band of *Ritterkreuz* holders.

Dönitz was dismayed at the outcome, for only two merchantmen had been sunk and he had not appreciated the full significance of the *U-571*'s action report.

Throughout 1941 the overall loss of merchant shipping in the North Atlantic and in British waters averaged about eight-three ships, totalling 300,000 GRT each month. At any given time, a further 1.9 million GRT (a figure which remained remarkably constant) was out of action, awaiting repair. Strenuous efforts to speed-up turnround times in British ports had met with some success but ships with bulk cargoes still averaged 12.5 days, and break-bulkers, i.e. those with general cargoes, eighteen days. Ships engaged in the North Atlantic run averaged 122 days for a complete cycle, thus making only three voyages a year, even without taking maintenance downtime into account.

Domestic ship-building could produce only some 1.5 million GRT of new construction annually and, with future large-scale military operations planned, an increasing tonnage shortfall was anticipated. This required to be addressed urgently.

It was, therefore, fortunate that in 1936, concerned about the deteriorating international situation and the generally run-down condition of their own merchant marine, the Americans had set up the United States Maritime Commission (USMC). This organization was, in 1937, charged with the effective replacement of the existing domestic fleet at the rate of fifty ships per annum. The ships would be passed to owners at advantageous rates and would be of four baseline designs, one tanker and three dry cargo. Contracts were placed for the first 100 ships of the eventual total of about 500, which would represent some 4 million GRT.

American shipyards responded rapidly to the prospect of modernization and guaranteed orders and, with Europe's descent into war, the USMC was able to double its target figure and, during 1940, to double it again.

It was against this background that a British mission arrived in the United States in October 1940 to identify suitable yards, there and in Canada, for the construction of eighty-six ships to an uncomplicated standard design capable of loading about 10,000 deadweight tons (dwt). A prototype, named *Empire Liberty*, was already under construction in Sunderland but would not be completed for another year.

Contracting for sixty ships in the United States and a further twenty-six in Canada, the British also financed new facilities for their construction. So commenced an enterprise that would eventually produce ships in their thousands.

Because of their less-developed technologies, the Canadians built in much the British fashion with framed erection and rivetted construction. The Americans, seizing the chance offered by new facilities, adopted the new techniques of all-welded structures, assembling ships from a number of prefabricated modules.

Quickly dubbed the 'Liberty Fleet', its individual vessels became known as Liberty ships although, strictly, this applied only to the so-called EC-2 design of which the first, *Patrick Henry*, was launched in September 1941.

Precipitated into war, Admiral Raeder had to scrap his Z-plan, now hopelessly beyond reach. A new Mobilization Programme gave priority to destroyers, torpedo boats, minesweepers and submarines. For the last-named an annual target of 108 was set, comprising twenty-four Type IXC, forty-eight Type VIIC and thirty-six Type IID. This nowhere near met Dönitz' requirement for a 300-boat fleet, to be maintained against an anticipated annual loss rate of 5 per cent.

The programme was thus quickly revamped to give greater priority to submarine construction. With the involvement of fourteen yards, and increasing the estimated annual loss rate to 10 per cent, it was hoped to reach a strength of 210 boats by the end of 1941, and the required 300 by the spring of 1943.

In practice, fewer boats were being lost than anticipated and overall numbers rose quickly. The total of actual operational boats was increasing more slowly, however, as the period of training and working up had to be considerably extended.

The great programme also encountered further difficulties. The severe winter of 1939–40 greatly affected open-air construction, although a growing shortage of materials was alleviated by the discovery of stockpiles in occupied France. The French collapse also permitted the release of skilled personnel from the German army, although the expansion of U-boat construction resulted in some production bottlenecks, notably in torpedo tubes.

Any flow of skills from the army was, however, quickly stemmed by the need to further expand that force following the Führer's decision to attack the Soviet Union. This disastrous strategic move was compounded by his rating it as a higher priority than the defeat of the United Kingdom. The blow finally landed in June 1941 and Dönitz once again found himself competing for resources.

He resurrected an earlier proposal for a new type of submarine for the re-supply of other boats to extend their cruises. Incorporating many components from the other standard classes, the Type XIV was popularly known as the '*Milch Kuh*'. Its main function was to assist operational boats that were low on fuel, for which service it carried 342 tons. With no torpedo armament of its own, a Type XIV carried four spares, difficulties in storage and transfer precluding more.

Only two dozen of these useful craft were ever ordered. Their operation inevitably generated radio traffic and the British ability to read much of it enabled both supplier and supplied to be targeted.

The Type VIIC was also improved. Experience showed that U-boats could often escape retribution by diving deeply to their 200-metre theoretical collapse depth. Depth charges took a considerable time to sink this far, while varying temperature and salinity layers made the escort's Asdic unreliable. Rigorous weight-paring made possible the strengthening of the pressure hull without increase in overall weight or dimensions, permitting a 300-metre collapse depth. This upgrade, also given an improved bow section to cope with surfaced conditions in the Atlantic, was termed the Type VIIC/41.

With increasing air activity around convoys, U-boats were also required to be faster, so as to spend less time on the surface gaining favourable attack positions. Escorts were also becoming noticeably more efficient, making a 500-metre capability desirable. More installed power and thicker pressure hulls of super-grade steel inevitably increased weight, demanding greater dimensions to compensate. A combination of Atlantic conditions and the danger from aircraft had combined to make a deck gun almost unusable and, to save weight, it was now omitted. The small dimensional increase allowed for a 30 per cent greater bunker capacity, extending the theoretical endurance to 10,000 miles at 12 knots. This second significant upgrade was known as the Type VIIC/42.

The signing of the Lend-Lease agreement in March 1941 marked also an increased American interest in the North Atlantic. Bases and garrisons appeared in Bermuda, Newfoundland, Greenland and Iceland, countered by the Germans' announcing of an extension to their War Zone to include waters around Greenland and Iceland.

Continuous AS escort for the more valuable, eastbound HX and SC convoys was now possible with some improvisation.

Canadian groups would shepherd a convoy to the so-called Mid-Ocean Meeting Point (MOMP) at about 35 degrees west. Here an Iceland-based British force would take over and cover as far as 18 degrees west. At this, the East-Ocean Meeting Point (EOMP), the responsibility passed to a Western Approaches group, which brought it to Scottish waters. Here, usually at Loch Ewe, ships bound for east coast ports were separated out and attached to the next northabout coastal movement under local escort.

Canadian groups returning from the MOMP would, wherever possible, do so having linked with a westbound OB convoy. A continuing escort shortage meant, however, that many such convoys had no cover in the western Atlantic. Improving AS measures on the eastern side was forcing U-boat activity ever further westward, so that dispersing, unescorted OBs offered easy pickings. Heavy losses in May 1941 led to the enforced provision of continuous escort. (It was in attacking OB.318 that the *U-100* ran foul of a British escort group with the results related earlier.)

Dönitz was now receiving many complaints, in the course of de-briefings, that escorts were making skippers' lives considerably more difficult. Given the admiral's single-mindedness, it spoke volumes that he now made escorts the primary target.

In August 1941, Prime Minister Churchill and President Roosevelt met secretly in Newfoundland. The main outcome was the woolly and idealistic joint declaration known as the Atlantic Charter but, more importantly for the course of events in the Atlantic itself, the US Navy assumed the role of convoy escort as far as the MOMP, the meridian of which was also moved eastward to 22 degrees west. By this new arrangement, Canadian groups would take HX convoys to a Western Ocean Meeting Point (WOMP) south of Newfoundland. From here, longer-ranged American destroyers would screen it as far as the MOMP. This was now situated sufficiently far east to allow Western Approaches groups to take over without having to divert to Iceland to refuel.

For the slow, eastbound SC convoys the existing arrangements between the British and Canadians were retained, but the scale of American assistance allowed the Royal Navy to release three escort groups to reinforce the inadequately-protected Gibraltar and Freetown convoys.

On 4 September 1941, even before the new arrangements took effect, the American destroyer *Greer*, en route to Iceland, was warned of a U-boat in the vicinity by a British patrol aircraft, which helpfully indicated the approximate position with depth charges. Behaving very un-neutrally the *Greer* obtained a sonar contact and harassed the submarine, *U-652*, for about three hours, during which period two torpedoes and several depth charge patterns were exchanged, with no result. In view of the American's rather ambiguous rules of engagement, it is not surprising that she acted less than decisively but her report drew a typically tart criticism from the acerbic commander of the US Atlantic Fleet, Admiral Ernest J. King. The incident did, however, give the President the opportunity to condemn an 'act of piracy' and to move hostility up one notch by ordering that, in future, American ships should fire first.

Admirals Raeder and Dönitz responded by unsuccessfully urging Hitler to extend the declared War Zone into Canadian and American waters.

On 16 September the Americans took up their new duties with the uneventful passage of HX.150. If this raised doubts about the dangers of working in the North Atlantic, these were dispelled when, on the night of 16–17 October, SC.48 was savaged. As tracking reports from *U-553* attracted nine other boats, Enigma intercepts warned the British that an assault was developing. In a 'fire brigade' response, reinforcements were diverted from other convoys. Although the resulting escort was numerically adequate, it comprised American, British, Canadian and French vessels which had had no opportunity to work together. Their cover was determined but lacked cohesion, resulting in the loss of nine of the convoy's ships, the corvette *Gladiolus* and the ex-American four-stacker *Broadwater*. The new American destroyer *Kearny* managed to survive severe torpedo damage.

If the US Neutrality Acts were already diluted, they became an effective dead letter when HX.156, escorted by five American destroyers, was attacked by *U-552* on 31 October. No merchantmen were lost but a torpedo broke the veteran destroyer *Reuben James* in two. She disappeared with the loss of 115 of her crew.

*   *   *

The Coastal Command of the RAF, which was eventually to prove such a potent obstacle to Dönitz' plans, enjoyed a painfully slow expansion. Until early in 1941, invasion was the primary threat to the nation. In denying the Luftwaffe the necessary air supremacy for such an undertaking, Fighter Command took an indisputable top priority. Bomber Command, with its deeply ingrained strategic bombing theories, could equally claim that it alone could strike directly at the enemy, reducing his capacity to continue the war through the destruction of his industrial base and the morale of his populace.

In July 1940, as Dönitz' boats extended their range by beginning operations from Biscay bases, Coastal Command had 500 aircraft, but only thirty-four of them were Sunderlands, capable of operation beyond a 500-mile radius. The enemy increasingly operated at the fringe of these limits.

Further to the all-important anti-invasion patrols, there were others to watch for attempted breakout by raiders, and the establishment of an AS reconnaissance line running north-westward from Cape Wrath. Patrols were gradually set up on a regular basis from Iceland, and then from Freetown, the busy southern terminal of the SL convoys.

For nearly two years, poorly equipped and lacking experience, Coastal Command spent thousands of hours patrolling, seeing U-boats aplenty but sinking none except in support of surface AS escorts. Then, on 27 August 1940, they captured one. With what appeared to be the most incompetent crew that ever sailed, the *U-570*, a Type VIIC, surfaced south of Iceland almost beneath a patrolling Hudson. Four shallow-set depth charges caused extensive superficial damage and created panic. With the boat unable to dive, the aircraft kept the crew below with strafing runs until further aircraft and, eventually, the Navy arrived. With some difficulty, the *U-570* was recovered and repaired. Although all sensitive material had been destroyed, the boat provided valuable operational data when re-commissioned with a Royal Navy crew.

Slowly, Coastal Command accumulated new aircraft – Sunderlands and Catalinas, Beaufort torpedo bombers, Blenheims and the new Beaufighter. As Bomber Command expanded its four-engined, heavy bomber fleet, it passed down some still-useful twin-engined aircraft – Hampdens, Whitleys and the versatile Wellington.

The useless AS bombs had been superseded by depth charges, modified for air drop but yet lacking a reliable ultra-shallow fuse. As U-boats were usually attacked while on or near the surface, this was an urgent requirement. To evaluate new weapons and to establish correct attack procedures a Development Unit was created.

Although the ASV Mark II, the first practical air-to-surface radar set, was introduced in August 1940, Bomber Command took first priority. When the development of the magnetron oscillator then facilitated a high-power centimetric radar, the discovery was shared with the Americans, who began production of sets with trainable antenna but small enough to be airborne. For these, Coastal Command's priorities ranked below those of the night fighters of Fighter Command.

Radar gave an aircraft the ability to surprise the U-boat, surfaced at night to recharge batteries and to refresh on-board air. Unfortunately, like Asdic-equipped ships, the aircraft was 'blind' over the very last stage of the approach, as the synchronously-switched transmitter and receiver units could not cope with near-simultaneous returns.

The solution was the brilliantly simple 'Leigh Light', a 24-inch naval projector mounted in a turret ring and controlled by the standard gun mounting servo system. When trials began in March 1941, a Wellington was required to accommodate the associated generator, but later variants were powered from a bank of trickle-charged accumulators. Entry into service of a device so important was inexcusably slow, it seeing action for the first time in June 1942.

From the middle of 1941, U-boats commissioned at an increasing rate while mercantile losses fell off considerably. This false dawn led to demands that Coastal Command's heavier aircraft be diverted to assist in Bomber Command operations. But this was to ignore that these same aircraft were a major reason for the improvement. Air cover extended some 700 miles westward from the British Isles, 600 miles eastward from Canada and 400 miles southward from Iceland. Within these limits, surfaced U-boat skippers found that they could be caught with little warning. Around the fringes life was safer, for the longer-range aircraft remained scarce and could not dally so far from base. The U-boats correspondingly congregated in what was known as the Gap, an aircraft-free zone, several hundred miles in width, occupying the central one-third of a line drawn from Iceland to Newfoundland. The Admiralty's Submarine Tracking Room thus sought to use intelligence to direct convoys in a great northerly arc, to avoid known submarine concentrations and to remain a maximum time within the limits of air cover.

Noting the decrease in interceptions, Dönitz initiated the first of several inconclusive enquiries to establish whether naval codes had been compromised, how to reduce the number of radio transmissions and to evaluate the accuracy of the known British D/F system.

By the end of 1941 a first Coastal Command squadron was converting to the American-built B-24 Liberator. This aircraft proved vulnerable as a daylight bomber over the Continent but was remarkably successful when converted for long-range maritime patrol duties, being well able to cover the Gap.

As the Bay of Biscay had to be traversed by every U-boat leaving or returning to its French base, it was divided into sectors by Coastal Command. These sectors reached down to Spanish coastal limits and each was covered in a planned patrol programme. Submarines increasingly had to submerge during daylight hours, slowing their progress and reducing their endurance.

Lest the enemy infer that Naval Enigma had been compromised, the British were unable to act on all such intelligence. From March 1941, however, it was apparent that the enemy was building a network of supply ships to extend U-boat endurance in the Central and South Atlantic. This was an important development and it was decided to nip it out. Cruisers rounded up seven such ships and, as a bonus, intercepted and destroyed the successful, homeward-bound raider *Atlantis*. This scale of loss convinced Dönitz that the British were acting on intelligence but an investigation proved nothing regarding its origin. The Admiral decided that only Type XIV supply boats could be used in future.

The diagrams (see pages 222–5) summarize the enemy's war against commerce until the end of year 1941; what might be termed the 'opening phase'.

Perhaps the most notable feature of Diagram 3 is the low rate of U-boats destroyed compared with new construction once the German programmes got into their stride. This had much to do with the insufficiency of Royal Navy AS escort ships, and that insufficiency with the unsuitability of the Hunt-class destroyer as an ocean escort, due to its poor endurance and, in early cases, to questionable stability. Although the Hunts proved effective in the Mediterranean and in home waters, their absence in the Atlantic caused the corvettes to shoulder the burden until alternatives became available.

Not designed as ocean escorts the Flowers, too, were short-legged and the low number of U-boats destroyed in this first phase reflects the fact that many simply operated beyond early escort limits.

Dönitz, in turn, suffered from too few boats (note that the number of operational U-boats was always considerably less than the total number) and an efficient British intelligence system that routed convoys clear of many ambushes. The timely arrival of the convoy was the highest British priority but the debit side was that the convoy was effectively the lure for U-boats and, if these were successfully evaded, then the escorts were also denied the opportunity to attack them, a further factor in keeping their loss rate low.

Despite severe losses, amounting so far to about 9.1 million GRT, the situation regarding cargo capacity engendered cautious optimism at the end of 1941. As Diagram 1 shows, the overruning of Norway, Denmark, the Netherlands and France between April and June 1940 resulted in much of their considerable tonnage coming under British control. This latter total actually stood at some 3 million GRT more than when the war began, a figure boosted further by purchase, new building and the seizure of many enemy vessels.

From June 1941 Germany's unwise assault on the Soviet Union diverted resources from the vital Atlantic battle, while their military campaign in North Africa, undertaken originally to underpin the shortcomings of their Italian allies, had developed to demand a concentration of U-boats, to Dönitz' displeasure. These had a devastating impact on the hitherto successful activities of the British Mediterranean Fleet, but their absence from the Atlantic contributed to the considerable drop in sinkings.

Chapter Four

Drumroll.
The Dark before the Dawn (1942)

Commonly viewed as craven appeasement to the dictatorships, the manoeuvrings of British politicians from Munich onwards had much to do with the urgent buying of time; time for rearming and rectifying the sins of omission of the blinkered lotus years.

The United States understandably had no wish to be involved in a further European fracas but it came as a profound shock when, in 1940, continental Europe collapsed so readily in the face of determined military aggression. With the United Kingdom also on the verge of invasion and subjugation, it came to responsible Americans that isolationalism in the face of such naked evil would be insupportable to the national conscience.

Already aware of the distant but growing threat from Japan, President Roosevelt embarked on his 'short of war' policy to keep Britain fighting and to buy time for American rearmament. In June 1940, Congress approved a 4 billion dollar expansion to the US Navy, to fit it for a 'two-ocean' war. From this, little real result could be expected within two years and, meanwhile, the first line of defence was the prevention of a British defeat. Such support would bypass all conventional rules of neutrality but the President adopted the robust viewpoint that Germany had already violated the neutrality of European states and could have no grounds for complaint. He gambled that Hitler would rage but stop short of declaring war because of it.

With the passing of the Lend-Lease Act of March 1941, Roosevelt declared 'the end of compromise with tyranny and the forces of oppression'. It was such a powerful statement of support for the beleaguered British that Hitler was moved, not to declare war, but to order the avoidance of any provocation that might bring the United States into the fray. His misgivings were not unrelated to his intention to attack the Soviet Union, a partner in alliance, in June 1941. Despite American distaste for Stalin's politics, Lend-Lease was then extended to assist the Russians.

Still the Germans did not respond, even when, in July 1941, a brigade of US Marines landed in Iceland to assume from the British its defence and to prepare facilities for American destroyers now engaged in the escort of Atlantic convoys.

Both the CNO, Admiral Harold R. Stark, and the US Atlantic Fleet's C.-in-C., Admiral Ernest J. King, were concerned at the general shortage of AS escorts. As, earlier, in the Royal Navy, it was considered a job for destroyers, with three divisions already detached to form the Newfoundland Support Force. Besides requiring the usual large number for fleet duties, King rightly insisted on powerfully escorting troop convoys, which carried highest priority. The resulting shortfall inevitably generated criticism at the President's earlier decision to transfer fifty veteran destroyers to Britain although, for the most part, it was in the Atlantic battle that they were already being employed.

With the urgent requirement to create a 'two-ocean-navy' there was a danger that less glamorous AS escorts might enjoy low priority. This was especially likely with the Navy's known preference for large, powerful ships, but destroyers took too long to build and were, simply, over-complex and too expensive for what was required. The President, one-time Secretary of the Navy, favoured large numbers of small craft but the admirals well understood the limitations of these so-called 'sub-chasers', good only for coastal waters and requiring more capable craft to complement them in deep-sea operations. A degree of presidential intransigence overcome, the final programme comprised a mix of 174-feet PCs (Patrol Craft, Steel Hull), 111-feet SCs (Submarine Chasers, Wooden Hull) and, what the fleet really wanted, 300-feet DEs (Destroyer Escorts). The last-named, of which hundreds would eventually be built, originated in a Lend-Lease order placed by the British in June 1941.

Because of the inadequacies of the corvettes, the Royal Navy had hurried an order for twenty-seven larger vessels from domestic yards under the 1940 Programme. Length is an important parameter in seakeeping and these new 'twin-screw corvettes' would be 301.5 feet overall compared with the Flowers' 268 feet. Also faster, these River-class ships were, from 1942, reclassified as frigates. Their extra length decreased the number of yards that could build them and, as numbers were still urgently required, Flowers continued to be constructed, later partly superseded by an improved Castle class.

It was the need for numbers that led to the British Lend-Lease order. A 20-knot speed was specified but where, due to production limitations, triple-expansion engines were fitted in many Rivers, the Americans employed four types of machinery fit. They were allowed a free hand with the design, which resembled a diminutive fleet destroyer. There was also an understanding that the Americans would retain the ships should the need arise. This they did in many cases, with neither fleet benefiting from DE deliveries until early in 1943.

The situation for the US Navy late in 1941 was not unlike that for the Germans in 1939, with the fleet's deficiencies awaiting solution through the realization of a massive construction programme that had, as yet, borne little fruit. Despite his own lack of suitable escorts, Admiral King predictably did not approve the British way of running convoys. The latter, their resources stretched paper-thin, operated with the benefit of experience, a strategy that statistics showed was working. King, however, disliked evasive routing, espousing a policy of streaming straight through, protected by an escort powerful enough to brush aside all opposition. The approach is interesting in almost exactly paralleling that of the US Eighth Air Force, vis-à-vis that of British Bomber Command, in the bombing offensive against Germany. But, as the air force had to await suitable aircraft, so King had to await the maturation of his own programme.

American policy was in accordance with Admiral Stark's Plan Dog, whereby the United States risked war with Germany, through overt support for the United Kingdom, while adopting a defensive stance in the Pacific. In that theatre the objective was to avoid provocation of the Japanese while maintaining a defence powerful enough to deter any Japanese adventurism.

That the deterrence was not credible was demonstrated on 7 December 1941 with the bold Japanese initiative against Pearl Harbor. Not being in formal alliance, Germany was equally surprised by the Japanese action but, following some agonizing, Hitler joined Japan by formally declaring war on the United States on 11 December.

The waters off the United States' eastern seaboard teemed with shipping, domestic traffic swollen by many deep sea vessels proceeding to and from convoy assembly and dispersal points. Dönitz had long badgered his leader to allow him to punish the Americans' unneutral behaviour by extending the declared War Zone to include their waters. Until now, the political consequences had been too daunting and the requests refused. Now, surprised by events, he needed to react rapidly.

His major problem was one of distance as, even from French bases, his boats were 3,000 miles from New York and 4,000 from Florida. His more numerous Type VIICs would be able to operate, unreplenished, only briefly off Nova Scotia and only the larger Type IXs had the endurance necessary for making the long return trip viable. Obviously, the new Type XIV re-supply boats would be of critical importance but the first two, *U-459* and *U-460*, were newly completed and not yet operational.

Dönitz also had a problem with availability. U-boats were being completed at an increasing rate but, mainly because of the need for intensive training and work-up, many fewer were actually operational. Just twenty Type IXs were available, of which only eleven were IXC variants with an improved theoretical range of 11,000 miles at 12 knots.

At an earlier Führer conference, Dönitz had anticipated events by explaining that, given sufficient warning, he would have a force ready to deliver what he termed '*einen kräftigen Paukenschlag*', a mighty drumroll presaging the entry of the full orchestra. Unfortunately, a number of his boats had been diverted, against his will, to support the military campaign in the Mediterranean. '*Paukenschlag*' as a result, took frustratingly long to initiate.

Only on 2 January 1942, over three weeks after the declaration of war, were six Type IXs, also destined for the Mediterranean, directed westward. Despite the obvious opportunity, higher authority held back six more to operate in the Gibraltar area. Seven Type VIICs, around or bound for the Azores were, however, also diverted to the United States.

The British Admiralty's Submarine Tracking Room was alive to the enemy's moves, if not his intentions. A single U-boat was noted as travelling considerable distances around the North Atlantic, transmitting on various frequencies to simulate a number of boats, probably three concentrations, with one positioned south-east of Newfoundland. A week later these groups were more exactly defined, with one of six boats near Cape Race and a second, of five boats, heading for the New York-Portland area, with an estimated arrival date of 13 January. Five further boats were detected as heading westward between longitudes 30 and 50 degrees W. This appreciation was shared with the US Navy.

Effective from 30 December 1941, Admiral King was appointed C.-in-C., US Fleet, giving him operational and adminstrative control of the Atlantic and Pacific fleets, together with the US Coast Guard. Within three months he would also have assumed the role of CNO, the first time in history that both posts were occupied by the same person.

King's jurisdiction extended also to the naval commands responsible for the nation's offshore waters. From the Canadian border south to Lake Maracaibo these were divided into four 'Sea Frontiers', respectively the Eastern, the Gulf, the Caribbean and the Panama.

Of these, the Eastern Sea Frontier was the most important, yet its senior officer, Rear Admiral Adolphus Andrews, had no warships under his permanent command. In the event of an attack, Andrews was dependent upon the Atlantic Fleet, but had used foresight in organizing an eclectic patrol force of some twenty craft whose only effective units, however, were one medium and six small Craft Guard cutters and four SCs.

The US Navy accepted that ships and aircraft were a more potent AS force when acting together than when operating separately, despite which Andrews also had no aircraft. King's requests for the loan of a force, to be manned by naval personnel tasked specifically with 'patrol, convoy and AS operations', met with obfuscation and foot-dragging. Inter-service friction and poor personal relationships between the irascible King and his peers contributed to the tragedy that was about to unfold, a situation from which the President decided to stand aside.

As part of its overall control of shipping, the British Admiralty maintained a worldwide network of Naval Control Service offices. Through the American office and their Naval Mission in Washington, the British were able to offer much useful advice born of long experience.

The mission would shortly be headed by Admiral Sir Andrew Cunningham, until recently C.-in-C. Mediterranean Fleet and indisputably Britain's finest naval commander of the period. Even he, however, found himself being reminded by King that, where the British had been managing world affairs for three hundred years, the US Navy now had something to say, palatable or not. King agreed that convoys were the best means of fighting U-boats but maintained, wrongly, that weakly-escorted convoys were worse than no convoys. As he lacked sufficient escorts, and coastwise convoys lacked the 'invisibility' of their deep sea counterparts, no immediate plans existed for them.

For whatever reasons, the Americans were, to quote their own historian, 'woefully unprepared, materially and mentally, for the U-boat blitz [shortly to be launched] on the Atlantic coast'. That there were no plans for the protection of merchant shipping, and that it then took several months to improve them, were due to 'unpreparedness [which] was largely the Navy's own fault'.

Operation *Paukenschlag* opened on 13 January 1942 with just five Type IXs operating between New York and Cape Hatteras. Seven Type VIICs were also grouped off Newfoundland, but were not part of the main operation.

The crews of the latter had endured considerable discomfort in embarking all possible fuel and stores, but arrived in a season of furious storms, bitter cold and fog. Although the boats had excellent hydrophone arrays, they lacked surface radar, and the fog greatly restricted their chance of attack. When surfaced, the boats were endangered by the intensity of the cold, which froze machinery such as engine exhaust valves. To this were added continuing torpedo problems and experienced Canadian AS forces. Results were not encouraging.

For the *Paukenschlag* boats, things were much different.

Following five weeks to anticipate such an attack, the defence was expected to be brisk, if inexperienced. Skippers were apprehensive that, with the continental shelf waters being wide and shallow, they would have to operate the big Type IXs in perhaps twenty fathoms, where a minimum of fifty was advisable. Only around Hatteras did deep water lie close to the coast and, with the Cape being a notable waypoint, the area became a favoured billet with boats lying submerged by day and moving inshore by night.

While on passage westward, the skippers had been under orders not to advertise their presence. On 12 January Reinhard Hardegen in the *U-123* defied instructions by sinking the British Blue Funneler *Cyclops* some 100 miles off Cape Sable. Then, for maximum effect, he approached New York and, in the small hours of the 14th, destroyed the Panamanian tanker *Norness* off Long Island. Like the *Cyclops*, she had been fully loaded and sailing independently.

Having laid low for the day, Hardegen dispatched the British tanker *Coimbra* on the following night. Expecting countermeasures, he then made southward for Hatteras, where he sank eight ships in twelve hours.

To his disbelief, there *were* no countermeasures. Navigational lights were dimmed but still obvious; many ships were fully lit. Despite warnings of U-boat activity, many ships still made their usual landfall. Radio communication was unrestricted, its chatter betraying both target disposition and the ineffectual defence. Air patrols were sporadic, inadequately armed (if at all) and with aircrews untrained in AS operations. So confident did Hardegen become that he conserved his torpedoes by using his deck gun close inshore, establishing his victims' identity by spotlight.

Returning safely, Hardegen claimed to have sunk ten ships, totally 66,000 GRT. Although this was some 30 per cent inflated, he received Admiral Raeder's warmest congratulations and a *Ritterkreuz* from an ecstatic Dönitz.

As two of the Type IXs decided to operate in Canadian waters, only three worked the more productive area farther south. Despite the teeming traffic here (Hardegen at one time reporting 'no fewer than twenty steamers' in sight) their score was not impressive. Postwar analysis credits the *U-123* with only four ships on the coast, seven in total. In addition the *U-66* sank five but the *U-125* only one.

Unusually, Japanese submarines were active at the same time off the western seaboard. Their success was of much the same order and led to the natural assumption that the two waves were coordinated, which they were not.

Despite their many problems, the Type VIICs sank eighteen ships in Canadian waters, with four more added by the two Type IXs. Operating at long range, fuel and torpedoes were generally quickly expended, obliging this first wave to return comparatively quickly. At no loss to themselves, they were credited with the destruction of 236,000 GRT, some of which was later salvaged. The sight of tankers blazing off the coast of New Jersey was more shocking to the population than images from a far-distant Pearl Harbor, and the massive outcry was predictable.

From their own slender resources, the British rallied to the Americans' defence with ten corvettes and two dozen AS trawlers. Technical missions offered advice when it was sought, particularly with respect to centralizing control of AS warfare and developing doctrines and weaponry.

Offsetting the limitations of existing organization and hardware, American electronic laboratories had made considerable progress in producing solutions to technical problems posed by earlier British requirements. The latter's prototype version of airborne centrimetric radar and shipborne high-frequency D/F ('Huff-Duff') sets had been engineered by the Americans to the point where both were about to go into quantity production. Although American depth-charges still contained out-moded TNT explosive and were limited to a 300-feet depth, research was well advanced on airborne magnetic anomaly detectors (MAD), expendable sonobuoys and air-dropped acoustic torpedoes.

By February 1942 the Americans had in place the organizational framework and had set up models of the Royal Navy's 'attack teacher'. In these, all aspirant AS escort commanders had first to qualify in a variety of simulated situations and under deliberately pressured conditions.

Even though they represented considerable sacrifice, the British escort contribution by no means solved King's problems. If he withdrew destroyers allocated to western Atlantic escort duties, it would throw a greater load on the still inadequate British and Canadian groups. Large numbers of American troops were also already being transported to the United Kingdom and their proper escort was King's highest priority. With escorts still too few, therefore, the CNO maintained his stance in not initiating a convoy system on the eastern seaboard.

When, finally, Army Air Force assistance was offered, there began a protracted dispute with naval air over how best to deploy it. The latter force well understood that convoys were the best means of attracting, detecting and sinking U-boats but the Army fell into the long discredited trap of proposing 'hunter-killer' squadrons, aggressively combing the seas in search of the enemy. The practical futility of this was lost on them and, for much of what would be an eight-month campaign, much available air support was misdirected.

Capitalizing on still-inadequate defences, Dönitz sailed his second wave during January 1942. In no sense concentrated, the 'wave' comprised twelve Type IXs and fourteen Type VIICs, departing in ones and twos over a space of four weeks.

Fortunately for the Allies, two British commando raids and, possibly, knowledge of a study commissioned by Churchill, had convinced Hitler that Norway would be invaded. This was never seriously contemplated as it ran counter to agreed Allied strategy, but the Führer ordered 'every available surface craft and U-boat' to Norway's defence.

Dönitz, trying to mount a maximum effort, was not pleased but, as his leader had expressed satisfaction with results so far off North America he was able, with some prevarication, to limit the number of boats affected to about sixteen. In spite of the bitterest Baltic winter of the century, he was still able to dispatch nine each Type IX and Type VIIC in February.

At about this juncture the Germans finally solved the problem of their deep-running torpedoes. Its correction reduced the number that needed to be fired and thus extended patrols, an advantage offset by the obvious fact that the defence was becoming more efficient. Reports mentioned shipping moving in informal groups, varying routes and using waters so shallow that U-boats had, on occasion, to attack in depths insufficient to permit submersion.

The British had been reading Naval Enigma so freely that it came as a major setback when, in January 1942, the enemy added a fourth rotor to all his machines. Theoretically, this increased the number of possible combinations by a factor of about ten and began a period of information 'black-out', with the OIC not able to evasively route convoys with its customary sure touch. Worse, the Germans had also broken the code common to American, British and Canadian escort forces.

American aircraft made their first U-boat kills when Hudsons sank a Type VIIC and a Type IXC on 1 and 15 March respectively. Both successes were, however, off Newfoundland. The first success further south was off Hatteras on the night of 13–14 April. Here the *U-85* was surprised by the radar-equipped four-stacker USS *Roper*. Surfaced in only sixteen fathoms of water, the boat had neither the time nor depth in which to submerge. Neither had she the speed to escape. Scuttling charges were blown but, as the crew scrambled clear, they were cut down by automatic fire. Such a procedure was sanctioned only to deter abandonment prior to boarding in search of intelligence material. This was retribution. As the submarine slid under she left half her crew in the water. These could have been rescued and the wreck searched at leisure by divers but the *Roper* exuberantly dumped a dozen depth charges on the spot. Over the next day, human remains were collected and at least a further half dozen valedictory depth charges dropped. No submarine was ever more sunk nor opportunity more wasted, for somewhere within that flattened hull was a desperately-needed Enigma machine and its associated documentation.

The *Roper*'s vengeful attack was undisciplined but understandable. Like so many others, she had spent weeks in fruitless patrolling and, more often, rescuing. In the shallow offshore waters, the gutted, broken hulls of many torpedoed tankers were marked for days by black columns of smoke. Slicks and charred débris surrounded them and rescue was limited too often to recovery of floating bodies and crewmen so badly burned that treatment seemed superfluous.

A fortnight earlier, the *Roper* had rescued survivors from the passenger ship *City of New York*, sunk by the *U-160* on

29 March. Some were too badly burned to be saved but the ship's doctor patched up those that could be patched up and even delivered a baby. The accumulated emotions of the men of the *Roper* mirrored those of hundreds of Allied crews, engendering an urge to repay those who could willingly spread carnage across peaceful waters for no good reason.

For their part, the U-boat skippers spoke contemptuously in their reports about the Americans' improvised defences and their obvious lack of training. This would not last, for the defenders had identified the dangerous choke points and were concentrating their assets. Following a careful debriefing of each returning commander, Dönitz curbed the earlier free-ranging in favour of allocating specific operational areas.

A large submarine hull, building to Turkish account, was taken over and converted as the first re-supply boat. Renamed simply *UA*, she appeared off the American coast during March 1942, a month ahead of the first purpose-built Type XIV, the *U-459*. The two were able to refuel seventeen operational boats, besides supplying spare parts, a little fresh food and some medical assistance.

During February 1942, U-boats sank seventy-one ships in the North Atlantic. Of these, sixty-five were independents sunk in United States coastal waters. In March the figures were worse, many of the ships being British, destroyed in waters where, to quote the Admiralty, 'the British writ does not run'.

By April the Americans had instituted their 'Bucket Brigade' system, whereby informal groups of ships travelled coastwise by day, escorted by any available means, but directed to a secure anchorage by night. This simple measure disrupted the U-boats' usual operating pattern of coming inshore and picking off targets silhouetted against the still-prolific shore lights.

Dönitz responded by shifting the centre of gravity of operations further south and exploiting a focal point discovered some 300 miles offshore. In the Command War Diary he noted that the defences had been stiffened, yet lacked concentration and fighting power, while their 'determination to attack and destroy [was] small'. He continued with a contemptuous 'those who fight are not sailors, but people who are being paid for their presence in the area endangered by U-boats'.

Moving southward, U-boats continued their second 'happy time' with no great interference. May saw forty-one ships, totalling nearly a ¼ million GRT, destroyed. Most were in the Gulf of Mexico and half the total comprised loaded tankers, urgently needed across the Atlantic but now so targeted that a temporary check was placed on them.

Further north, U-boats were now finding empty seas. The *U-352*, one of those replenished by the *U-459*, finally encountered a small Swedish tramp but failed to sink her with four faulty torpedoes. Next day, her frustrated skipper attacked a small Coast Guard cutter, the *Icarus*, while in very shallow water. One torpedo prematured, providing the *Icarus* with a useful attack datum. A couple of five-charge patterns later, the *U-352* broached, her crew abandoning, again under a hail of automatic fire. Half were rescued but, although the wreck was subsequently located in only nineteen fathoms, it was not searched for intelligence purposes.

Their success occurred on 9 May off Cape Lookout, another dangerous focal point south of Hatteras, and put great heart into the little ships that had worked so long and so fruitlessly against an opponent who appeared to hold all the aces. Just two days later, in the same waters, one of the very active seconded British AS trawlers, HMS *Bedfordshire*, latched onto the *U-558*. The U-boat responded lethally with a single torpedo, sinking the trawler with all hands.

Cape Lookout was becoming something of a bogey area for the British AS craft as the *St Cathan* had been sunk in April by collision with a ship that she was escorting, while the British-manned *Senateur Duhamel* had gone down off Wilmington on 6 May after the American four-stacker *Semmes* mistook her for a surfaced U-boat in darkness and rammed her.

Forced southward, Dönitz' forces concentrated off the southern part of the Florida peninsula and along the broad sweep of the Keys, where deep water conveniently approached the land. Shipping here still moved independently and was punished accordingly. Some friction is evident at this time between Dönitz and his C.-in-C. Raeder. The latter was keen to exploit the political impact of striking at specific areas, but Dönitz, as ever, insisted that he 'should continue to operate the U-boats where they can sink the greatest tonnage with the smallest losses, which at present is in American waters'. He was correct for, in all areas, his forces destroyed a massive 576,000 GRT in May alone.

This situation would have been yet worse had not the U-boat force expanded more slowly than planned. Another hard Baltic winter had delayed commissionings, so that only sixty-nine new boats joined the flag during the first half of 1942. Of these, twenty-eight were sent to Norway or the Mediterranean. Forty-one were directed to the Atlantic, but these had to be set against twelve losses in this theatre, resulting in a net increase of only twenty-nine.

German intelligence had also confirmed that the reported American shipbuilding programmes were rather more than morale-boosting rhetoric, and were beginning to take shape. Preliminary forecasts indicated that, if the issue were not resolved quickly, U-boats would eventually be required to sink an impossible 700,000 GRT, even 900,000, per month.

During the first eight months of 1942, however, 188 deep sea Allied tankers had been sunk in Atlantic waters, 143 of them off the eastern seaboard. The Americans responded typically by initiating the construction of pipelines, a massive project which, in time, would reduce the dependency upon tankers by nearly 30 per cent.

As he migrated southward, the enemy left small, but widely scattered, minefields. These proved surprisingly ineffective, causing little disruption.

Operations in the Caribbean were brief but profitable. During February and March 1942, with the main effort still in the north, thirty-one ships were sunk. In April and May this rose to forty-one, with a further forty-two in June and July. No U-boats were lost. A convoy system was then initiated and sinkings immediately declined. By September they had dropped to the point where it was again more profitable for submarines to concentrate on the ocean convoys.

Dönitz left a few boats to worry the coastal traffic from Panama, via Trinidad, to Brazilian ports but, over the next year, the exchange rate became an unprofitable seven U-boats for thirty-five merchantmen. For the final three months of 1942 the only ships sunk were in the eastern Caribbean. All were convoyed and, although they represented only a minute percentage of the total convoyed, the losses reflected upon the inexperience of the escort crews and the unsuitability of their ships. In the earlier war, small AS craft had proved unequal to the task and the President's insistence on them only saw history repeat itself.

In summarizing the whole, seven-month *Paukenschlag* campaign it is apparent that the Americans, like the British in the earlier war, paid a heavy price for viewing convoys as a 'defensive' measure and not adopting them immediately.

In exchange for approximately 360 ships sunk south of Halifax, Nova Scotia, the enemy lost just eight U-boats. Only eleven ships had been sunk in convoy, for the loss of three submarines to escorts, a ratio of about four to one. One U-boat had been sunk on passage, meaning that about 350 independents had been destroyed for the remaining four boats, a massive eighty-eight to one.

Over the same period, within the arc of Newfoundland-based air cover, only twenty-six ships had been lost from ocean convoys for the destruction of six U-boats, again an exchange rate of about four to one.

Of the 184 submarine patrols conducted in United States waters during the campaign, eighty were by Type IXs, the remainder by the smaller Type VIICs. Although the Type IXs were at a disadvantage in the shallow waters, they were responsible for two-thirds of the merchantmen sunk.

Over 3 million GRT was lost in the course of the campaign, representing about 21 per cent by numbers and 14.5 per cent by tonnage of all shipping sunk by U-boats in the entire war. In return, Dönitz lost twenty-two U-boats. Truly a happy time.

The fully interlocking convoy system initiated following the German onslaught linked the western terminals of the transatlantic convoys with coastwise routes proceeding to the Gulf ports, and direct routes via the Windward Passage to Panama, and to Trinidad/Brazil. Both Halifax and Sydney ceased to be termini in favour of the more convenient New York. Such changes were gradual, however, and modifications continued throughout the war.

Although they had cut their teeth in what experienced Atlantic escort personnel would consider little better than a shooting gallery, a new generation of U-boat 'aces' had emerged, confident and dangerous, to succeed the original experts who, one by one, were being eliminated. Nonetheless, it was already apparent to analysts that the total sinkings per submarine ocean patrol had stabilized, even if they had not yet really started to decline. In the rapid expansion of any service, months of hectic training, however thorough, could never supplant years of experience, and standards were bound to drop.

Paradoxically, escort performance improved with the steady introduction of new ships, new weapons and technologies, and evolved tactics, married to the exploitation of air power. A further factor was that escort commanders targeted U-boat commanders, whereas the latter targeted merchantmen. Escort commanders thus had a greater expectation of survival and, thus, accumulation of experience.

Paukenschlag, although highly successful, was mounted at the expense of the ongoing effort against the North Atlantic convoys. For each of the first four months of 1942 there had been lost an average of about seventy ships, aggregating 400,000 GRT. In May and June, as operations in American waters began to be scaled down, boats were redirected to ocean warfare and the average rocketed to a peak of 122 ships of 600,000 GRT. This was about the figure that Dönitz calculated would, if sustained, knock Britain out of the war. That it was not sustained was due to the continued steadfastness of the merchant navy crews and to the dedication of the escort groups, themselves increasing in strength and in technical quality.

Selected tankers were now fitted by the British with Replenishment-at-Sea (RAS) equipment. Whenever possible, one accompanied each convoy and, weather always permitting, considerably reduced the escorts' time-consuming diversions to Iceland for refuelling. By extending their sea-time, however, the operation added to the often extreme exhaustion of their crews. Oiling at sea still did not mean that an escort group would accompany its convoy for the complete crossing. The organization was a complex business, relying greatly on American, British and Canadian liaison groups working permanently in each other's headquarters.

Having been slowed during the *Paukenschlag* offensive, the

A group of early German submarines and torpedo craft, seen in 1916 berthed ahead of the specialist submarine salvage vessel *Vulkan*.

A merchantman awaits destruction by gunfire. Observance of the prize rules by U-boats increased their risks by obliging them to operate surfaced, but had the added advantage of conserving torpedoes.

Crewmen aboard *U-35*. During her career this boat was commanded by two 'aces', de la Perière and Kophamel who, between them, were credited with sinking 590,000 GRT of Allied shipping.

THEY KEPT THE
SEA LANES
OPEN

INVEST IN THE VICTORY LIBERTY LOAN

This fine American poster of 1918 shows to good effect a Cassin-class 'four stacker' destroyer, very similiar to those that proved so valuable during the Second World War.

Surrendered German
U-boats at Harwich in
1919.

Most of Germany's 154
minesweepers were
disposed of in 1921-2. A
few remained with the
fleet, serving in various
capacities. The *M113*
became tender to the new
1936 U-boat flotilla.

Inspecting the fast battleship *Gneisenau* prior to the Second World War, Hitler is seen here with Grand Admiral Raedar. The Führer had little grasp of the functions of seapower.

Befehlshaber der U-boote (BdU), Karl Dönitz advanced from Commodore to Grand Admiral during 1939-45. He briefly became Germany's last Führer.

Grand Admiral Erich Raedar.

Intended as 'U-cruisers', the Type I proved to be totally unsatisfactory. Only two were ever built.

Designed for coastal and near-sea operations, the Type II was also valuable for training.

Continuously improved, the Type VII was the workhorse of the German submarine arm.

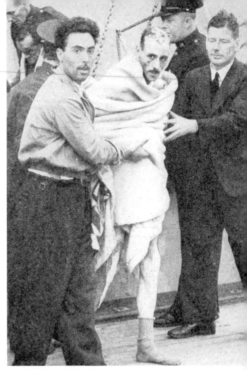

International outrage followed the sinking of the liner *Athenia* just hours after the declaration of war. The culprit was *Kapitänleutnant* Lemp in *U-30*.

A survivor from the *Athenia* being helped ashore at Galway. Of the 118 persons killed by the torpedo strike, twenty-eight were American citizens.

Convoy protection. A flight of Avro Ansons and a British destroyer flotilla.

Left and above: HMS *Courageous* sunk by *U-29* whilst on anti-submarine operations. Using large fleet carriers for these operations was stopped.

Below: A German S-Boat. Effective in both direct attack and for minelaying.

Below: Contact mines being loaded aboard a small combatant. Note the side screen.

The *U-564* departs the French Atlantic base at Lorient. She was sunk in the Bay of Biscay by Coastal Command aircraft during June 1943.

An early picture of a 10 Squadron Sunderland flying boat. Note the abraded paintwork.

Ships in this early convoy still show their peacetime liveries. The nearest vessel is of typically German build, possibly a prize.

Operating an Enigma encoding machine aboard a U-boat. The continued ability to read transmissions was of incalculable value to the Allies. While Dönitz often suspected its compromise, he could never prove it.

A U-boat commander, identifiable by his white cap cover, works at his charts as a fellow officer maintains periscope watch.

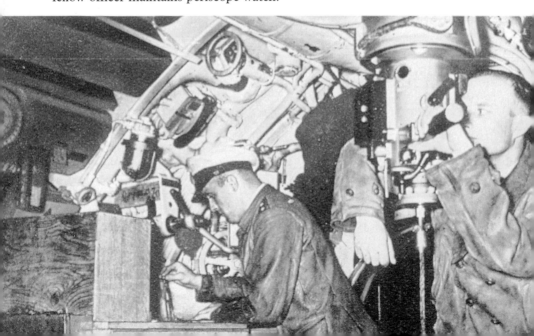

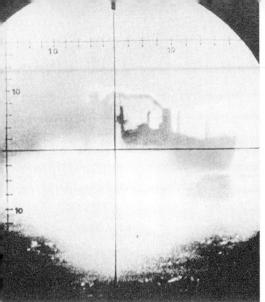
On target... *Torpedo los*!

Vital supplies sent to the bottom.

A stricken merchantman is finished off by the surfaced U-boat's 88mm gun. Note the number of shell cases.

Coastal Command HQ at Northwood in Middlesex. Air Marshal Sir John Slessor, Commander-in-Chief of Coastal Command (leaning on desk) with his Air Staff Officer, Air Vice Marshal Durston (on his right) and Senior Naval Staff Officer, Captain Peyton-Ward (on his left), were part of the team that began to win the war against the U-boats. The WAAF working on the Operations Chart is plotting air patrols (white box) over the Bay of Biscay. Air operations, flying out of the south of England, were successful in keeping U-boats submerged, forcing them to operate on their batteries at the start and end of their missions.

The B-24 Liberator proved to be the most potent of Coastal Command's anti-submarine aircraft.

Caught on the surface.
Depth charged.

Struggles to remain afloat.

Oil slick...Gone to the bottom.

Two in one day. The Philadelphia Navy Yard launches the destroyer escorts *Scott* (DE214) and *Burke* (DE215) together on 3 April 1943.

Canadian destroyers shepherding their convoy safely into an English port.

Captain Frederick 'Johnny' Walker, on the bridge of HMS *Starling*, directs a fourteen-hour Asdic chase of *U-202*. He died from overwork before the end of the war.

Six U-boats are destroyed in one patrol by the Second Support Group led by Captain Walker. Crowds cheer them into Gladstone Dock, Liverpool.

The Allied bombing offensive played its part in the Battle of the Atlantic. Three Type XXI U-boats amidst bomb damage at the Blohm & Voss yards, Hamburg, being given the 'once-over' by British soldiers in May 1945.

A German U-boat, *U776*, with a British crew, on the Thames at the war's end.

Atlantic convoy cycle quickly regained its rhythm, with about a dozen movements per month, each of some fifty ships. Large convoys were more economical on escorts than small, because the length of periphery to be guarded increased only linearly as the enclosed area increased as the square.

A typical escort group comprised three destroyers and six corvettes. Allowing for one or two ships to be undergoing repair or maintenance at any time, the remainder were the minimum necessary to cover a fifty-ship convoy. To maintain coverage at the above rate, a total of twenty-six groups were required.

By mid-1942 there were eight British and Canadian groups based at Halifax and Boston. These shepherded convoys from their port of origin in New York, via the optional Ocean Meeting Point at about 61 degrees west, to the WESTOMP at about 40 degrees west. From here, air cover was sparse or non-existent for the extent of the Gap and a mid-ocean escort from any of the three navies, based on Newfoundland, delivered the convoy to the Western Approaches escort at the EASTOMP.

Of about 450 British and Canadian AS escorts, nearly half were the ubiquitous Flower-class corvettes which, for all their failings, had been produced rapidly and cheaply. Also operational were the first ten River-class frigates.

Where the use of hunter/killer groups to comb the ocean for U-boats had been thoroughly discredited, the same did not wholly apply to aircraft, with their ability to scan immense areas in a relatively short period. Mid-1942 saw the strength of RAF Coastal Command stand at over fifty flying boats (Catalinas and Sunderlands) and nearly 500 other aircraft. These included Hudsons, Wellingtons, Whitleys and Hampdens for general reconnaissance but only two squadrons of B-24 (Liberator) and B-17 (Fortress) Long Range Maritime Patrol aircraft. As the Luftwaffe was now operating Ju88 and Me110 heavy fighters over the Bay of Biscay, there were also deployed eight squadrons of Beaufighters and the more vulnerable Blenheims.

In addition, four naval squadrons were attached to the Command, together with specialist units for photographic, meteorological and air-sea rescue duties. Based around the British Isles (with Group headquarters at Liverpool, Chatham, Rosyth and Plymouth), at Iceland and Gibraltar, the Command's aircraft were complemented by those of the US Navy and the Royal Canadian Air Force (RCAF) operating from Iceland, Newfoundland and the Canadian mainland. Despite increasing offensive capacity, however, the Gap yawned as wide and as deadly as ever.

With the reduction in scale of submarine attack, it became the practice to reduce the degree of evasive routing and to follow more closely the shortest Great Circle routes. There came also an inevitable relaxation in vigilance, so that it came as an unpleasant surprise when Dönitz set up the occasional pack attack. This he did in order to prevent the transfer of escorts to assist the beleaguered Americans.

One such attack fell on HG.84, a twenty-three ship convoy which sailed northbound from Gibraltar on 9 June 1942. Barring its route were the nine U-boats of Group *Endrass*, named for the 'ace' lost in these waters some six months earlier. The group itself contained one ace skipper in Erich Topp of *U-552*. It was he that had earlier sunk the American destroyer *Reuben James* and, by virtue of surviving the war, would accumulate a 'score' of 185,000 GRT, earning him the *Ritterkreuz* with Oak Leaves and Swords.

By coincidence Endrass' nemesis, Captain F.J. Walker, was again the Senior Officer of the escort, although EG.36 was at a reduced strength of Walker's sloop *Stork* and three Flowers. Included in the convoy was the fighter catapult ship, *Empire Morn*.

Enemy agents in Spain duly reported HG.84's departure. Twenty ships sailed from Gibraltar, the final three joining from Lisbon on 11 June. These were tracked by Kondors, which thus discovered the main convoy. The reported position proved to be thirty-five miles in error, prompting a tart comment from Dönitz.

With the convoy's slow progress, Dönitz was able to deploy his boats in two search lines and it was Topp himself that made the first sighting on the afternoon of the 14th some 400 miles west of Cape Finisterre.

In vectoring-in the three colleagues, Topp generated radio traffic that was noted by the rescue ship *Copeland* at the rear of the convoy. Rescue ships did not enjoy any special immunity and were equipped with 'Huff-Duff', the existence of which was suspected by the enemy but not yet confirmed. The *Copeland* alerted Walker who ordered away the *Empire Morn*'s solitary Hurricane to disperse the snoopers while his four escorts pursued three separate contacts.

With darkness, Topp had worked himself into an attacking position. He launched a full, four-tube bow salvo, then swung to fire the stern tube. Three ships went down, the Norwegian tanker *Slemdal* and two British ships, Moss Hutchinson's *Etrib* and MacAndrew's *Pelayo*. Reloading rapidly, he was able to repeat his attack, this time destroying two Ellerman ships, Hall Line's *Thurso* and the Papayanni vessel *City of Oxford*. The four British ships aggregated barely 8,500 GRT but typified the valuable little Mediterranean traders which, working cargo with their own equipment, could use the most minor ports.

Despite the number of boats in contact with the convoy by the 15th they were kept at a safe distance by the escort, Topp and one other receiving sufficient damage to cause them to break off.

On the following day the escort was reinforced by three fresh ships, including two of the new River-class frigates. The convoy also came within the range of Coastal Command Liberators. Continuous air cover and calm conditions caused the remaining enemy to abandon the operation. Topping-up from a pair of U-tankers, they resumed their interrupted passage to the United States.

Rapid expansion of the U-boat force was not matched by techno-logical improvements. German scientists not only did not develop suitable surface- and air-search radars but appeared to believe that the appropriate level of miniaturization was impossible. Returning submarine skippers, however, spoke regularly of AS escorts appearing on cue following radio transmissions, and of aircraft materializing out of poor visibility in which a boat's own lookouts were ineffective. The Allies were obviously using elec-tronic aids.

The British had long noted that U-boats reported to BdU, i.e. Dönitz' centralized control organization, by high-frequency (H/F) radio but homed-in their colleagues with medium-frequency (M/F) beacon signals. Shipborne Huff-Duff (H/F D/F) first went operational in July 1941 and, following the solution of problems of mutual interference, was joined afloat by ten centimetre radar. Huff Duff gave an escort commander an accurate bearing on a transmitting U-boat and the ship could run down this line of bearing until the radar registered a precise range. The urge to follow on to a 'kill' must have been overwhelming but the speed superiority of a corvette over her convoy was not great. Prosecuting a contact could result in her falling far behind her convoy, leaving a gap in the screen for hours as she consumed large quantities of fuel in racing to catch up. As the safety of the convoy took precedence over U-boat killing, it was sufficient to drive an enemy down long enough to ensure his losing contact. Many U-boat commanders were greatly relieved when an apparently developing attack was suddenly abandoned.

That the enemy was thus being 'let off the hook' was of great concern to the Admiralty which, as soon as suitable vessels could be mustered, initiated the Support Group concept. This comprised an independent group, accompanied by its own oiler, which could be directed to reinforce the escort of any threatened convoy. First tried in September 1942, the idea immediately faltered with the need of every available ship to cover the North Africa landings in the November. Requirements here consumed not only every possible AS escort but also the first escort carriers (CVE) that were coming forward. It was thus a further six months before Support Groups would become a reality, for which reason the Admiralty initiated the emergency Merchant Aircraft Carrier (MAC) programme. This, however, would produce no result before May 1943.

Deployment of escort carriers pitted U-boats against that most unlikely of killers, the Fairey Swordfish. Often portrayed as an obsolescent stopgap, the aircraft was nothing of the sort, having entered service with the Fleet Air Arm only in July 1936. Designed to handle well at very low speeds, it could lift off a short flight deck with a relative wind speed of only 55 knots. A rare example of a successful multi-purpose design, the Swordfish could deploy torpedoes or mines, and even engage in divebombing in the face of light opposition. Fitted with ASV radar, it carried depth charges or, later, hull-piercing rocket projectiles, to deadly effect against submarines. Often 'superseded', it nevertheless remained operational throughout the war.

Although ASV Mark II radar had first been flown in March 1941, Fighter Command's night fighters enjoyed higher priority than Coastal Command, and it was June 1942 before the enemy became convinced that his surfaced submarines were being surprised because of airborne radar rather than poor watch-keeping. In this same month came a further alarming report of a U-boat, surfaced at night in the Bay of Biscay, being surprised by a sudden illumination and almost simultaneous bombing. The Leigh Light had arrived.

From their French Atlantic bases, all U-boats had to deploy and return across 'the Bay' and the growing attentions of Coastal Command were a matter of concern to BdU. Where early 1942 had been casualty-free, June had seen three boats damaged sufficiently to abort their deployments and return. Unusually, Dönitz over-reacted, ordering boats to remain submerged at night, surfacing by day only to recharge and refresh. This was intended to be only a stopgap measure, pending the improvisation of a suitable radar warning receiver. Its result, however, was to more than double the number of sightings and to begin a slow attrition as odd boats were picked off.

Following complaints about lack of Luftwaffe cover, two dozen fighter versions of the Ju88 were transferred to Lorient and Bordeaux. Additional automatic weapons began to appear on U-boats, starting a trend to growing topside clutter that had a cumulative and adverse effect on surfaced stability and submerged manoeuvrability.

Ironically, a couple of French firms, Metox and Grandin, were already producing electronic equipment which, with the addition of a crude antenna, could receive signals over a bandwidth that included the frequency range of ASV Mark II. Known simply as 'Metox', the first sets were rushed to completion within six weeks. On surfacing, boats so equipped would hoist a wooden-framed antenna (the 'Biscay Cross') and submerge again hastily on the reception of a train of signals at around 200 MHz. Metox-equipped boats escorted those without and, once again, sightings dropped almost to zero.

During May 1942, two long-ranged Type IXC40s, *U-506* and *U-507*, made pilot patrols into the Gulf of Mexico. They found the defences as lacking as anywhere along the eastern seaboard and sank a joint total of seventeen ships aggregating about 85,000 GRT, several of them boldly by gunfire off the very mouth of the Mississippi.

The *U-507* returned home for a quick refit, following which she was sent in the July as a component of a group, supported by three U-tankers, to raid West African waters. Her skipper Harro Schacht, had little luck and requested to be allowed to try Brazilian waters. Earlier sinkings of neutral Brazilian shipping had already led this state to sever diplomatic relations with Germany in the previous January, and permission was given subject to special care being taken not to molest Argentinian or Chilean ships. Within a week, Schacht had expended all his torpedoes in sinking seven ships of some 18,000 GRT. Six were Brazilian-flagged. This gratuitous act of aggression advanced Germany's cause not one jot but promptly brought Brazil into the war on the Allied side.

Although Brazil's armed forces were slender, her geography was of major significance, enabling the Allies to exercise control of the central Atlantic narrows from either side. The central organization for shipping control could also be extended well south toward the important focal point of the River Plate.

Following intensive trials, the Hedgehog AS weapon had gone into production at end of the 1941 but had been far from a popular success. The weapon's twenty-four bombs were fitted onto spring-loaded rods, or 'spigots'. These were angled, relative to each other, to spread the bombs in a circle of forty metres' diameter. Acting as a firing pin, the spigot was reset by the downward force on firing. At the same time, it absorbed some of the recoil force, but this was still so great that the bombs needed to be fired in pairs, in rapid sequence.

Over 100 ships had been fitted with Hedgehog by the end of 1942 but, what with minor faults, poor maintenance and inadequate documentation the weapon was little used if depth charges were available. British commanders eventually had to be ordered to use the weapon, but it was long before its deadly potential was fully exploited.

Equally disliking Hedgehog's massive recoil forces, the US Navy adapted the principle to fire rocket projectiles. This version

94

was called Mousetrap, and could be deployed by smaller craft.

The Royal Navy's trial ship for Hedgehog was the veteran destroyer *Westcott* but, when she sank her first submarine (*U-581*) in February 1942, it was through a combination of depth charges and ramming.

As already noted, U-boats were increasingly able to dive deeper. Early depth charges took thirty seconds to sink to 300 feet, time sufficient to allow an alert submarine to manoeuvre beyond their lethal radius. Better design saw charges able to sink to 500 feet in the same time.

Air-dropped depth charges, by contrast, were aimed at surfaced or barely-submerged targets. In these weapons, the sink rate had to be *retarded* in order to allow their shallow (twenty-five feet) hydrostatic fuse to function correctly. Air-dropped weapons were standard, drum-shaped charges with ballistic fairings added to improve the predictability of their trajectories.

A further expedient worthy of note was the Mark X depth charge. This monster contained one ton of explosive and was usually launched from a torpedo tube. It caused the escort more anxiety than the target.

With their superior electronic industrial base, the Americans were keen to apply technology to AS warfare. Airborne magnetic anomaly detectors were shown to work in principle but the distance from detector to the ferrous mass of the target could not exceed 600 feet. Even the lowest and slowest of aircraft could thus detect a transient lasting only milliseconds.

Expendable air-dropped sonobuoys appeared to be more promising. Released around a suspected target position, these detected target noise, amplified it and re-transmitted it to the circling aircraft. By the end of 1942 they were in use by both US Army Air Corps and US Navy aircraft, and were about to go into mass production.

As sonobuoys could give only an approximate position for the target, precision-dependent weapons such as depth-charges were not appropriate. For this purpose, the self-homing acoustic torpedo was developed. For submarines, too, this was a useful weapon for, launched against a threatening escort, it allowed a skipper to concentrate on a convoy. The Germans had been working on the device since 1933 but progress had been slow.

Targeting depended upon matched pairs of sensitive and highly-directional hydrophones. As these, in a fast torpedo, would be swamped by self-generated noise, the weapon was electrically-propelled at about 25 knots. Wrongly assuming that the Allies were already using acoustic torpedoes, German scientists managed to deploy them operationally during 1943.

During November 1942 Admiral Sir Percy Noble, who had been C.-in-C., Western Approaches since February 1941, was succeeded by Admiral Sir Max Horton. Starting with miserably inadequate resources, Noble had done a magnificent job in creating a viable AS defence for the convoys. Churchill, however, found him lacking sufficient aggression, wanting a man who would use the Allies' growing strength to carry the war to Dönitz. In Horton he made the perfect choice. A career submariner, he had been in command of the whole Royal Navy submarine force and well understood Dönitz' problems and weaknesses. Horton was ferocious with erring subordinates yet knew that the war against the U-boat was one of patience, for which the maintenance of morale was top priority. In pursuit of this he regularly sailed on operational cruises and flew with Coastal Command crews.

The introduction of the four-wheel Enigma machine by the enemy resulted in a protracted intelligence blackout for the British, who sought a solution in a further capture. At the end of October 1942 the Submarine Tracking Room estimated that the enemy had concentrated nineteen U-boats in the western Mediterranean prior to Operation Torch. Only one had been left in the eastern basin, being the *U-559* which was due for a refit. On a final patrol, she was hovering hopefully around the busy British Port Said-Haifa convoy route when, on 30 October, she was detected by a patrolling Sunderland. Her position being so close to the Mediterranean Fleet's Alexandria base, three fleet destroyers and a pair of Hunts were quickly mustered.

The *U-559*'s skipper, Hans Heidtmann, was experienced and elusive. Only after ten hours and 150 depth charges he was finally forced to surface. He attempted to run for it in the darkness but was detected by radar and illuminated.

Standard procedure was now to use automatic weapons to deter a U-boat crew from scuttling and abandoning. Despite this, the *U-559*'s scuttling charges were blown and the crew suffered several fatalities, including Heidtmann himself, in baling out.

The closest British destroyer was the *Petard*, whose eccentric commanding officer, Thornton, had planned for this eventuality. Sending away one whaler to rescue survivors, he had the other put a boarding party on the stricken submarine. A mass of documentation was quickly recovered but the Enigma machine itself was well secured. Two of the *Petard*'s men were still struggling to free it when the boat suddenly up-ended and foundered. Both men were lost.

All the new data was passed to Bletchley Park where, following three weeks of furious activity, a first message was decrypted. The work showed also that the enemy operators were being lazy, tending to use the fourth rotor only in fixed settings. Remastering German naval codes would still require some months, but the *Petard*'s action in the distant waters of the Levant had enormous significance for the Atlantic convoys and their evasive routing.

It was the *Petard*'s good fortune to make another haul of valuable documentation some six weeks later, this time from the Italian submarine *Uarsciek*. The strains of war were beginning to tell, however, and the *Petard*'s captain had to be transferred ashore. Another temporary casualty of overwork at this time was Rodger Winn, one of the mainstays of the Submarine Tracking Room, whose continuous experience over three years had given him an almost intuitive feel for Dönitz' intentions.

With the scaling-down of *Paukenschlag*, Dönitz concentrated increasingly on the ocean routes. The OG and HG convoys, running to and from Gibraltar, were now considered to be of secondary interest, comprising as they did a proportion of smaller ships. In addition, both these and the Freetown (SC and OS) convoys generated little radio traffic, causing the *B-dienst* problems in detecting their movements. Their cycle was a comparatively long ten days and, provided that they kept to the east of meridian 12 degrees west, air cover was practically continuous.

Loaded, east-bound Atlantic convoys remained the priority

target. Despite the increase in escort strength and extension of air cover, these still kept close to the shortest, Great Circle route. This remained a puzzle to the enemy who, still lacking an operational search radar and reliable air reconnaissance, found it of great assistance. Their task was further eased by the considerable inroads made by German intelligence into British ciphers, unchanged for two years. Fortunately, the level of compromise was appreciated and new codes were issued in May 1943, from which date they remained effectively secure.

Increasing numbers of Type IX boats and Type XIV tankers prompted Dönitz in August 1942 to stage another major raid into the central Atlantic and beyond. Of three U-boat groups the first, *Iltis* (Polecat), comprising an early Type IX and five Type VIIs, was to cover the nearest area of Azores-Freetown. The second, Group *Eisbär* (Polar Bear), of four longer range Type IXCs, was to work as far south as the Cape and, if profitable, the near Indian Ocean.

There was a further, unnamed group of four so-called 'U-cruisers'. The type IXD2 was based on a Type IX pressure hull, extended to accommodate an auxiliary diesel-electric cruising propulsion system which, with increased bunker capacity, gave a theoretical endurance of 23,700 miles at 12 knots. Despite their increased size, however, they carried only twenty-four torpedoes, just two better than a standard Type IX. As the Type XIV re-supply boats carried fuel rather than spare torpedoes, several captured Dutch 'Far East' boats were converted to torpedo carriers, two accompanying this incursion. Five other German and three Italian boats were also operating independently in the central Atlantic.

Only two British merchantmen were encountered on this general move southward, which attracted little attention from the Submarine Tracking Room. Then, during the forenoon of 12 September, the *U-156*, one of the *Eisbär* group, sighted a large liner proceeding independently about 900 miles south of Freetown. Only with dusk did the submarine close the vessel, the 19,700-ton Cunarder *Laconia*. Armed, blacked-out and zigzagging, the *Laconia* was a legitimate target that Werner Hartenstein, *U-156*'s skipper, had no hesitation in torpedoing. Hit twice, the big ship came to a halt and began to develop a severe list.

So large an addition to his tonnage score would qualify Hartenstein for his *Ritterkreuz* and he remained surfaced, watching developments. It was soon apparent that there were large numbers of people aboard, in considerable disorder because the list prevented the launch of half the lifeboats. Those in the water were already under attack by sharks attracted by the disturbance.

There were, in fact, 2,700 people aboard, comprising 1,800 Italian prisoners of war, guarded by 100 Poles, and some 350 British service personnel, women and children in addition to the crew.

Hartenstein soon discovered that he was faced with the political disaster of killing hundreds of Italian allies. Rescuing as many as possible, he radioed BdU. Dönitz immediately directed seven other boats, one Italian, to the scene. On then informing Berlin, Dönitz was directed by Raeder to rescue only Italians, while Vichy French warships would be requested from West Africa.

Panicking, swamped with survivors, knowing nothing of Berlin's involvement, Hartenstein broadcast *en clair* that he would not attack any vessel that could come to assist. Not yet knowing of the *Laconia*'s end and suspecting the transmission to be a ruse, the Allies did not at first respond.

One by one, other submarines arrived. They remained surfaced, displaying large improvised Red Cross flags, taking aboard many, assisting others. When the *U-507* reported towing lifeboats full of British and Polish survivors, her skipper was ordered by Dönitz to slip the tow.

On 15 September the unusual concentration of craft was overflown by an American aircraft based on Ascension Island. The result was a B-24 Liberator, ignoring all signals and banners, making four unopposed bomb runs. Hartenstein's boat was damaged by near misses (and reported as sunk).

Dönitz was infuriated by what he saw as Allied perfidy, but would not abandon the Italians. Two days later, the B-24 returned, depth-charging the *U-506* which put down hurriedly with about 150 survivors aboard. The Liberator captain modestly claimed the U-boat as 'probably destroyed'.

At last, five days after the sinking, Vichy French surface

warships arrived taking aboard about 1,100 survivors, of whom about 800 were Italians.

The angry Dönitz issued a directive to all boats that no future attempts were to be made at rescuing or assisting survivors. The only exceptions were to be captains or chief engineers, who were likely to have useful knowledge or special skills better denied to the Allied cause. Finally: 'Be harsh . . . the enemy takes no regard of women and children in his bombing attacks on German cities'.

This, the so-called Laconia Order, would eventually be used as evidence against Dönitz when, three years later, he was on trial for his life.

Resuming the offensive against the ocean convoys, Dönitz' men discovered that the defences had improved. Metox radar detectors could not be produced quickly enough to meet demand, leading to the situation where one Metox-equipped boat would shepherd a non-fitted group or where boats would meet at sea to transfer both equipment and operator.

Reception of a radar pulse on Metox did not necessarily mean that it had the reflected power to be detected by the transmitting aircraft. Submarine skippers could not take that chance, however, and regular submergences and the sense of being watched did much to erode the early sense of invulnerability enjoyed by U-boat personnel.

Skippers began to report more encounters with aircraft beyond 800 miles from known bases. If detected and forced down, they were also now faced with the prospect of a follow-up by AS ships, the advent of support groups having been noted. Considerable concern followed the first British aircraft being observed to be dropping sonobuoys. The German conclusion was that these were active devices that simulated Asdic transmissions in order to encourage boats to remain submerged, where their lack of mobility left them relatively impotent.

Promising concentrations of boats against four convoys came to little, due to the activities of aircraft. While the convoys were not entirely unscathed there were ominous signs that the defence was getting the measure of the attack. There would be many more U-boat successes, but the happy times were past.

One of the four convoys referred to was the north-bound

SL.118, which had left Freetown with thirty-four ships on 4 August 1942. Even after three years of war the convoy's only anti-raider protection consisted of the AMC *Cheshire*, one of the stately liners built during the 1920s for Bibby's Rangoon service. There were also four AS sloops, whose senior officer complained of lack of speed margin over even this, a slow convoy.

Across the path of SL.118 lay the six Type VIIs of Group *Blücher*, of which *U-653* first made contact. Refraining from immediate attack, the boat transmitted beacon signals for the remainder of her group. These were D/Fed by the escort, the sloop *Folkestone* detecting the *U-333* and, in a rapid series of passes, damaging her to the extent where she was obliged to abandon her patrol.

On the 17th, east of the Azores, the *U-566* fired first at the convoy, expending three torpedoes in sinking the Norwegian freighter *Triton*. Although chased away, the U-boat did not lose contact.

The next day brought the convoy to within extreme air range from England and two boats were quickly surprised by aircraft and forced down. Despite this, *U-124* worked herself in a firing position by afternoon. Her full salvo of four torpedoes ran true, sinking the Dutch *Balingkar* and the British *Hatarana* while badly damaging the AMC, which survived. Again, however, aircraft intervened, suppressing the *U-124*'s mobility to the extent that she was unable to make an 'end run' and attack again.

The aircraft concerned were Liberators of the RAF's 120 Squadron whose leader, Terence Bulloch, would later become a leading U-boat killer. He was experimenting with dropping shallow-set depth charges in a tight cluster along the length of a surfaced target rather than across it, as standard doctrine prescribed. Catching the surfaced *U-653* he caused her considerable damage, even blowing a crew member overboard but, as in earlier cases, the Type VII's tough design saved her. Again, however, she had to abort her patrol. In her case, BdU would allow her to return only when she had used her now excess fuel to top-up other boats.

Next for a working-over, this time by the escorts, was the *U-509*. She sustained minor damage but, unable to communicate, her skipper requested another to ask BdU for leave to break off.

This was refused, the incident hinting at an increasing lack of determination.

By the 19th SL.118 had crept far enough northward to attract continuous air cover. Despite this, the *U-406* managed to penetrate the screen and sink the British ship *City of Manila*, although paying a price with a persistent and damaging depth charging.

Although the convoy had still not reached the latitude of Cape Finisterre, Dönitz ordered the attack to be broken off. None of his boats had been sunk but three had been fortunate to survive, and there were distinct signs that he was becoming greatly dissatisfied with the progress of the whole campaign.

The four ships that had been lost from SL.118 underlined the heavy toll being exacted from the major companies. Laden with grain, wool and general cargo from Australia, the 6,600 GRT *Triton* was one of Wilhelmsen's extensive Tønsberg-based fleet. The *Hatarana* was a British India vessel of about 7,500 GRT, while the *City of Manila* was one of Ellerman's Hall Line ships which had loaded in West Africa. The *Balingkar* had been captured from the enemy. Previously the *Werdenfels* of the Bremen-based Hansa Line, she was now operated by Rotterdam-Lloyd and had been given one of their customary 'East Indies' names. Fortunately, and unusually, only three lives had been lost in the sinkings but four fine, fully laden ships, aggregating 27,899 GRT, had joined the melancholy list of marine casualties.

The action around SL.118 was fairly typical and showed yet again that slow convoys suffered more than fast, and that escorts, however resolutely fought, remained too slow and too few.

With so many U-boats and so many skippers it was inevitable that fortunes would vary, some being lost in short order while others, boats and commanders, bore seemingly charmed lives. In the latter class fell the *U-333* and Peter Cremer.

Their first mission was as one of the groups of Type VIICs dispatched to the northern sector during *Paukenschlag*. They arrived in ferocious winter weather in January 1942 but, by moving southward, Cremer sank one ship from each of three convoys. With 14,000 GRT to his credit, he headed back for France. En route, he encountered an independent on 31 January, north of the Azores. Having duly sunk her with his last two torpedoes, he was informed by BdU that the ship was the disguised German blockade runner *Spreewald*, arriving from the Far East with a vital cargo of raw rubber and eighty-six British prisoners of war. In contrast to the *Laconia* incident, fifty-five British survived but only twenty-five Germans. Cremer found himself close to being court-martialled for his error before being exonerated.

A second patrol to the United States took the *U-333* to southern waters. In brilliant moonlight, off the coast of Florida, he lined up his first target, the tanker *British Prestige*. She was zigzagging, and Cremer's first shot missed. Unaware even that she was under attack, the tanker made a further radical change of course. Reloading at periscope depth, Cremer was caught unawares, the deep-draughted tanker raking his upper casing from end to end.

With wrecked upperworks, no periscopes but with a still-intact pressure hull, Cremer dared not return in further disgrace and continued his patrol. Operating in shallow water on the night of 5–6 May he sank three tankers in the space of six hours. One was later salvaged but the last, laden with highly volatile naphtha, exploded in a gigantic fireball which led to the boat being hunted for eighteen hours. Slowly working his way to deeper water, Cremer escaped and sank a British Clan liner while on his way home. Although his confirmed sinkings were still only about 30,000 GRT, his high-profile activities now brought Cremer his *Ritterkreuz*.

Following considerable repair, the *U-333* was one of the Group *Blücher* boats which attacked SL.118 in the August. As related above, the attentions of HMS *Folkestone* sent him home again, this time with a bent propeller shaft.

Patched up again, the *U-333* was sent south to the central Atlantic during September, part of the large-scale movement that resulted *inter alia*, with the *Laconia* sinking. The forthcoming North African landings had seen many escorts withdrawn temporarily. Shipping movements had, therefore, been minimized and targets were few.

Cremer closed the anchorage off Freetown on the night of 5–6 October, only to be caught on the surface by the radar-equipped corvette *Crocus*. With no time to submerge, the U-boat was caught in a dogfight during which she was twice rammed but survived due to her superior speed. With her topsides shredded by the corvette's gunfire, she managed to put down with several of her crew dead and her skipper badly injured. Bottomed in only ten fathoms and already leaking, the boat was then depth charged.

Facing the apparently inevitable, Cremer surfaced and prepared to scuttle, only to realize that the injured *Crocus* had lost contact. Gratefully, Cremer crept away in the darkness.

As the boat headed for a rendezvous with a re-supply boat, *U-459*, Cremer's chief engineer used pliers to remove eight shell fragments from his skipper. With the latter incapacitated and his first lieutenant dead, the *U-459* transferred an officer to bring the boat safely back to her French base.

As Cremer convalesced and took a temporary shore appointment, his boat, duly repaired, made a patrol under a replacement skipper. On 5–6 March 1943 (to anticipate briefly) the boat was surprised by a Leigh Light Wellington which, before it was shot down, actually hit the submarine with two depth charges. One lodged in the casing, necessitating clearance before the boat could submerge. Beyond sinking a straggler, the boat otherwise had a fruitless patrol.

In the May, Cremer returned to the *U-333*. His replacement was given the *U-440*, which was destroyed a few weeks later by a Sunderland. There were no survivors.

Neither he nor his boat fully fit for service, Cremer was sent south again to the central Atlantic. He sank nothing but, in company with three other Type VIIs, ran out of fuel. All were topped-up by a redirected Type IX.

Although a survivor, Cremer was a far from competent skipper. During November 1943 he was one of a group searching for a particularly large convoy off Portugal. He sighted it but was driven down by an escort, then waited an unnecessary eighteen hours before reporting it. The position he gave was incorrect, the planned attack failed to materialize and he was censured.

A fortnight later, acting on a Luftwaffe sighting, a chastened Cremer was first to attack a further convoy. He was immediately detected by two escorts and an aircraft. The veteran boat survived yet another pounding by depth charges and further material contact with the enemy, in this case the frigate *Exe*, which sliced across the barely submerged boat, breaking off her attack periscope. Cremer, having achieved nothing, had to abort.

With the pattern of the U-boat war greatly changed, boats were again operating in hazardous United Kingdom waters. In March 1944, spotted by an aircraft, Cremer lay doggo, becoming one of the few boats fortunate enough to escape the attentions of Captain F.J. Walker, by then commanding a support group. Only after ten anxious hours could Cremer creep away.

Deemed too old for modernization, the *U-333* was one of a dwindling number of boats operating in Biscay waters following the Normandy landings. Attacked on successive days by Sunderlands, of which she destroyed one, the boat was again damaged sufficiently to oblige her return.

With their long experience, Cremer and the bulk of his crew were then transferred to a new boat. The battle-weary *U-333* was handed over to another skipper, Hans Fiedler, who, ominously, had already survived the loss of two boats. Off the Scillies, on his very first patrol, he again encountered Walker's SG2 and was sunk without survivors by Walker's own ship, the *Starling*, and the new frigate *Loch Killin*. The *U-333* had been the first victim of the new Squid AS mortar but, ironically, Walker himself was not present, having died from a stroke just three weeks earlier. Cremer survived the war.

To revert to correct chronology, Operation Torch, the Allied landings in North Africa in November 1942, had to be a success. First of their kind, they were on a scale that caused significant disruption to other theatres. In addition to over fifty minesweepers, the Royal Navy alone had to muster a total of 125 escorts. Convoys were necessarily suspended on the Gibraltar (OG/HG) and Sierra Leone/Freetown (OS/SL) routes, in addition to those to North Russia. On the southern routes, disruption began as early as August 1942 and, when resumed in the following year, the convoys lost their original identities.

An average of some 350 ships shuttled between Freetown and the United Kingdom each month and these had to be rerouted for their protection. Most kept to the coast of now-allied Brazil, thence to Trinidad to link with the new interlocking convoy system operating along the United States eastern seaboard, and onward to the United Kingdom in an HX or SC convoy. Some, coming around the Cape or originating in the River Plate, were actually routed via the Strait of Magellan, up the west coast of South America and through the Panama Canal.

This great increase in shipping density in the Caribbean meant that control over Dönitz' activities in the theatre had been achieved none too soon. A significant side effect was that shipping concerned was steaming much further, reducing its utilization factor and the volume of imports urgently required in Britain.

Although the initial onslaught was over, however, the enemy had not entirely deserted the region. Convoys gathered in Port of Spain or Aruba, which were yet weakly protected and vulnerable. While not quite realizing the implications, BdU did not fail to take advantage and, in the five weeks beginning early in October 1942, twenty-five ships were lost around Trinidad for the loss of just one U-boat.

Involving about 800 ships of all types, Torch generated so much prior activity that the enemy could not fail to notice. Not for the first time, fortunately, his intelligence summaries began with an assumption, then placed too much credence on subsequent information that supported that assumption.

The actual landings thus came as a complete surprise to the German Naval Staff. Dönitz was informed only after the assault had begun and immediately ordered fifteen U-boats to Moroccan waters. Many had to be withdrawn from the South-West Approaches to the British Isles and from waters west of Ireland.

This was all to the Allied advantage. Despite the open and unprotected nature of roadsteads offshore from the landing beaches, the landings had already been accomplished, and in the face of minimal resistance. Many U-boats which, otherwise, would have been worrying at North Atlantic convoys, had now been diverted, too late, to the area of the highest concentration of AS vessels. Seven were thus destroyed during November 1942, with skippers reporting that radar and aerial activity kept them submerged for twenty hours in twenty-four.

With only nine boats on the North Atlantic routes at this point, and most of these already deficient in torpedoes or fuel, Dönitz needed to take steps to reinforce operations in the most productive areas, some 600 miles west of Iceland. The tanker *U-460* was ordered to the region but, with continuous storm conditions, virtually the whole group (*Kreuzotter*, or *Viper*) was, at one stage, queuing for fuel. Most were totally dry, riding out the storm surfaced, with no electrical power. This emergency saw fuel having to be transferred in drums by line, a process so slow that boats drifted considerable distances, generating much further radio traffic in bringing the tanker to them. It was the Germans' good fortune that Allied patrols were equally affected by the storm.

Even with no fuel problems a surfaced U-boat was most uncomfortable in a storm, her very low centre of gravity giving good stability at the cost of a rapid roll, often to dramatic angles (which, incidentally, made them poor gun platforms). With the watch topside, and the need to ventilate the boat, the conning tower hatch had to be open, admitting copious quantities of ocean to further the general squalor within. Driven hard to reach an operational area or to attack a convoy, the boat would be awash from end to end, with topside personnel totally reliant upon their safety harnesses.

The series of violent storms which marked the close of 1942 contributed to a lower level of mercantile loss, grievous though it remained. In the conditions, the usual line of search was not always feasible and some convoys were located by hydrophone, although maintaining contact proved to be difficult. No fewer than twenty-two U-boats closed on HX.217 but only two ships, totalling 13,500 GRT were lost in exchange for two U-boats. Next in sequence, HX.218 was betrayed by decrypted British radio traffic. Although located on cue, few boats were able to fight their way through the heavy seas in time to intercept it. In searching, they came across ONS.152, itself broken into two groups. This slow convoy was thus in a vulnerable position but the enemy was still unable to achieve more than to pick off one straggler.

In a quieter spell of weather the following ONS.153 lost two ships and an escorting destroyer but the year ended with a savaging for ONS.154. This comprised forty-six ships and had sailed from Liverpool on 18 December. For escort it had one destroyer and five corvettes of the Canadian C1 group. Because

107

of the violence of the weather, the convoy was routed unusually far to the south, reducing the period over which it could expect long-range air cover and setting it on so long a track that escorts would need to refuel from a specially modified tanker en route.

Timely *B-dienst* radio intelligence enabled Dönitz to position two patrol lines across the convoy's expected track. These comprised ten U-boats of Group *Spitz* (Sharp) and eight of Group *Ungestüm* (Violent). Due to its southerly track and extra slow progress, ONS.154 almost evaded the barriers, only to be spotted by the wing boat of Group *Spitz*, U-664, on 26 December. It was still only 600 miles out.

Three more boats quickly closed. One, the *U-346*, attacked immediately, sinking three British ships and damaging a Dutchman so severely that she fell easy prey to another boat. Although the likely position of the *U-346* was well plastered with depth charges, the Canadians had to move on. Only after the war did records show that they had evened the score somewhat by destroying her.

On the 27th while actually engaged in refuelling a corvette, the critically important oiler, *Scottish Heather*, was herself torpedoed. While not sunk, she incurred damage that obliged her return. Escorts thus had to be detached in turn to refuel in the Azores at a time when thirteen U-boats had made contact. During the night of 28–29 December, nine ships were lost. The action included an early use of the enemy's new pattern-running torpedo which, by circling or zigzagging within a convoy, had a greater chance of finding a target.

Two British destroyers arrived on the 29th, which kept the enemy at a greater distance during the following night. Unfortunately, they had been diverted from another convoy and were already low on fuel. On the 30th, therefore, they and two corvettes were obliged to leave. The long pursuit had, however, left the U-boats in much the same condition and only one more ship was lost. By the 31st no submarine remained in contact.

Fourteen ships had been lost from ONS.154 for, it was believed, none of the enemy. While they had done their utmost in unusual circumstances, the Canadians took harsh criticism from the British, who withdrew all Canadian escort groups for intensive training at the Western Isles base. They were replaced by ships released through the successful conclusion of Operation Torch.

For the Canadians, the battle had been a depressing experience. Their historian rightly bemoaned the continuing deficiency in assets and that U-boats were entering service faster than they could be sunk. 'The long hoped-for support groups, the merchant aircraft carriers and the land-based Liberators had still not materialized, and without them the battle we could look forward to in 1943 would be grimmer than ever.' It is not to the credit of the Royal Navy that it invariably left the Canadians with second-best, particularly in newly-developed equipment.

Canadian pessimism seemed to be well founded. Of the score of convoys suffering the highest losses, fourteen sailed in the six months between September 1942 and March 1943. Operational U-boat strength was increasing at about five times the rate of U-boat losses (see Diagram 3). To the Canadians, their magnificent effort in expanding their fleet so rapidly had resulted in escort groups being formed at a rate that outstripped their ability to fully train them, resulting in the humiliating temporary withdrawal for intensive battle practice.

The British were mesmerized by the near 8 million GRT of Allied-controlled shipping lost during 1942 (see Diagram 1), a horrifying total by any yardstick.

With the benefit of hindsight, however, it is difficult to explain why plain statistics were not more taken into account. As the data was freely available, the only conclusion is that it was officially politic to maximize the threat. For instance, from Diagram 4 one appreciates immediately that the number of operational U-boats increased rapidly from the beginning of 1941 (Curve B). Using the crude relationship of dividing tonnage (Curve A) or numbers of ships (Curve C) sunk per quarter by the average number of operational U-boats in that quarter, it is apparent that, except for the peaks of the two 'happy times', the score per boat was decreasing with time. The Germans, in fact, were suffering the same problems with inexperience as were the Canadians.

Diagram 2 then shows that, over this same period Dönitz was getting even further from his objective. The diagrams account for the British pessimism in that, although there had been a creditable output of new building, losses outstripped it by about 50 per cent. Looking at American-controlled tonnage, however, it is striking how quickly the production of standard ships got into its stride. Even the savage losses of *Paukenschlag* did not prevent the expansion of their fleet during 1942. Offsetting British losses against American gains, it can be seen that tonnage available to the Allies increased by some 1.3 million GRT over the year. As long as the Americans undertook to maintain the level of British imports, vital to their war effort, there was no prospect even at this early stage, that Dönitz could prevail.

Chapter Five

Climax in the Atlantic
(January – July 1943)

When, in June 1941, Germany suddenly turned on her ally, the Soviet Union, it meant that the western powers, by force of circumstance, themselves became allies of a régime as repellent to them as it was to the Germans. In terms of both size and manpower, however, Stalin's union was a colossus. Fired by a genuine hatred it would, if properly armed and equipped, spell ultimate disaster for Germany.

Russian armed forces were inadequately equipped in every sense and, although they, too, were striving to build up their strength, the democracies had every incentive to support them. Even as his armies reeled from the German onslaught, Stalin was assured by Prime Minister Churchill that 'we shall do everything to help you that time, geography and our growing resources allow'. The United States at this time was, of course, not yet a combatant but was pursuing the President's 'short of war' policy.

The sprawling geography of the Soviet Union allowed shipments of aid to be directed via Pacific coast ports, through the head of the Persian Gulf or to the north Russian ports of Archangel and Murmansk. Liable to be vigorously opposed, convoys to the latter region much involved the British Home Fleet and, through the latter's material requirements, affected resources that would otherwise have been directed at the Battle of the Atlantic.

Although the British dispatched the first Arctic convoy as early as August 1941, supplies started moving in earnest only after

October when Congress, having swallowed hard, accepted the political practicality of supporting Stalin. Thus began the famous PQ/QP (later JW/RA) convoy cycle that would be maintained for the duration of hostilities.

Convoys to north Russia, like their counterparts to Malta, were effectively naval operations. Neither offered much scope for variation in route, both were flanked by enemy-held territory. Both were bitterly contested.

The strategy governing the operation of the German Navy's remaining heavy units was rather foggy. Their small number precluded any real trial of strength with the Royal Navy. As solitary raiders they were less cost-effective than auxiliary cruisers and their threat to ocean convoys had been largely eliminated through the accompaniment of convoys by veteran capital ships.

Lacking any real role, they were increasingly based in Norway, where they both offset the Führer's fears of invasion and were well placed to break out into the Atlantic. They also menaced the flank of the Arctic convoys. By adopting the age-old stance of 'fleet-in-being', therefore, the enemy was able to tie down the greater resources of the British Home Fleet.

As the usual policy was to cover outward and homeward movements with a distant escort of heavy units, including a fleet carrier, enemy naval forces based in Norway made few and, usually, half-hearted forays. That of the end of December 1942 promised to be different, however.

On the last day of the year, northbound JW.51B was intercepted by a powerful enemy squadron comprising a 'pocket battleship', a heavy cruiser and six destroyers. In a protracted and confused action, the six destroyers and five smaller ships of the British escort kept the enemy at bay until the arrival of two British light cruisers brought about his withdrawal. The convoy was unscathed.

Although the indecisive handling of the German heavy units was due in great part to their orders to avoid risk, Hitler nonetheless summoned Grand Admiral Raeder, the Fleet C.-in-C., berated him at length on their uselessness and demanded their removal from service. The relationship between the two was already cool and now the Admiral insisted on tendering his resignation. It would be effective from 30 January 1943 on which date he would conveniently have completed ten years as Supreme Commander of the German Navy. To soften the inevitable blow to the service's morale, Raeder was granted the sinecure appointment of Inspector General, while his post was taken by Admiral Dönitz. The appointment underlined the primacy of the U-boat arm but, ironically, within the month, Dönitz successfully argued a reprieve for the heavy ships.

In addition to being supreme commander of the whole fleet, Dönitz remained Flag Officer, U-boats (*Befehlshaber der U-Boote*, or BdU). Although the U-boat war remained his highest priority, it was now inevitable that a greater portion of its conduct would now be assumed by his Chief of Staff, Rear Admiral Eberhard Godt, and a small, hand-picked team.

Direction by Dönitz of submarine operations had also become more distant in the geographical sense. In the heady days following the fall of France, he had established his headquarters in the château of Kernevel, hard by the U-boat base at Lorient. In March 1942 the powerful British commando raid on St Nazaire suggested that BdU could, itself, be targeted and, for its own safety, the organization was relocated to Paris. Now it shifted to Berlin, where Dönitz needed to divide his time between fleet headquarters in one suburb and U-boat headquarters in another. As the Atlantic struggle approached its climax, such upheaval cannot have been beneficial.

During September 1942 Raeder and Dönitz had met with Hitler to review the overall situation in the war at sea. Dönitz highlighted the serious effect of growing Allied maritime air power on U-boat operations. At this point there were some 700 aircraft so engaged, of which barely one third could be termed 'long range'. Nonetheless, U-boats required to spend considerable periods surfaced and were becoming increasingly vulnerable. Still ignorant of the full significance of seaborne Huff Duff, Dönitz tended to credit most interceptions to aerial intervention. Both navy men made a strong case for a new-style U-boat, fast when submerged yet more independent of surface operation. They required also a long-range maritime aircraft to replace the few and inadequate FW200 Kondors. The yet unproven Heinkel He177 was proposed as a possible candidate.

113

Over-influenced by Göring, Supreme Commander of the Luftwaffe, the Führer made no commitment on aircraft but fully agreed a new approach to submarine design. It was probably on this date that the new-generation U-boat was conceived.

The vision at this time was based on the ideas of Professor Hellmuth Walter. To minimize a submarine's size, it is necessary to minimize her weight. On the other hand, battery cells for submerged propulsion were bulky, numerous and heavy. Walter's concept was to remove these from the equation by using a lightweight, closed-cycle turbine when submerged. The energy to drive this unit would be derived from burning diesel oil in an oxygen-rich atmosphere, the oxygen being produced through the breakdown of stored hydrogen peroxide. This compound, in terms of volume and density, is the most efficient means of storing oxygen, but its very readiness to change its chemical state made it unpredictable and dangerous.

The German Navy's technical department had been interested in the concept since 1934 and had built a successful shoreside system in great secrecy. By 1939 Walter's design bureau had produced drawings for a diminutive testbed submarine, whose second major feature was a return to the clutter-free, clean-lined hull of pioneer submersibles. Built during 1939–40 this 80 ton test vehicle, named *V80*, made better than twenty-eight knots submerged.

Despite Dönitz' enthusiastic endorsement, however, there had already been sufficient problems to leave doubts, while the very success of the technically simpler Type VII and Type IX earlier in the war had led to the obvious course of building these in the greatest possible numbers. By 1942, Walter's office had overseen the construction of four larger 'one-offs' and had also investigated the application of the system to torpedo propulsion. Problems continued, however, and Walter's brainchild did not survive infancy. His greatest contribution was to highlight the advantages of the protuberance-free submarine hull, optimized for submerged hydrodynamic efficiency.

Aware that the Allies were gaining the technological edge, Dönitz began to show a slight despondency. Besides the ever-present need to speed-up production, there were several technical shortcomings that required to be addressed.

114

In the deep field, more and better, radar-equipped very long range (VLR) aircraft were operating into the Gap and making life difficult for surfaced U-boats closing in on convoys. While radar search receivers were a major safeguard, they told a skipper no more than that he was probably under observation. What he needed in addition was an active search set that would identify both range and bearing of the threat.

Asdic, when used at moderate speed and in the hands of an experienced operator, was usually very effective. While the operator would be cursing false echoes and the distortion caused by salinity and temperature layers, those in the target below, creeping away in silent routine, were all too aware of the probing beam as they awaited the apocalyptic crash of a depth charge pattern. Although the Asdic's acoustic energy might well be impacting the target, however, it did not necessarily follow that sufficient energy was reflected to allow the AS ship to detect it. To reduce the level of reflected energy even further, BdU requested the development of absorbent hull coatings.

A further concern for Dönitz was the increasingly aggressive patrolling of the Bay of Biscay by British aircraft. While night attacks had, for the moment, been countered by radar search receivers, boats were finding themselves caught by day and, not daring to dive, were having to fight it out. The transfer of Junkers Ju88 fighters to western France had only resulted in Coastal Command deploying Beaufighters and Mosquito aircraft. They carried no depth charges but a formidable array of cannon and rockets. Ranging the Bay in groups they could give a surfaced U-boat a most deadly strafing, often causing an abandoned patrol due to crew casualties alone. The useful payloads of submarines thus had to be reduced to compensate for the weight of extra guns and armour plate to protect bridge personnel.

A last problem concerned the increasing ability of AS escorts to surprise surfaced U-boats in darkness or fog. Skippers thus encountered had very little time in which to react and had an obvious requirement for a self-homing acoustic torpedo with which to occupy the frigate's attention while the submarine took evasive action.

To address the first of these requirements a surface search radar set was already being hurried into production. Designed

FuMo.30, it proved to be unsatisfactory and, as an alternative, a Luftwaffe radar was adapted as the FuMo.61. Known as *Hohentwiel U*, it could detect a freighter at seven kilometres in good conditions. Production was, however, slow and the set came into service as the growing air threat was requiring that U-boats remain submerged as far as possible, in which condition *Hohentwiel* was, of course, useless.

In order to reduce a U-boat's Asdic signature, two types of hull coating were developed. The first, known as *Alberich*, was an aerated rubber paint. Although effective when freshly applied, water pressure slowly collapsed the foam structure, degrading its absorbent properties. An alternative, *Fafnir*, resembled tiles of rubber 'grass'. It proved too fragile in service and, like *Alberich*, had difficulty in adhering to the hull.

Attempts were also made to fool Asdic operators with decoys. Widely used was the *Pillenwerfer*, or Bubble Ejector. Once released, this device hovered at a depth of about thirty metres. Sea water reacted with its calcium hydride filling to produce a dense column of hydrogen bubbles. These gave a solid Asdic return but, by remaining stationary, deceived only inexperienced operators.

By way of enhanced anti-aircraft (AA) armament, U-boats acquired what was available. This included single, twin and quadruple 20mm cannon, single 37mm cannon or twin Breda 13.2mm machine guns. To compensate, all Atlantic boats landed the 8.8cm deck guns which, by now, were rarely used. The increased topside clutter did nothing for submerged manoeuvrability and also increased radiated noise.

A total of eight Type VIIs were converted as special 'flak boats', whose powerfully enhanced armament was designed to trap unwary attackers or to allow the craft to escort others.

For use against escorts the early T-3 *Falke* acoustic torpedo was entering service. Limited in speed, range and homing ability, it was only a stopgap, pending the introduction of the greatly superior T-5 *Zaunkönig*, which was tuned to home directly onto a frigate's high-revving propellers.

Thus Dönitz (or, more correctly, Admiral von Friedeburg, who had succeeded as BdU in February 1943) was acquiring solutions to his major sources of concern but, as Allied technologies were also advancing rapidly, most were soon found inadequate or even, in some cases, nullified.

In January 1943 President Roosevelt and Prime Minister Churchill met again, this time at Casablanca. Their purpose was to agree future strategy and their mood was one of qualified optimism. On land, the Japanese tide had been stemmed in the Pacific, the Afrika Korps defeated at El Alamein and Paulus' 6th Army captured at Stalingrad. Only at sea was there major cause for concern, with the adverse shipping situation and a pressing need to defeat the U-boat.

Although American shipbuilders were confident of more than compensating for losses, this was not yet the case and even the staunchest optimist could not fail to be influenced by the 1,600-plus ships lost during 1942. The Allied shipping pool had been diminished by some 1.3 million GRT, of which 70 per cent had been sunk by submarine. Allied campaigns from North Africa to the Western Pacific consumed further large quantities of tonnage. The net result was that United Kingdom imports had fallen to about 45 per cent of their pre-war level, with the population increasingly short of staples as priorities were accorded to war matériel. From a comfortable distance the Americans, however supportive, could never fully appreciate that, while the Atlantic battle was to them just one more aspect of a complex struggle it was, to the British, literally a matter of life and death. British insistence, which frequently irritated its ally, should be considered against this situation.

The Casablanca conference made far-reaching decisions. Keen to invade northern Europe during 1943, the Americans agreed to delay the operation for a year and reluctantly to become more deeply involved in the sideshow of Sicily and Italy. More pertinently, re-supply convoys to support any northern European invasion could not be considered until the U-boat was beaten.

A huge and sustained Anglo-American bombing effort would be mounted against the French submarine bases and against factories producing components vital to submarine construction. The Bay offensive would be stepped up, with US Army aircraft operating jointly with those of Coastal Command. Centimetric radar sets destined for Bomber Command would be reprioritized for Coastal Command aircraft.

Controversially, the eight-day cycle of the all-important HX convoys would be opened out to ten days from February 1943, releasing escorts sufficient to form at least five support groups. These, as soon as was practicable, would each incorporate an escort carrier (CVE). Tasked to reinforce the escort of any threatened convoy, their objective would be to kill, rather than merely suppress, U-boats.

A further controversial decision was that the Axis partnership would be beaten into unconditional surrender. While this would avoid a rerun of the problems consequent upon ending the earlier war by armistice, it would encourage the enemy, with nothing to lose, to fight to the bitter end. In the case of Dönitz' submarine arm, this was all too true.

A combination of diminished imports and the demands of Operation Torch had greatly reduced Britain's oil fuel stocks. Beyond the Admiralty's emergency reserve there remained sufficient for about ten weeks. To redress the situation and to build up stocks against the eventual European invasion, a new tanker convoy route was initiated, linking Curaçao with New York and the United Kingdom.

Standard-built American tankers, both the turbo-electric T2 type and the steam turbine-driven T3s, were unusually fast for the day and the resulting UC/CU convoys ran at 14 knots. They were an American responsibility and received an American escort. Because of their speed, they were often accompanied by faster merchantmen which, otherwise, would have been constrained to a slower convoy or obliged to run riskily as independents.

Commenced as the Atlantic battle neared its climax, the CU series was highly successful, running in an eventual 1,500 shiploads with the loss of only five ships, three to submarines and two to collision. They illustrated, once again, the advantages of fast convoys over slow.

A vexing problem for the Allied high command was whether their burgeoning Atlantic operations would be more efficiently conducted if made a unified command. While wasteful duplication could obviously be thus avoided, the issue decided itself because none of the Allies could countenance the delegation to others of the responsibility for their strategic waters. Admiral King was also adamant that US naval forces would not serve under British direction, and assumed that, with the United States now the dominant partner, the appointment of an American supreme commander was axiomatic. Although the Admiralty Board professed itself broadly in favour of a 'step-by-step' approach to deeper integration, the First Sea Lord, the very able Sir Dudley Pound, stood firmly against it.

While small improvements were continuously made, therefore, the proposed overall aim was not pursued. In Churchill's words, matters were best left to 'separate commands working in close cooperation and unison on either side of the Atlantic'.

In making major commitments at Casablanca the leaders paid but scant attention to that Cinderella issue, the availability of shipping. The British Minister of War Transport and very experienced shipping man, Lord Leathers, attended the conference as technical adviser but his opinions, vital to the formulation of policy, were of but ancillary interest. Neither the American nor British Chiefs of Staff considered the Ministry to be concerned with military questions yet, even as they drew up their plans and timetables, that same Ministry could have told them that, in their fulfilment, shipping would need to be in more than one place at the same time.

Operations to date had been on a modest scale and tolerably close to home. After Casablanca, objectives included re-opening the Burma Road (Operation Anakim), to shipping over a further 1 million American troops (Operation Bolero), shipments to Free French forces in Africa and more to Soviet Russia via the Persian Gulf. In addition, Admiral King was pressing to increase the tempo against Japan in the Pacific.

In support of these far-flung objectives leaders of both sides seemed beguiled by the pending flood of American-built standard tonnage. Pending, however, remained the operative word for, as we have seen, 1942 had seen a net reduction of 1.3 million GRT in Allied-controlled shipping.

Crucial to the whole war effort was keeping Britain supplied with at least the minimum level of essential imports. Yet Anakim alone, it was calculated, would cost the United Kingdom the equivalent of 0.5 million imported tons during the first half of

1943. Leathers put it later to the Chiefs of Staff: 'We must cut the cost of our strategy according to the cloth of our shipping.' Enormous concerns remained with the British, Churchill being advised that 'It is impossible to plan ahead as long as we are at the mercy of the day-to-day moods [of the Americans] and can only extract last-minute promises, wrapped up in provisos [and] only covering a few months at a time.'

As agreed, the joint bomber offensive against U-boat related targets was greatly increased, but with embarrassingly little result in relation to resources committed and losses sustained.

Following First World War precedent the Germans, having secured the Biscay ports, quickly began the construction of bomb-proof facilities for whole submarine flotillas. Those at Lorient and la Pallice were operational by the end of 1941. That at Bordeaux was nearly complete, with others at Brest and St Nazaire following. During the early stages of their construction, the structure's enormous groundworks, impounded by water-tight caissons, were highly vulnerable to heavy bombing, but the Admiralty failed to recognize the opportunity and requested no special effort of Bomber Command.

Once in place, the roofs were proof against even one-ton bombs, unless dropped from a height that guaranteed poor accuracy. Because of this, the British War Cabinet was driven to the controversial decision to area-bomb the surrounding districts, where lived the forced labour vital to the bases' functioning. The French thus suffered terribly because of their unwelcome guests, while the enemy U-boat crews were unaffected for, between cruises, they were accommodated in hotels along the coast.

As was usual, the British bombed by night, the Americans by day. Over the first five months of 1943, some 7,000 bomber sorties were divided between the U-boat's building yards and their Biscay bases. About 18,000 tons of explosives and incendiaries were released at a cost of 266 aircraft. Not one shelter was penetrated, nor one U-boat directly damaged. The whole offensive became deeply unpopular, as much with the bombers as with the bombed.

Air Marshal Sir John Slessor, about to assume command of Coastal Command, was desperately keen to acquire ASV MkIII centimetric radar sets for his aircraft so as to mount a major effort against the U-boats before they could be provided with a successor to Metox.

Before Casablanca, Bomber Command had enjoyed priority and, as H_2S, the set had been issued to two Pathfinder squadrons as a blind marking aid. It had yet, in January 1943, to be used over enemy territory.

One decision at Casablanca was to allocate Coastal Command the next forty sets. As Slessor awaited these, he requested that the fact of their existence was not compromised, in short that Bomber Command should delay their operational debut. The Prime Minister ruled otherwise.

Early in February, on its second mission, an H_2S set was recovered by the enemy from a bomber shot down near Rotterdam. Scientific examination informed enemy scientists that it worked on a wavelength of only 9.7 centimetres. It confirmed what had been suspected, and why Metox-equipped submarines were being surprised. Work began urgently on a replacement radar search receiver.

January 1943. In the North Atlantic storm succeeded storm, hindering convoys and U-boats alike. Only one HX convoy was attacked during the month, the *U-268* taking one ship out of HX. 222. Her prize was the 14,500 GRT whale factory ship *Vestfold*, whose considerable size enabled her to carry three Landing Craft, Tank (LCT) as deck cargo. These, too, were lost.

To improve matters, Dönitz redirected Group *Delphin* a considerable distance southward to intercept convoy TM.1 between the Azores and the Canaries. The short-lived series of TM convoys ran tankers directly from Trinidad to the Mediter-ranean, post-Torch. This, the first, comprised nine slow tankers with a British escort of one destroyer and three corvettes. Over a period of four days twelve U-boats made contact. Against a defence slated by Dönitz as 'unpracticed' and 'lacking persever-ence', they sank six loaded tankers aggregating 48,360 GRT. This represented some 80,000 tons of oil.

In an empty, gas-free condition, or when loaded with high flashpoint cargo with little ullage space, tankers can, by virtue of their sub-division, be very difficult to sink. Several tankers here were thus torpedoed by more than one submarine, leading to inflated enemy claims of fifteen tankers of 141,000 GRT.

Some 400 U-boats were now in various states of service. Numbers based in French Atlantic ports rose from 145 to 186 between October 1942 and May 1943, an increase of some 28 per cent.

On 24 January 1943 the sixty-one ships of convoy SC.118 left New York. Their escort varied between ten and twelve ships but long-range aircraft, despite being radar-equipped, were much hindered by darkness and the poor conditions. Twenty U-boats of two separate groups worried the convoy between the 4–9 February. The resulting running battle saw ten merchantmen lost. From thirteen attacks on U-boats, escorts sank three and seriously damaged two more.

There were also lessons for the defence. Firstly, large numbers of escorts did not compensate for their never having worked as a team. The unavailability of a support group was critical. The prodigious expenditure of depth charges led to the practice of carrying spare outfits aboard ships of the convoy.

A particularly sad loss was that of the *Toward*, a convoy rescue ship which went down with fifty-eight personnel, many of them already survivors. Overall loss of life on this convoy was particularly heavy, the 464 fatalities being swelled by 272 from the American ship *Henry R. Mallory* alone.

Despite the number of ships destroyed, the enemy war diary noted that 'only the most experienced attackers could achieve results in face of the formidable defences'.

This opinion appeared to be well justified when, on 17 February, the slow convoy ONS.165 was located. Several returning U-boats of Group *Hardegen* were well placed to intercept but, although several made contact, they found the British B-6 escort group well practiced. In exchange for two lost merchant vessels the destroyers *Fame* and *Viscount* sank the U-201 and U-69 respectively. One of the convoy's losses had been caused by the new Type IX40, *U-525* which, in turn, was surprised by a Leigh Light Wellington as she crossed the Bay of Biscay. Badly damaged, she was fortunate to reach her base at Lorient.

Two U-tankers, *U-460* and *U-462*, refuelled no less than

twenty-seven boats at this time, which helped in keeping a larger number than usual on patrol. Despite being evasively routed, ON.166 was discovered and closed by no less than nineteen of the enemy. Thirteen were able to attack over several days, sinking fourteen ships of 79,000 GRT. This contributed greatly to the large increase in tonnage lost during February and was typical of the, mercifully few, convoy disasters that so exercised the minds of those in high authority to the exclusion of the many convoys that passed without incident.

Escorting ON.166 had been the American A-3 group which, despite its title, comprised five corvettes, four Canadian and one British, headed by two American Coast Guard cutters. Greatly occupied in protecting their charges, they were able to account for only one U-boat.

As it happened, the Allies concerned met on 1 March 1943 in Washington for the Atlantic Convoy Conference, the purpose of which was to take the broad overview of the struggle and its implications. For over a year the Americans had exercised authority over the western Atlantic, although the escorting forces were primarily Canadian and British. While for the most part there was harmony, the situation made for what the Canadian historian called 'an imbalance between authority and force levels, [making] for complexities which sometimes led to contradictions'.

Admiral King expressed a strong dislike for mixed-nationality escort groups, where differing procedures lowered efficiency in time of crisis. Such ad hoc grouping had arisen from the original chronic shortage of ships but now, with increasing numbers, the Americans decided to withdraw completely from the more northerly convoy routes and become entirely responsible for those from New York and ports south to the Mediterranean. As this placed considerable extra burden upon the other two navies, the Americans agreed also to cover the CU/UC tanker convoys between the Caribbean and the United Kingdom.

Having started almost from scratch, the Royal Canadian Navy (RCN) was now a full partner and responsible for waters west of longitude 47 degrees W and north of the latitude of New York. To assist in this extra responsibility, all RCN corvettes were returned from other commands and the Royal Navy transferred half a dozen destroyers.

Five support groups, each eventually to be built around a dedicated CVE, would be contributed by both the Royal and US Navies. As, however, the British CVEs would stem from American yards, the Royal Navy's contribution was hostage to factors outside British control. As compensation, the Americans agreed that their first such formation, based on the USS *Bogue*, should operate within the Anglo-Canadian zone of responsibility.

Coastal Command's pioneer B-24 Liberator squadron, No. 120, was based on Iceland. Its aircraft had been stripped in order to accommodate a maximum fuel load and were classed as Very Long Range (VLR). A second squadron, No. 224, operated over the Bay with aircraft in the standard condition.

The B-24 was the best AS aircraft of its time but although Casablanca agreed a further eighty VLR-modified versions to work over the Gap, none had yet materialized. It was early established that the bulk of B-24 production passed to the US Navy and, of 112 on the current inventory, seventy operated over the Pacific. In this theatre they were employed on tasks of lower priority than obtained in the Atlantic. Aircraft and new production were thus diverted with the firm objective of establishing eleven further B-24 squadrons (five US Navy, four US Army, one RAF and one RCAF) in the Atlantic theatre by the end of 1943.

The month of March 1943 was one to test the strongest of Allied constitutions. Several factors were in favour of the enemy. A wild early spring kept Iceland-based VLR aircraft grounded at critical times. There was a ten-day break in Ultra intelligence which greatly affected the evasive routing of convoys at a time when the enemy's *B-Dienst* was freely reading associated Allied radio traffic. Over sixty U-boats were at sea in the North Atlantic and, in the absence of 'special intelligence', D/F fixes placed them over a wide area.

In a rare patch of fine weather, convoy HX.228 was closed by eighteen U-boats of Group *Neuland*. Effective and continuous air cover combined with an aggressive surface escort to limit losses to four ships. In return the escort, the British B-3 group, sank two of the enemy.

The B-3 leader, the destroyer *Harvester*, surprised and rammed the *U-444*. Both were so damaged as to be left dead in the water, in which condition the *Harvester* was easily dispatched by the *U-432*. Arriving too late to prevent the destroyer's loss, the Free French corvette *Aconit* returned the compliment by sinking the disabled *U-444*. As she then closed to rescue the *Harvester*'s survivors, the *Aconit* detected the victorious *U-432*, which she promptly blew to the surface with two accurate depth charge patterns before finishing the job with gunfire and ramming. With the *Harvester* was unfortunately lost Commander A.A. Tait, an 'outstanding' group leader.

Portents were ominous as the Submarine Tracking Room's weekly summary noted that two large convoys, SC.122 and HX.229, were placed to unavoidably cross an area heavily populated by the enemy.

Eventually comprising fifty-one ships, SC.122 had left New York on 5 March 1943. Three days later, the thirty-eight ship HX.229 departed the same port. For the early part of their passage, their routes were divergent, but were almost coincident at the Gap. As the later convoy was the faster, it brought the two masses of ships into dangerously close proximity at a particularly hazardous point.

East of Newfoundland, Group *Raubgraf*'s location was known to the British, who signalled both convoys to take a more southerly track to avoid it. The signal was decoded by the *B-Dienst*, enabling BdU to place two more groups on lines of search along the newly projected convoy track. By the evening of 15 March both convoys, then some 120 miles apart, had been located and a total of thirty-eight U-boats were closing.

During the following night HX.229 took the first onslaught. Badly hit, it lost ten ships, with six others torpedoed and abandoned. Large numbers of survivors required assistance and, in the absence of a dedicated rescue ship, this duty fell on the escort. Itself only six strong, it was thus greatly diverted from its primary task, rendering the enemy's task the easier.

Rather scattered by the customary stormy conditions, SC.122 now also became a target. A first probe by *U-338* sank three ships and damaged one more from a single torpedo salvo. Urgently requested escort reinforcement sailed from Iceland and Newfoundland but, in 70-knot winds, made slow progress. Their eventual arrival did no more than replace others that had left to refuel.

Fortunately, B-24s from Iceland and Northern Ireland were able to maintain a presence throughout the 17th. They made numerous contacts and carried out several attacks, preventing several submarines from making 'end-arounds' for further attacks.

Including three more sunk during the night of 17–18 March, HX.229 lost a total of thirteen large vessels, aggregating over 93,000 GRT. A similar slaughter to SC.122 was averted by its arriving more quickly under air cover, B-24s being supplemented by B-17s, then Sunderlands. A total of fifty-four sorties were flown in the convoy's support, resulting in thirty-two sightings and twenty-one attacks. One U-boat, *U-384*, was destroyed and, again, several more were made to lose contact. With nine escorts present, the convoy still lost nine ships of 53,000 GRT.

As his skippers reported sinking thirty-two ships of 186,000 GRT from what they assumed to be a single convoy, Dönitz was understandably elated. The true figures were, however, grim enough and, with only one submarine claimed in return, caused considerable despondency at the Admiralty.

The welcome entry into service of the long-awaited support groups was frustrated by truly appalling weather. In February a British group, based on the CVE *Dasher*, had to leave the North Russian convoy JW.53 when the little carrier was damaged by heavy seas. Then, early in March, the American *Bogue* group was obliged to leave HX.228 and make for Newfoundland.

A first quartette of CVEs had been delivered to the Royal Navy during the autumn of 1942 but had been diverted by the requirements of Torch. Engaged in these duties, the *Avenger* was torpedoed by the *U-155* west of Gibraltar on 15 November 1942. Splinters from the explosion penetrated her magazine and she blew up. On ships this small, based on C-3 mercantile hulls (i.e. between 450 and 500 feet on the waterline) it was difficult to provide protection in depth but, where the US Navy accepted this as a wartime risk, the Royal Navy now insisted on locating the magazine inboard of new longitudinal bulkheads, sited ten to fifteen feet from the side shell plating.

Then the *Dasher* was lost, suffering a catastrophic avgas explosion while exercising in the Clyde and sinking with over two-thirds of her crew. In British opinion, fuel stowage and handling arrangements were far too basic and a major difference arose with the Americans when the Royal Navy insisted upon a further six-week programme of modifications before acceptance. The results almost halved fuel stowage and added considerable weight.

The British were also unhappy with the initial stability of the CVEs, and their stability range. A further 1,000 tons of ballast were added, while void wing spaces were filled with sealed oil drums. While these modifications restored British confidence in small carriers, the Americans looked upon the delays as wholly unacceptable at a time of great emergency.

Of the original group of four, therefore, only two CVEs (*Archer* and *Biter*) were able to assume Atlantic convoy support in April 1943. The designed air wing was six Grumman F4F Wildcat fighters (called Martlets in British service) and nine Grumman TBM Avenger torpedo bombers. The fitted catapult was not compatible with British aircraft such as the Swordfish and Hurricane. American CVEs employed deck parks to increase their aircraft complement to a typical nine F4Fs and twelve TBMs.

In Fleet Air Arm service, the versatility of the Avenger was fully exploited. In its internal weapons bay it could carry bombs or mines, acoustic torpedoes or depth charges. Eight of the new sixty-six-pound rocket projectiles could be accommodated in external, underwing racks. These weapons featured a solid, twenty-five-pound semi-armour piercing (SAP) head, capable of punching through the toughest pressure hull. Simple and reliable, the rockets could equally well be carried by fighters or by the Swordfish.

Captain F.J. ('Johnny') Walker now commanded the Second Escort Group (2EG), comprising seven *Black Swan*-type sloops. Already proven as excellent AS ships, they were deadly when under Walker's control.

Walker's speciality, and ever being refined, was his 'creeping' attack. Having driven a U-boat deep, its usual evasive tactic, he would put a sloop on its tail. This ship would use her Asdic which, being clearly audible by the enemy, encouraged him to keep ahead of his tracker. As his submerged speed was low, it was then simple to have a second sloop slip silently past the first and take station, unsuspected, *ahead* of the target. At a given signal, the leading sloop would release twenty-six deep-set depth charges in pairs at nine-second intervals. Only exceptionally alert U-boat skippers escaped the trap.

Gritty battles fought around a few unlucky convoys were responsible in part for the total of 120 ships of 693,000 GRT lost in March 1943. Taken in isolation, these dour struggles gave an entirely distorted view of the success or otherwise of the overall convoy system. The appalling loss in lives and ships greatly affected the weary men directing operations, some even doubting the continued viability of convoy in the face of growing U-boat strength.

The following table lists the total number of each of the major North Atlantic convoys, arriving and departing during the month of March 1943.

Convoy Designator	Number Sailed And Arrived	Ships Convoyed	Ships Destroyed	Tonnage Destroyed
HX	6	301	19	111,000
SC	6	276	15	79,000
ON	12	458	14	103,000
SL	2	57	4	29,000
OS	3	122	6	26,000
Totals:	29	1214	58	348,000

As can be seen, about half the month's losses from all causes had occurred from the critical North Atlantic convoys. Eighteen of the twenty-nine convoys listed, however, suffered no loss. Less than one-third of the total had, therefore, borne the loss of fifty-eight ships which, a savage enough price, represented a just-sustainable loss rate of about 4.8 per cent of all ships convoyed. The general despondency arose because, at that point, there was no reason to assume that matters would improve.

Although a record 170 U-boats were deployed in the Atlantic by the end of March 1943, they were being significantly punished, with most of the nineteen sunk in February and fifteen in March being lost in this theatre. Most went down without survivors; the crew that did survive were captured. There was, therefore, a continuous stream of raw skippers and crews squaring up to an increasingly experienced and better-equipped Allied defence.

Many patrolling U-boats never even sighted a potential target. During February 1943, for instance, thirty-six of sixty-nine North Atlantic patrols sank nothing. In the critical month of March it was worse, the proportion being twenty-nine in forty-nine.

Following a steady decrease since the beginning of hostilities, U-boat losses in the North Atlantic, expressed as a percentage of the actual number of boats at sea in that theatre, had begun to rise. The enemy's own figures record 13.4 per cent in 1940, 11.4 per cent in 1941, 7.0 per cent in 1942 but, for the first three months of 1943, 9.2 per cent. At this stage, only straws in the wind, but the wind was freshening.

Coastal Command, the value of whose ASV Mark II had been degraded by Metox since the previous autumn, was set to make a comeback in the Bay of Biscay. In a maximum effort to assist convoys directly in the early spring of 1943, the Bay had been left only lightly covered and it was significant that, during the February, the only U-boat destroyed transiting these waters was by a US Army B-24 equipped with a new 10-cm radar. Two squadrons of these invaluable aircraft had been moved to south west England but, before they had been allowed to make much impact, had been redeployed to Morocco. Reluctantly, Dönitz had moved a force of U-boats to these waters to attack post-Torch support shipping. The greater proportion of this tonnage was American and the B-24s remained under American authority.

The Anglo-American bombing assault on French U-boat bases had begun on 14 January 1943. By the end of February Dönitz reported the surrounding districts of St Nazaire and Lorient destroyed – 'No dog or cat is left . . . nothing but the submarine shelters remain'. U-boats within the completed pens were indeed secure but, along with the homes of thousands of hapless French citizens, essential services to the facilities were destroyed. They

129

could always be reinstated, and indeed were, but the regular disruption to both workforce and services had a definite, if unquantifiable, effect on refit programmes.

To use these bases, however, the submarines still had to navigate the waters of the Bay of Biscay, and here they were vulnerable. Although the number of Coastal Command aircraft equipped with ASV Mark III was yet small, their ability to surprise Metox-equipped boats greatly concerned Dönitz, who correctly inferred its existence. A score of sudden attacks resulted in only two sinkings but had the effect, at the end of April, of BdU again ordering boats to remain submerged by night in these waters, surfacing in daylight only long enough to recharge.

German scientists were working to produce a practical search receiver (*Naxos*) but, three months after the recovery of the *Rotterdam Gerät*, had not yet been successful. U-boats caught on the surface by aircraft were ordered to fight it out rather than risk themselves during the vulnerable phase of submergence. This played into the hands of the fliers because although older aircraft were, singly, no match for a U-boat's firepower, they were increasingly flying in pairs or groups and were able to overwhelm the enemy gunners whose firing arcs were, in any case, limited.

Naval direction of the resources of the RAF's Coastal Command usually worked very smoothly. Submarine losses began to increase in May, and included that of the first U-tanker, *U-463*, outward bound on her fifth mission. Direct input from the Admiralty's Submarine Tracking Room indicated convoys most threatened and requiring priority air cover. Like the Americans, the British accorded troop movements the highest priority. Most were by small groups of fast passenger liners but other comprised the so-called 'Monsters'. These ships, the largest and fastest, usually proceeded alone, relying on their great speed and subtle zigzagging for protection. In this they were largely successful against submarines but the early loss of the 42,350 GRT *Empress of Britain* had demonstrated their vulnerability to even single enemy maritime aircraft. Air cover in near waters thus became a further priority. With the major tasks addressed, Coastal Command's remaining resources could be directed at the Bay.

These waters were the purlieu of Plymouth-based 19 Group. Its commanding officer, Air Vice Marshal Geoffrey Bromet, took advantage of Dönitz' new instructions by saturating the Bay of Biscay with day patrols, even including the usually nocturnal Leigh Light Wellingtons.

Often proceeding in groups to concentrate their firepower, U-boats presented a considerable risk to pilots, but loss was accepted for the occasional success. A flight of Polish Mosquito aircraft found a group of five surfaced boats and, by cannon fire alone, caused two of them to abort their patrols. Facing facts, Dönitz again ordered his boats to risk submerging if discovered. This, however, also increased time submerged, slowing transit rates and reducing time spent in operational areas.

As the answer to group defence by U-boats was group attack by aircraft, patrol patterns were reorganized along the lines of Dönitz' own 'wolf pack' tactics. Three times each day, seven aircraft would fly on parallel tracks, fifteen miles apart. Any sighting a target would orbit and summon the remainder. The potential weakness of this system was its regular pattern. Dönitz knew to the minute when these flights would get airborne and made repeated requests for Luftwaffe intruder patrols, but to no avail.

Encounters between aircraft and submarine were often marked by great determination on each side. A Leigh Light Wellington of 172 Squadron discovered a special prize in the U-tanker *U-459*. The latter's eight 20mm cannon far outgunned the bomber but left the pilot, Flying Officer Jennings, undeterred. Heading straight and low into a wall of metal, the Wellington was mortally hit. Out of control, it sliced through the enemy's conning tower, disintegrating in the process. Crew members fought their way from below to move the dead and dying, and to disentangle the wreckage. They then discovered two or three live depth charges in the debris. Rather than risk defusing them in their damaged state, the veteran German skipper, Georg von Wilamowitz-Möllendorf, decided to increase to full speed and to roll them overboard. Unfortunately, they were fused on the ultra-shallow twenty-five feet setting and the resulting explosion all but disabled the *U-459*. Settling aft and slowly circling, she fell easy victim to a second aircraft, probably summoned by Jennings. The second pilot radioed a call for assistance and a Polish destroyer was able to rescue forty Germans and one of Jennings' crew. Following evidence given by the enemy survivors, Jennings was awarded a posthumous Victoria Cross.

Resourceful U-boat skippers discovered that they could defeat 'Johnny' Walker's creeping attacks by making continual small changes of course. Equally astute, Walker responded with the 'plaster' attack. The directing ship again followed the submerged target, but at a slightly overtaking speed. Close on either beam, two other sloops kept station. At such low speed, their joint noise was easily mistaken by the enemy for that of one ship. At a given signal, all three ships would accelerate and 'plaster' their track with depth charges set for 500 feet and released at five-second intervals.

This form of attack was first tried out by 2EG in June 1943 as it steamed to support convoy HX.241. The very experienced *U-202* actually withstood a total of 250 depth charges before broaching and being destroyed by gunfire.

Walker's view that explosives were cheaper than submarines was not necessarily shared by the authorities and work had been done on 'fixing' a submerged target in three dimensions, i.e. bearing, range and depth. To measure depth, a second Asdic transducer, known as the 'Q Attachment', was added. This produced a narrow beam at a steeper angle than the main beam and which could maintain target contact up the point of attack. The apparatus was refined as the Type 147, which generated thin, fan-shaped beams and which could be tilted through a vertical forty-five degrees. With the target's position well-defined, the forward-firing Hedgehog was about to prove deadly.

As depth charges were still employed in large numbers, there was still a problem with 'dead' time, reduced by making the weapons faster-sinking. Statistics again, however, soon began to tell their own story. Hundreds of depth charge attacks had resulted in a comparatively steady kill rate of about 6 per cent, or one in every sixteen attacks. Once initial difficulties and preju-dices had been overcome, Hedgehog's success rate slowly climbed to near 30 per cent, almost one in three. In 1943, however, this level of competence still had to be achieved.

* * *

Extensive operations during March 1943 saw an unusually large number of U-boats heading home for rest and refurbishment. To fill the resulting vacuum, Dönitz ordered north all of the larger Type IXCs that were already deployed in the more distant waters of the central Atlantic and, by a considerable effort, sailed no less than ninety-eight further boats during April, seventy of them to the North Atlantic.

One of these boats, *U-262*, was directed to the St Lawrence. Many surviving U-boat men, including the ace Otto Kretschmer, were incarcerated in Canadian prisoner of war camps close by and, using a crude code in personal letters, a breakout had been arranged.

En route to her rendezvous, *U-262* encountered the fifty-seven ship HX.233 on 15 April. Obeying procedures, she remained long enough to vector-in seven other boats before proceeding. These, later coded Group *Specht* (Woodpecker), had little luck. Four managed to attack but conditions were calm and the eight ships of the American A-3 escort group were quickly reinforced by the British Support Group 3 (SG3). Only one ship was sunk, a new Canadian-built standard, the 7,100 GRT *Fort Rampart*. Her loss was balanced by that of a Type IXC, the *U-175*, destroyed by the US Coast Guard cutters *Spencer* and *Duane*. The German history noted that the escort commander was aware of the relatively small number of assailants and permitted his ships to make persistent hunts.

As for the *U-262*, her mission was unsuccessful. She loitered for five days in the St Lawrence, without result. Having incurred ice damage, she withdrew to refuel from a U-tanker before returning to France.

During April 1943 many Atlantic U-boats were concentrating in the north as Group *Meise* (Titmouse) and convoys were being routed to the south to avoid them. On 21 April, however, two of their number separately sighted convoys HX.234 and ONS.3, and the group's coherence was necessarily broken. Although two ships were taken from HX.234, rapid reinforcement by VLR aircraft saw a B-24 compensate with the destruction of *U-189*.

It should be explained that, with New York becoming very congested as a convoy terminal, Halifax became the western terminal for slow convoys from March 1943. Eastbound movements continued to be coded 'SC' but westbound began a new ONS series, beginning with ONS.1 which sailed from Liverpool on 15 March.

On 28 April Group *Meise* fastened onto convoy ONS.4. This was screened by the British B-2 escort group, commanded by another noted U-boat killer, Captain Donald MacIntyre, in the destroyer *Hesperus*. Also on hand was the support group SG5, centred on the CVE HMS *Biter*, whose slow-flying Swordfish soon caused problems to U-boats trying to gain attack positions.

Hesperus opened proceedings by eliminating the *U-191* with a combination of Hedgehog, depth charges and one of the terrifying, tube-launched Mark X one-ton depth charges. Pinpointed and held down by a Swordfish, the *U-203* was then dispatched by the destroyer *Pathfinder*.

As the enemy continued to probe fruitlessly, the already powerful escort was further strengthened by the arrival of SG1 and more VLR cover. Accepting realities, Dönitz called off the attack, concerned at the loss of two boats yet exhorting the remainder to greater effort and to increased risk-taking.

Good use of Ultra intelligence then allowed planners to thread convoys SC.127 and HX.235 through no less than thirty-two U-boats, but these were then reorganized. One section, Group *Star* (Starling) located ONS.5 on 28 April 1943. Its forty-three ships were escorted by another experienced British group, Peter Gretton's B-7. From HMS *Duncan* he commanded two destroyers, a frigate and four corvettes but, although a RAS tanker was in company, unremittingly foul weather conditions prevented any refuelling. To shorten the route, ONS.5 thus kept close to the Great Circle track.

Group *Star*'s boats were already at the end of their resources and were dispersing but one of its number, *U-650*, dogged the convoy until it hit the middle of the search line of the thirty-boat Group *Fink* (Finch). The British were experiencing one of their periodic 'Enigma blackouts' but, while the Submarine Tracking Room was consequently operating at below customary levels of efficiency, it knew of the presence of a further line beyond Group *Fink*. This was known as *Amsel* (Blackbird). Support Group SG3 was sailed urgently from Newfoundland, meeting the convoy, which was all but hove-to in the conditions, on 2 May.

The convoy had, meanwhile, suffered its first loss when, on 29 April, the *U-258* put a single torpedo into the veteran American tanker *McKeesport*. In ballast and gas-free she, typically, refused to sink. In normal times she would have been salvaged but, with no ocean-going tug accompanying the convoy and a major battle looming, she was finished off by the escort.

With the convoy much scattered, the escorts, too, had problems. The *Duncan* had to fall out with a severe leak, while SG3's destroyers had used so much fuel in labouring against the heavy seas that they, too, had to leave. On 4 May, with a deteriorating situation, SG1 was ordered out from Newfoundland.

No less than fifty-three U-boats were now in a position to molest ONS.5 and a maximum air effort was laid on. This quickly paid off with a Canadian PBY Catalina surprising the *U-209* on 4 May and dispatching her economically with just four shallow-set depth charges.

At this stage, the convoy comprised a main body of about thirty ships, a further group of six and the remainder straggling. In this vulnerable state it took the main assault by both enemy groups. Although *U-630* was also destroyed on 4 May, her loss was quickly offset as dusk fell. During the hours of darkness, five ships were picked off from the main group, together with one straggler.

As conditions improved on 5 May the badly depleted escorts began to refuel from the tanker. The situation was now eased by the convoy's track crossing the Newfoundland Grand Banks, notorious for fogs. Visibility shut down, blinding surfaced U-boats but leaving them open to being surprised by radar-equipped escorts. Engaged in rounding-up stragglers, the corvette *Pink* thus caught and sank the *U-192*.

As SG1 arrived during the 5th, other escorts had to leave, and matters remained very much in the balance. Two boats, *U-264* and *U-266*, successfully penetrated the screen and sank three ships apiece from the main group. Four others each took one ship. For this savagery they, however, paid. The corvette *Loosestrife* ran down and sank the *U-192*, while *Vidette*'s Hedgehog accounted for the *U-531*. Another destroyer, *Oribi* of SG3, rammed and sank the *U-125*. The newly-arrived SG2 sloop *Pelican* detected the *U-438* in thick fog, surprised and sank her. Another corvette, *Sunflower*, accounted for the *U-638*.

Many attacks by the escorts had been curtailed by the need to rejoin their charges. Several U-boats had, however, been damaged to the extent that they had to abandon their patrols. One, the triumphant *U-266*, was then caught and sunk by a Coastal Command Halifax as she crossed the Bay of Biscay.

Early on 6 May the enemy hauled off as ONS.5 came within the area of the western local escort. Some 62,000 GRT had been lost but the enemy had paid with seven submarines.

This setback was thoroughly analysed by Dönitz. The disproportionately high number of Type IXs lost pointed to their greater size and inferior manoeuvrability being detrimental to their continued deployment against convoys. Four boats had been surprised out of thick fog, two with fatal results. Metox had been reported as useless and BdU ascribed the incidents to the escort's radar. Even with the inflated claims of 90,000 GRT destroyed, a general feeling of gloom was hard to dispel.

In truth, the situation was worse than even Dönitz thought, for no escort carrier had participated and VLR flights had been badly disrupted by weather. The success was due simply to an experienced surface escort, reinforced by support groups when under pressure.

Dönitz wasted no time in determining whether or not it had been an unrepresentative 'one-off'. *B-Dienst* predicted two east-bound convoys, HX.237 and SC.129, which were also routed well southward of normal. Remaining boats of Group *Amsel* were reorganized in two searchlines, coded Groups *Elbe* and *Rhein*. The exact position of HX.237 for noon on 11 May had been decoded and it was duly sighted by *U-359*. Western Approaches Command recognized the threat and directed SG5, including the CVE HMS *Biter*, to reinforce the convoy escort, the Canadian C-2 group.

Swordfish from the *Biter* caused two shadowers to lose contact, but four more succeeded in closing the convoy. Three ships, two Norwegian and one British, were sunk but for their total of 21,000 GRT the attackers lost a similar number. All were destroyed by noticeably smooth cooperation between various elements of the defence. Thus, the veteran *U-89* was marked by a Swordfish and depth-charged to destruction by two escorts, of which one was an ex-American four-stacker. The *U-456* was disabled by an acoustic torpedo dropped by a B-24, making her easy meat for a destroyer. Finally, the *U-753* was damaged by a Canadian-crewed Sunderland, to be finished off by two escorts, one Canadian, one British.

Once again, Dönitz had received a poor return on his investment, but the Fleet Air Arm had discovered that Swordfish were very vulnerable to return fire, and single aircraft were thus forbidden to attack surfaced U-boats.

Group *Elbe*'s twenty-one boats were now divided into two forces, one of which located SC.129 on 11 May. With HX.237 now out of trouble it was possible to divert SG5 to meet the new threat, although it could not arrive before the 13th.

The attack opened on the evening of the 11th, when *U-402* slipped through the screen to sink two ships with one torpedo spread. Quickly locating the firing point, the corvette *Gentian* damaged the submarine sufficiently to enforce her return.

Once again, the escort was the veteran British B-2 group, headed by Donald MacIntyre in the destroyer *Hesperus*. With one of his speciality Mark X depth charges he brought the *U-223* to the surface but had insufficient time to complete her destruction. Wrecked internally, she reached her French base.

MacIntyre made no such mistake with the *U-186*, running down a D/F bearing and blasting her with conventional depth charges. As usual, there were no survivors. In total, B-2 had made over a dozen attacks and had kept the enemy at bay. With the arrival of SG5 the escorts could begin to refuel from their tanker.

As we have seen, good intelligence gave the British an accurate picture of U-boat dispositions, enabling convoys to be evasively routed around the marauding groups of enemy boats. For the benefit of escort commanders and convoy commodores, however, the Admiralty transmitted regular 'U-boat situation' signals. Its cipher had long been broken by the German *B-dienst*, allowing the enemy to occasionally accurately predict a convoy's waypoints.

Thus, in mid-May 1943, convoy SC.130 found itself heading into Groups *Iller* and *Donau*, divided into four tactical units, with Group *Oder* disposed beyond, along the convoy's projected track. The usual enemy radio traffic warned of the developing threat, however, and Peter Gretton's B-7 escort group was reinforced by SG1. Regular B-24 cover was mounted from Iceland and it was one of these aircraft that opened proceedings by dropping two acoustic torpedoes into the swirl left by the submerging *U-954*. She was never seen again and among her lost crew was Dönitz' own younger son.

Twelve experienced escorts and effective air cover frustrated every attempt by the enemy to gain an attacking position, his persistence costing him two more submarines. Gretton's report bemoaned the poor communications still existing between surface escorts and aircraft. The enemy blamed the continuous presence of aircraft although, in fact, there were never more than two circling at any one time.

Just a few days later, Groups *Mosel* and *Donau* found ON.184 and HX.239 passing in fairly close proximity. Each convoy had an escort group and a support group in company. Aircraft from two CVEs, the USS *Bogue* and HMS *Archer*, were able to frustrate all attempts at attack. In the course of these, the Americans destroyed the *U-569* and the British the *U-752*. The latter was the first unaided kill credited to a British CVE.

Further depressed by bereavement, Dönitz contemplated defeat. Thirty-one U-boats had been lost in the first twenty-three days of May 1943 (by the end of the month it would be forty). In just one month this meant a loss in personnel, dead or captive, of about 1,600. In return, his force had sunk just six ships in convoy, some 35,000 GRT.

Pending the availability of a centimetric radar detector, reliable anti-escort acoustic torpedoes and further AA weapons, Dönitz decided to abandon operations against North Atlantic convoys and concentrate on those areas where defences were less effective. To conceal this temporary withdrawal, a dozen boats were directed to act as rearguard, transmitting radio messages to simulate the missing groups. Even this ruse rebounded, the transmissions leading to three being ambushed and sunk, two by aircraft and the other 'carpet-bombed' by 'Johnny' Walker's SG2.

Beneath its bland, top-secret cover, the exchange of Ultra information between Great Britain and the United States was far from a smooth process. An early and enthusiastic prime ministerial

138

decision to pool resources was followed by the reality of British experts acting coyly in the actual release of information, a source of continual friction.

In fairness, the British valued Ultra as a precious asset, never to be jeopardized by allowing the enemy to suspect that his security had been compromised. 'Need to know' was rigorously preserved and only an absolute minimum were party to the secret. Once the existence of Ultra was passed into foreign hands, those safeguards could no longer be guaranteed. Safeguards included deliberately not acting on much useful information where the resulting action could not be attributed by the enemy to a logical cause other than a security leak.

Admiral King, again typically, argued that British caution was exaggerated and pushed to employ Ultra information more aggressively. An example was a round-up of the enemy's U-tankers but, while nobody on the British side would have argued against the huge advantage accruing from the liquidation of these maritime filling stations, no suitable 'cover story' was acceptable and the proposal was vetoed.

King, however, was not entirely wrong. The US Navy depended much on the output of decrypts from Bletchley Park, and the rate of throughput from this establishment depended in turn on the number of operable 'bombes'. These complex machines deduced the Enigma rotor order, together with interconnections. Laborious to construct, ever in short supply, bombes were required to work also on Army, Rail and Luftwaffe Enigma traffic. With a degree more candour from the British, American resources could have ensured an adequate number and, in King's opinion, 'shortened the war considerably'. The British were equally convinced that such a procedure would inevitably have led to the loss of secrecy. The enemy would have responded by changing his methods and prime intelligence would have been lost to both Allies.

American and British leaders met again in Washington during 12–25 May 1943 for the so-called Trident Conference. Timetables were agreed for the invasions of Sicily, Italy and continental Europe. Also approved was the scope and magnitude of support for the Soviet Union and China. It was recognized that, until the U-boat menace was subdued, a European invasion was at risk due to the vulnerability of essential supply convoys. An important outcome of Trident was, therefore, a resolution to further intensify anti U-boat measures.

Firstly, Britain would exert diplomatic pressure on neutral Portugal to enable facilities for VLR aircraft and AS escorts to be established in the Azores. (This objective would be realized in the following October). An all-out offensive by Coastal Command in the Bay of Biscay would be supported by the British-based US Eighth Air Force specifically targeting German building yards.

Just before the Trident Conference, Admiral King had taken an important initiative in his creation of the US Tenth Fleet. During seventeen months of war, the American organization for Atlantic AS operations had developed haphazardly, reflecting the eclectic range of assets initially available. At last the 'jeep' carriers (as American CVEs were commonly termed), destroyer escorts (DEs) and VLR aircraft were about to appear in numbers and a coherent fleet structure was required to employ them to best advantage.

Although, ultimately, the Tenth Fleet was commanded by King, its effective head was his Chief of Staff, Rear Admiral Francis S. Low.

An important question now resolved was that of who controlled the AS aerial effort. King succeeded in having it assumed by the Navy and the Army's contribution, twenty-seven squadrons of adapted aircraft, were exchanged for a similar unmodified number.

For Coastal Command the Bay offensive had not been altogether satisfactory. Operation Enclose of 20–28 March 1943 had resulted in the sighting of twenty-six of the forty-one U-boats transiting the waters. Fifteen of these had been attacked but only one sunk.

Enclose II of 6–13 April was even less successful in that only eleven of twenty-five U-boats were sighted, four attacked and, again, one sunk. The aggressive chief of Coastal Command, Air Marshal Sir John Slessor, then conferred with 19 Group's head, Air Vice Marshal Geoffrey Bromet. Responsible for the Biscay area, Plymouth-based 19 Group was now tasked with Derange, an operation to run from 13 April until 6 June.

Two squadrons of Wellingtons, with up-rated engines, Leigh

Light and ASV Mark III centimetric radar, would run saturation patrols over the Bay by night, forcing U-boats to remain submerged and, thus, to surface by day in order to recharge. With CVEs now operating in the Atlantic it was possible to 'borrow' a squadron of the precious B-24s. These, together with two squadrons of Halifax aircraft, all with ASV Mark III, would reinforce Sunderlands and older, ASV Mark II-equipped, aircraft for a daylight blitz.

During May, four U-boats were destroyed by aircraft in the Bay and many more harassed and damaged, six so badly that they had to return. With this promising start, and wishing to further intensify effort, Slessor flew to Washington to see King. His objective was to secure the services of some of the B-24 squadrons being transferred by the US Army. In this he was successful and, between July and September 1943, five squadrons were moved to southern England and placed under British control.

Admiral Dönitz, meanwhile, was urgently looking to improved technology to assist his force in re-establishing the initiative. While the great hopes placed on the revolutionary Walter hydrogen peroxide boat were increasingly appearing to be misplaced, the spin-off high-speed hull packed with extra battery power looked highly promising. From May 1943, development proceeded in earnest on the Schnorkel, a concept going back to the twenties.

Despite the solid evidence of recovered H_2S equipment, German scientists continued to doubt the practicality of airborne centimetric radar. A crystal detector, 'Naxos', was expected to be available 'some time before the end of the year'. Before then, a new search receiver which could sweep a frequency band, code-named Wanze, would be available.

A false report had convinced Dönitz that Metox emitted radiation powerful enough for Allied aircraft to home on. Restrictions, later an outright ban, were therefore placed on its use. Wanze was intended as a non-radiating substitute but, as its median wavelength was about 80cm, it was never likely to be effective in detecting the pulses for ASV Mark III.

Also introduced at this time was an ingenious, non-electronic means of extending a U-boat's search horizon. The Focke-Achgelis Fa330 knock-down wind-powered helicopter could loft an observer to 500 feet in a relative windspeed of only 15 knots. As it was tethered by line and winch, however, the observer had to be viewed as expendable in an emergency.

Despite improvements in technology, the loss of skilled workers to the armed forces meant that submarine maintenance work slowed considerably. At the outset, a U-boat would spend six months at sea for every four in dockyard hands. By 1943 this ratio had been reversed. In 1941, working-up took three weeks; two years later it required six.

The latest programme of naval construction, submitted for the Führer's approval in April 1943, reflected the greatly changed priorities of the *Kriegsmarine*. There was no plan to build anything larger than torpedo boats and destroyers. The only other 'offensive' surface craft were E-boats (termed 'S'-boats by the Germans). The remainder comprised substantial numbers of minesweepers, mine destructor vessels and coastal escorts, a response to the beleaguered state of German shipping.

Of major priority was the programmed construction of twenty-seven to thirty U-boats per month. Interestingly, this production rate extended into 1944, indicating a realism with regard to how long it would take to introduce the new *Elektroboote*, upon which all would ultimately depend.

As neither skilled labour nor raw materials could be further diverted to realize the plan, it was approved only on condition that it was subsumed into the overall programme of Albert Speer's Armaments Ministry. If Dönitz entertained misgivings at thus relinquishing a large measure of control, these were quickly dispelled by Speer's renowned efficiency. With losses mounting Dönitz was encouraged to request an increase to forty boats per month, and received a favourable response. He noted also the reduced time necessary to take a new project from concept to practical application.

Even Speer, however, would have been dismayed could he have seen at first hand American ship production, which really began to get into its stride in mid-1942. By January 1943 it had produced sufficient tonnage to offset that sunk by U-boats alone. In the July it was at a level that exceeded losses due to all types of enemy action and, by September, it would exceed all losses from enemy action and all other marine causes combined. Short of a total breakdown in the morale of mercantile seamen, there was no way from this point that Dönitz, however determined, could resolve the outcome of the war by submarine operations alone.

The United States were doing what they did best and, in truth, their citizens and High Command had never doubted the eventual outcome. But now, even the British, their Commonwealth brethren and the limited forces of 'free' Europeans, all of whom had suffered so much, could permit themselves that rise in spirit that presaged the beginning of the end.

Chapter Six

The Battle Won
(August – December 1943)

As a measure to boost Allied morale, the enormous American shipbuilding programmes were accorded maximum publicity. Purpose-built ship assembly facilities (hardly shipyards in the then accepted sense) with six or more slipways turned out 7,000-tonners as alike as peas from a pod. Cinemas and magazines carried powerful images of rows of identical hulls, ranged for launch or packing the fitting-out berths. Newsreels of grim-faced soldiers, bound for the re-conquest of Europe, were counterpointed by those of smiling, even glamorous, female welders working on the ships that would support them. The impression was one of a nation fully mobilized, fully committed.

As intended, the message was not lost on the enemy. Indeed, it was so effective that Admiral Dönitz believed that the Allies had stemmed the shipping haemorrhage by the beginning of 1943 which, as we have seen, was not the case. Together with the rest of the German High Command, however, he knew that the U-boat campaign would have to continue on the basis of 'maximum effort', not only to keep the growing Allied strength within bounds but also to keep tied down the extensive Allied resources devoted to anti-submarine (AS) warfare. Any relaxation would see such resources reorganized and directed unpredictably, perhaps decisively, at other theatres.

The Admiral's discussions with Speer developed a new urgency. For the moment, the priority had to be the construction of maximum numbers of what he now referred to as 'surface

144

U-boats'. In parallel, concentrated effort was directed at the development of new-style craft, optimized for high-speed submerged operation, whose Schnorkel equipment would make them largely independent of surface operation. Although work on Walter's hydrogen peroxide boats was never fully abandoned, the near future obviously lay with the *Elektroboote*, whose basic technology was already available, fully proven and reliable.

Practicalities demanded that two types be built. Because of the weight of the greatly enhanced battery capacity the ocean-going boat, designated the Type XXI, would require to displace about 1,600 tons surfaced and 1,800 tons submerged. Tight design kept dimensions to little more than those of the existing Type IX, but such big boats would be vulnerable in what Dönitz referred to as the 'inner ocean zone'. A 234/258-ton diminutive, the Type XXIII was, therefore, defined for operations around the British coasts, in the North Sea and the Mediterranean.

The design proposal for the Type XXI was submitted to Dönitz in June 1943. Its hull design owed much to the projected Walter Type XVIII, which maximized internal volume by adopting a 'figure eight', i.e. '8', cross-section. Although unhappy at the craft's bulk, Dönitz could not fail to be impressed by its predicted ability to sprint submerged at 18 knots for ninety minutes, or at 12 knots for ten hours. At 6 knots, it would be possible to travel for two days without snorting. Because lines were optimized for submerged efficiency, the Type XXI would be nearly 3 knots slower on the surface than a standard Type IXC. It was the first submarine design since the revolutionary British 'R' class of 1918 to travel faster submerged than surfaced.

In July 1943, senior staff from seventeen yards engaged in U-boat construction came together to discuss a production programme for the new boats. Their resulting two-year draft plan envisaged the first group of craft completed by the end of 1944, with evaluation then necessarily being undertaken alongside production. A total of seventy-five completions appeared possible by the late summer of 1945, with production rate increasing as the Type VII and Type IX programmes tailed off.

With the Atlantic campaign already faltering, Dönitz considered this timescale 'intolerable'. To shorten it, he conferred urgently with Speer, who then appointed Otto Merker to take a broad view of the requirement. Merker was a director of the Magirus factory and his experience was with heavy vehicles. Although he had never built a ship, he knew all about series production. His conclusion was that building times for submarines could be little improved as long as they were assembled and launched in the traditional manner from building ways.

Tendered in August 1943, Merker's proposal was to assemble Type XXIs from pre-fabricated modules. These would be widely sourced and delivered to a purpose-built facility in a fully fitted-out state. If final drawings of the Type XXI were to be delivered by 1 December, and maximum resources of the submarine yards were to be suitably allocated, Merker promised a first prototype by April 1944 and a production rate of thirty per month by the autumn.

Conscious of the effect of depth charging on submarine hulls, Dönitz had misgivings about changes so radical but, faced with realities, he agreed with Merker's proposals. Type XXIs would be assembled from nine sections, built by non-shipbuilding engineering companies. These would be distributed widely to minimize the impact of the Allied bombing campaign which, by mid-1943, was becoming a serious problem. Specialist assembly facilities, to be constructed similarly to the bomb-proof submarine pens, would be built in three established yards, at Hamburg, Bremen and Danzig. Necessity had thus driven the Germans to adopt much the same approach to submarine production as the Americans had to standard merchant ships.

The origins of the German *Schnorkel* (or 'Snort' in Allied terminology) lay in a patent taken out by the Italian Navy as far back as the 1920s. Desultory interest was maintained for at least a decade, but it was the Dutch who progressed the concept, equipping several of their 'overseas' submarines with a practical arrangement by 1940. With the country's invasion in the May of that year, several boats escaped to Britain, others were taken by the invaders. Technical staff from both navies were thus able to evaluate the device but neither force had an application for it at the time. Only with the later emergence of air power as a mortal threat to the submarine was the idea again examined by the Germans as a means of allowing a submarine to recharge batteries while safely submerged.

Hellmuth Walter, aware of developments abroad had, during the 1930s, suggested an air induction and exhaust tube for his hydrogen peroxide boats, and now, with his considerable contribution to the Type XXI, resurrected the idea. An initial discussion with Dönitz was followed by a draft proposal in May 1943, a finalized design in the following month, and the beginning of trials in training boats in the August. By the end of September, 160 kits had been ordered for retro-fitting to existing boats, and all new craft were to be so equipped.

Admiral Sir Max Horton, at the end of May 1943, sent a congratulatory signal to all American, British and Canadian units in his sprawling command. It included that 'quite apart from the spectacular kills which have been achieved by Escort Groups and Support Groups, many notable victories have been achieved by the safe and timely arrival of a number of convoys in the face of heavy enemy attack'. It was a useful reminder that the 'safe and timely arrival' of escorted shipping remained the paramount objective of this huge cooperative effort.

Later, in a letter to a colleague, Horton wrote: 'The great point to me is that *we know now* what strength and composition of forces . . . is necessary to deal with the U-boat menace against convoys. He may wriggle as much as he likes, but the inherent disabilities of the submarine, if properly exploited, will reduce our losses in convoy to a small factor'. He had been appointed to head the Western Approaches Command because of this thorough appreciation of the workings and weaknesses of the submarine arm. He was now confident that he was getting the measure of that other veteran submariner, the opponent that he had yet to meet, Grand Admiral Karl Dönitz.

As far as U-boat men were concerned the most hazardous area was the Bay of Biscay. Nine boats had been sunk there during May and a further seven so badly damaged that they had been obliged to return. Their air cover comprised the upgraded C6 version of the Junkers Ju88, itself hardly a match for the heavy firepower of Allied four-engined aircraft. It could however, inflict unpleasant shocks, as on 1 June, when twenty-three were sent to support a reportedly damaged U-boat, failed to find her but shot down four British AS aircraft which they encountered operating independently.

Again the enemy concluded that submarines were being lost by endeavouring to dive when approached by aircraft, rather than fighting it out surfaced. During June, therefore, outward-bound groups were formed, comprising five or more boats, disposed so that their augmented lookouts and firepower covered all sectors while their, admittedly inadequate, radar search receivers shared the monitoring of a wide waveband.

Single aircraft certainly found such formations difficult to attack, although the enemy was impressed at their determination. On 13 June for instance, a 228 Squadron Sunderland was lost with its complete crew when attacking *U-564*, one of a group of five. The flying boat's depth charges damaged the submarine to the extent that the group's senior officer had to order the *U-185* to escort her to Spanish waters for emergency repairs.

Coastal Command believed in 'on the job' training and the elderly Whitleys of Operational Training Units (OTU) flew regular patrols. On 14 June an Australian-manned aircraft from 10 OTU sighted the two U-boats. Observing correct procedure, it radioed for assistance but when, after two hours, this had not materialized the Whitley, its fuel running low, attacked alone. Its depth charges completed the destruction of *U-564* but, badly shot up by her consort, the bomber had to ditch. The crew were rescued by a French trawler but were made prisoners on its return to port.

The enemy's group procedure was soon defeated by Allied aircraft themselves working in groups and, once again, U-boats were ordered to proceed submerged as far as was practicable. It became practice to hug the Spanish coast, where the continuous high ground behind a surfaced boat made her difficult to distinguish on airborne radar.

This general shift to the southern waters of the Bay meant that the smaller aircraft could operate for only a short space of time, while all were open to flank attack by enemy fighters working from French airfields. As the threat to the Atlantic convoys had, for the moment, diminished, Admiral Horton was able to assist by transferring 'Johnny' Walker's 2EG to police the area in co-operation with 19 Group's aircraft. As half-a-dozen enemy destroyers shared the U-boat's base at la Pallice, Walker's sloops, and those that succeeded them, needed to be provided with cruiser cover.

The ploy quickly met with success. On 24 June an aircraft sighted the big, inward-bound minelayer *U-119*. Following up immediately, 2EG located both *U-119* and the smaller *U-449*. Walker's own ship, *Starling*, brought the former to the surface with depth charges and, despite the ready availability of the group's combined firepower, the *Starling* was badly damaged in dispatching his larger adversary by ramming. This procedure, popular with AS commanders, was deprecated by the Admiralty as it invariably put valuable escort vessels in dock for a considerable period.

The *U-449*, meanwhile, went deep, but the old hands of 2EG were very patient. Four sloops hunted for six hours before the fatal attack was made. Neither submarine had survivors.

As the Allied grip on the Bay tightened, the enemy sought to strike at the resident escort group. The la Pallice destroyers were dedicated to submarine escort and, almost certainly lacking adequate air support, would have run foul of the lurking British cruiser cover.

Air attack was thus the only practical option but for this, the few available FW200s would have been too vulnerable in the face of the sloops' high-angle armament. The new Messerschmitt Me410 had made an appearance, primarily to counter the hard-hitting Beaufighters but, while it could have acted effectively in the fighter-bomber role, it had been quickly withdrawn to convert to the night fighter role in the growing battle over the German cities.

Fortuitously, the Luftwaffe's long-awaited heavy bomber, the Heinkel He177, had proved a failure in its planned role, and some of the few built were made available for maritime operations. For this, they were fitted to deploy the new Henschel Hs293 glider bomb. This could be steered to its target using the several radio channels that gave it its German name of *Kehlgerät*.

In the anti-shipping role, the missile's first use was probably on 11 July 1943, when a British troop convoy was hard hit some 300 miles west of Vigo. Unusually lightly escorted by only two destroyers and a frigate, the 20,020 GRT Canadian Pacific liner *Duchess of York* and Anchor Line's 16,790 GRT *California* were both destroyed and the valuable refrigerated cargo liner *Port Fairy* badly damaged. Fortunately the loss of life was small.

At the end of July, Dönitz had to accept that, of seventeen U-boats that had sailed from French bases during the month, ten, including three of the invaluable U-tankers, had been sunk and another severely damaged. Although analysis showed that casualties from groups were less than from those proceeding independently, the trend clearly showed that groups only attracted more attackers, the number of which was causing concern. Sailings were, therefore, suspended pending the delivery of the first *Wanze* receivers, due at the end of August. All returning boats were ordered to hug the Spanish coast.

Any reduction in submarine activity was not reflected by a scaling-down in the offensive. On 25 August 1943, Support Group 5 (SG5), comprising two British frigates and three Canadian corvettes, was the resident patrol off Cape Finisterre when it was attacked by fourteen Dornier Do217 bombers, escorted by seven Ju88 fighters. Another recently-introduced aircraft, the Do217 also deployed the Hs293 but, on this occasion, the little ships escaped by virtue of radical manoeuvres, barrage fire and the general inexperience of the enemy bombardiers. Several ships were, however, severely shaken.

Two days later, when SG1 had assumed the patrol, the Luftwaffe struck again with sixteen Do217s. Hit squarely, the British sloop *Egret* blew up, leaving only thirty-five survivors and becoming the first warship to be destroyed in action by an air-to-surface missile. Very nearly suffering the same fate, the Canadian destroyer *Athabaskan* had a bomb pass clean through the forward superstructure, badly damaging her as it exploded on coming clear.

Bletchley Park was having difficulty coping with four-rotor Enigma traffic, and admitted so as efforts were intensified to develop the necessary high-speed bombe. Fortunately, with the requisite facilities and expertise, the Americans had revolted in September 1942 and had gone their own way. As a result their first two bombes, very much prototypes, were delivered in May

1943. By the end of August, the first production model was in operation, albeit haltingly.

In this same month, Dönitz was warned that his naval ciphers were compromised. He had, of course, regularly suspected that this was the case but this information had reportedly come from within the US Navy Department. Amazingly, a new investigation again concluded that the warning was unfounded, but further mechanical changes were made to complicate code-breaking.

Paradoxically, this scare in the enemy camp came at a time when the British were themselves experiencing considerable problems. Because of the temporary withdrawal of U-boats from the North Atlantic, radio traffic had been greatly reduced. In consequence, there were fewer transmissions on subjects such as weather statistics, positions or fuel situations which, sent in standard short form, were easily recognized by codebreakers. They could then be used as 'cribs', or starting points for attacking the current cipher setting.

In June 1943, the situation had deteriorated to the extent that enemy messages in the simpler 'home waters' code had to be broken before the more important 'Atlantic' code could be tackled. This caused unacceptable delays. Sinkings in the Atlantic, at an agreeably low level, began to rise again as the Submarine Tracking Room had to evasively route convoys mainly on the basis of direction finding. From below 100,000 GRT in June 1943, losses rose to over ¼ million tons in July.

The huge American effort resulted in no less than seventy-five of the more complex four-wheel bombes being in operation by the end of 1943. Cooperation proved fruitful and, despite the greater risk of the secret being compromised, the system worked commendably smoothly. By the autumn of 1943 there was, in fact, more codebreaking capacity than there was coded traffic to break, although this situation obtained because enemy operators were lax in not exploiting the full potential of the four-rotor machine.

During the four months to the end of July 1943, the enemy lost 109 U-boats, twenty-five of them to Coastal Command's saturation coverage of the Bay of Biscay. Those permitted to sail were forbidden to use Metox, proceeded singly and surfaced only at night for a period sufficient to recharge.

Following the loss, in late July and early August, of six of the U-tankers, Dönitz was obliged to reduce submarine operations in distant waters. Some boats experienced difficulties when they were not able to top-up for their return passages. They were to rendezvous with operational boats but these, having transferred much of their own fuel, had then to abort their own patrols.

Defences in distant waters had also been considerably strengthened. For instance, the Type IXC boat *U-161* sailed for Brazilian waters on 8 August. En route, as instructed, she met up with a Japanese blockade-running boat and the homeward-bound *U-198*. To each she transferred a *Wanze* radar detector and, from the latter boat, she took on spare fuel. She sank just two ships, totalling 10,500 GRT, before being destroyed by a locally-based American flying boat.

In mid-August, the veteran *U-123* and *U-523* sailed together for the American eastern seaboard. One week out, the latter was unsuccessfully attacked by a Leigh Light Wellington which, however, reported her position. A measure of the growing strength of convoy escorts was that the nearby Gibraltar-bound convoy OG.92 could detach two destroyers and a corvette to hunt her down and destroy her.

Her colleague, although herself briefly attacked, successfully reached her operating area around Trinidad. She enjoyed no luck and, because of the unavailability of U-tankers, was recalled early. On 7 November, as she crossed the Bay of Biscay, she was caught on the surface by a Canadian-piloted Mosquito. The aircraft in question was a Mark XVIII, nicknamed the 'Tsetse', which was armed with a centreline 57mm gun. Automatically loaded, this weapon fired a six-pound, armour-piercing shot every 1.5 seconds. Badly holed, the *U-123* was left unable to dive yet struggled back to St Nazaire. She had been at sea for eighty-four days, during which she had destroyed nothing.

Bent on a propaganda coup, BdU tried again to spring the veteran skipper Otto Kretschmer and others from captivity in Canada. Again, the crude code used in routine mail betrayed the plan. During August 1943, the *U-669* was duly dispatched to the

St Lawrence but never arrived, probably falling victim to a Canadian Leigh Light Wellington.

Nothing daunted, BdU redirected *U-536* to the task. There developed the slightly farcical situation of this boat lying doggo in the St Lawrence, waiting for escapees who never escaped, while Allied forces hunted vainly with the intention of capturing her. Finally admitting defeat, BdU ordered *U-536* to withdraw but, homeward bound during November, she was directed to join an attack on the combined SL.139/MKS.30G convoy. This north-bound accumulation of fifty-seven merchantmen was screened by three groups and enjoyed continuous air cover, some mounted from the Azores.

Thirty U-boats were arranged in three search lines but, having located their target without great trouble, found themselves unable to penetrate the outer defences. For the minor achievement of blowing the after end off a British sloop with a T5 torpedo, the cost was six submarines. Of the three sunk by surface escorts, one was the redirected *U-536* while another, *U-648*, was probably an early victim of American-built DEs that were now operating under the White Ensign.

With the escorts preoccupied with the submarine attack, the enemy had high hopes for the success of a coordinated strike by twenty-five He177s armed with guided bombs. Twenty aircraft, launching two bombs apiece, actually attacked but only two ships were hit. Of these one, the elderly Strick freighter *Marsa* (4,405 GRT), was sunk. In the course of the 1,600-mile round trip, three of these unreliable aircraft came down in the sea.

During August, when *U-536* sailed on her ill-starred final patrol, BdU had dispatched nine boats to distant waters. Their sinking of just three merchantmen cost the loss of four boats and the near-loss of a fifth.

In this same month, overall mercantile losses fell to twenty-five ships totalling under 120,000 GRT. Of these, sixteen of 87,000 GRT were claimed by submarine attack. Significantly, however, the majority were in the Mediterranean and the Indian Ocean. Only two were sunk by U-boat in the North Atlantic during the month, yet there was no complacency on the part of the defence, which faced an opponent known to be both adaptable and resourceful. There was every expectation that 'they' would be back.

Earlier in this narrative it was stressed how useless was the policy of creating AS hunting groups to act 'offensively' in roaming the seas looking for submarines. This was because the quarry could not be located in the immensity of the ocean and needed to be lured by a convoy for there to be any chance of discovery. The evolving nature of ocean warfare in the Atlantic now demanded that this principle be modified.

Firstly, the ability of the VLR aircraft to cover extended areas of ocean in comparatively short time exploited the U-boat's weakness of needing to spend considerable periods surfaced. Random patrols by aircraft were quite capable of surprising U-boats, whereas those by surface forces were not.

Secondly, there was now the priceless gift of precise Ultra intelligence. Anti-submarine surface groups, centred on an escort carrier (CVE), now had the information and the means to strike accurately where, three short years before, a group could only grope blindly.

With more available carriers, the Americans were particularly adept at exploiting the latter option. At this time they deployed four hunting groups, based on the CVEs *Bogue*, *Card*, *Core*, and *Santee*, soon to be joined by the *Croatan* and *Block Island* groups. Between June and August they accounted for at least fourteen of the enemy. Their very success concerned the British guardians of the Ultra secret, for this aggressive application of special intelligence made BdU ponder just how the whereabouts of its boats could be so accurately predicted. It strains credulity that the Germans still concluded that the primary cause of location was radiation due to unauthorized use of Metox or through some, as yet unspecified, quality of Allied radar.

Prefacing the invasion of Sicily and Italy, many of the UGS convoys between the United States and the Mediterranean were very large, UGS.10 of June–July 1943 comprising a near-record 129 ships as it passed Gibraltar. The convoys' usual track was so far to the south that air cover could be furnished only from Bermuda until the agreement to use the Azores was finalized. Themselves forced southward, Dönitz' forces thus looked to this service for targets. In response, the Americans here deployed their first CVE-based support groups. These each comprised a carrier and, usually, three destroyers. Their orders gave them a free hand and their intelligence was good. Their customary tactic was to use Wildcats to suppress enemy return fire while an Avenger went for the kill with depth charges or an acoustic torpedo.

As the enemy's submarines were largely using Spanish 'friendly neutral' waters to access the open ocean, Coastal Command aircraft enjoyed, by their standards, a quiet August. Their patrols were increasingly challenged by the Luftwaffe, however, and the month saw the loss of seventeen AS aircraft and six fighters.

During September, Slessor was able to reduce the pressure on his hard-worked crews as US Navy Fleet Wing Seven went operational, deploying Catalinas (PBY) and Liberators (B-24 or PBY4Y) from south-west England. Professional, keen and hard-working, the Navy fliers nonetheless never established the rapport enjoyed by their Army predecessors. The latter had learned 'on the job', along with their allies, and their easy working relationship was the result of triumph and disaster mutually shared.

Dönitz was, by no means, asleep. One by one, his U-boats were slipped beyond Cape Finisterre and assembled to make a surprise comeback in the North Atlantic, breaking a three-month lull. Eighteen boats from French bases were joined by three that had come directly from Germany. Organized as Group *Leuthen* their objective was to strike hard and suddenly in mid-September. Convinced that earlier reverses had been due entirely to superior Allied technology, Dönitz had ensured that each of these boats had received the latest German equipment. All carried the T5 *Zaunkönig* for use against escorts, and various fits of 20mm cannon, including quadruples, to counter aircraft attack. Conformal acoustic sensor arrays could detect convoys beyond visual range. The *Wanze* radar detector, of which so much was expected, was complemented by a radar decoy (*Aphrodite*). There was also an improved sonar decoy (*Bolde*). The group was accompanied by *U-460*, one of the greatly-diminished band of U-tankers.

On 21 September 1943 Prime Minister Churchill made a major speech to a packed House. For the four months ended

18 September, he stated, no merchant vessel had been lost through direct enemy action in the North Atlantic. Since the outset of the year, moreover, new construction had exceeded losses from all causes by 6 million GRT.

The speech was greeted enthusiastically, both at home and abroad, but the Premier was speaking from a sense of relief and was also choosing his words very carefully. Relief stemmed from the safe passage of the first UT convoy, transporting the initial batch of a planned 600,000 soldiers for the planned invasion of Europe. Also significant was his quoted date of 18 September for, on the following day, Group *Leuthen* had begun to make its presence felt in what was still, in many respects, the Gap.

Because of changes in Allied codes, the enemy's *B-dienst* had lost a valuable means of locating convoys. Stragglers were, however, still given specific courses to steer to enable them to link with any following convoy. Such transmissions were of great use to the enemy who also reasoned, correctly, that after several months of negligible threat, convoys would be speeded-up by keeping close to the shortest, Great Circle route and, probably, with a reduced escort.

On 19 September, therefore, *U-270* made contact without difficulty with the slow, westbound ONS.18. This was about to be joined by the overtaking ON.202, to make a total of sixty-five merchantmen. Their escort, fortunately, had been in no way reduced, comprising two escort groups (the British B-3 and Canadian C-2) and the Canadian support group SG9. Although there was no CVE present, there were four Swordfish aboard the MAC *Empire MacAlpine*.

As the enemy pack surfaced to close on *U-270*'s signals, it became fair game for the now omnipresent B-24s. A Canadian-manned aircraft dispatched the *U-341* on 19 September and, the next day, the *U-338* disappeared, probably following the attentions of a Liberator of Coastal Command's veteran 120 Squadron.

Each U-boat skipper had at least two T5s and was instructed to first hit the escorts with these, creating a path to the convoy itself. Even before the pack had fully concentrated, *U-270* was cleared to attack. Hit by a T5, the British River-class frigate *Lagan* suffered what was to become almost 'trademark' damage,

156

her after end wrecked but the ship still safely afloat with the nearest transverse bulkhead holding. As part of a developing strategy, considerable numbers of deep sea salvage tugs were being constructed, these either accompanying convoys or being stationed so as to be able to bring in severely damaged ships that, otherwise, would have to be destroyed. The *Lagan* was thus salvaged, only to be declared a constructive total loss (CTL). Her departure from the scene, together with the necessary AS trawler escort, reduced the escort strength by two, soon increased to three when a destroyer suffered an on-board Hedgehog explosion.

During the 20th, two U-boats made attacks on the convoy proper but only one, the *U-238*, was successful, destroying two of the new Liberty ships. Eight more boats claimed to have attacked in the course of the following night, but the sum total of their efforts amounted only to two more of the escort. First hit was the Canadian destroyer *St. Croix*, an ex-American four-stacker whose elderly structure could not withstand two T5s from the *U-305*. The second, the Flower-class corvette *Polyanthus*, was too small to accept the scale of flooding caused by another T5 from the *U-952*. Eighty-two survivors, from both ships, were fished from the ever-chill Atlantic by the *Itchen*, another River.

Although the enemy probed continually throughout the 21st, the screen remained aggressive and, well supported by aircraft, damaged five submarines sufficiently to oblige them to break off and make for home.

In the early hours of 22 September the destroyer *Keppel*, now senior ship of the escort, D/F-ed a shadower and dropped back, catching *U-229* on the surface at first light. Racing in shooting, the old destroyer rode clear over her target's after end, dropping ten depth charges with zero settings. From the submarine there were no survivors.

A comparatively uneventful 23rd was followed by an unpleasant night as BdU exhorted skippers to maximum effort. Only two merchantmen had, so far, been lost, but the *U-238* again managed to thread her way through the screen, sinking three ships from a single, four-shot salvo. Tragically, the frigate *Itchen* then took a T5 from the *U-666*. Crowded with survivors, she blew up. From three ships' companies, just three men survived.

As daylight strengthened, the *U-952* struck again, sinking a 6,200-ton American freighter and hitting a second with a dud torpedo. Gratefully, the sorely-tried convoy then edged into the shallows and fogs of the Grand Banks, and the enemy disappeared.

Buoyed by hugely-inflated claims by his skippers, Dönitz proclaimed a significant victory of no less than twelve escorts and nine merchant ships in exchange for two U-boats, the early loss of *U-341* as yet being unknown.

Because the T5 torpedo required a very short arming run, there existed the danger that the submarine firing it might prove a more attractive noise source than the intended target. Doctrine provided, therefore, for the boat to dive to sixty metres immediately after firing, then to proceed quietly. This was not an easy proposition if the target were missed, it then becoming within seconds an instrument of revenge. Because so many boats fired at escorts (twenty-four T5s were expended in all) and then dived, any nearby explosion, particularly of the many depth charges, was taken as evidence of a hit.

The main outcome of the operation was, therefore, an over-inflated appreciation of the standard T5 acoustic torpedo which, in truth, was a capricious and over-sensitive weapon, easily de-calibrated by shock. Crews of the hard-worked escorts could, nonetheless, not fail to be concerned at what was a very real threat.

Fortunately, in designing their own acoustic homing weapons, Allied scientists had also considered suitable antidotes. Silence, of course, would defeat it and, for every 50 per cent reduction in ship speed, there was an 80 per cent reduction in the effectiveness of a torpedo's homing system. Alternatively, as a T5's maximum speed was only 25 knots, a faster escort could outrun it. Neither option, however, was usually available.

Early efforts at masking propeller noise with a bubble screen were not very successful and the only practical means left was to tow a device that made more noise than the ship. A 'pipe noise-maker', already devised for detonating acoustic mines, was quickly adapted for use by escorts. It comprised no more than a pair of pipes in a frame which, when towed, were free to hit each other randomly, emitting a high-frequency racket. Generally known as 'Foxers', their design varied between navies but, following trials in October 1943, all escorts were so equipped within months. Although effective, the Foxer was hugely unpopular, being difficult to stream and recover, while also seriously degrading the efficiency of the ship's own Asdic. Only with the later recovery of T5s from sunken U-boats could more scientifically-based noise sources be developed.

For reasons unspecified, *Wanze* was pronounced a success during these operations. It was increasingly found, however, that large Allied aircraft, a principal source of U-boat discomfiture, could absorb a considerable amount of 20mm cannon fire without incurring critical damage. New single and twin 37mm mountings were, therefore, put into urgent production for the submarine service.

To build on the modest success of the attack on ON.202/ ONS.18, BdU reinforced the twelve still-operational boats of Group *Leuthen* with nine more from France and Germany. Reconstituted as Group *Rossbach*, the twenty-one U-boats were disposed on a line to locate the next-scheduled convoys, ON.203 and ONS.19.

Allied appreciation of U-boat strength and disposition was very precise and the situation of the *Rossbach* line was quickly verified by aircraft sightings. As ON.203 was successfully directed around its northern extremity, Iceland-based aircraft hounded the would-be ambushers. A rocket-equipped British Hudson disposed of the *U-221* and an American Ventura (an improved successor to the Hudson) sank the *U-279* with depth charges. A B-24 of the ever-industrious 120 Squadron then totally demolished the *U-389* with a shallow-set depth charge salvo of pinpoint accuracy.

As the *Rossbach* line was manoeuvred by BdU to locate the elusively-routed convoy, seven more of its boats were attacked. Four received damage sufficiently serious to compel their return.

Thanks to continuing British instructions to stragglers, the remaining boats were confident of intercepting ONS.19. Indeed, on 2 October several boats reported distant activity. So effectively, however, did air cover suppress their freedom of movement that this convoy, too, was successfully ghosted through.

Nothing daunted, the fourteen remaining *Rossbach* boats were ordered to sweep south-westward to comb the predicted tracks of the two eastbound HX.259 and SC.143 convoys. On 8 October several boats sighted escorts, all heading eastward and, for a time, their search was assisted by a large Blohm and Voss Bv222 flying boat. Although the fast convoy was diverted safely to the south, SC.143 was sighted by the aircraft. This successful cooperation, at so distant a location, then went awry because the aircraft's transmitted signals were ahead of their expected time and were not received by any of the U-boats.

Western Approaches Command read all the signs that SC.143 was heading for trouble and its escort, the Canadian C-2 group and the MAC *Rapana*, was quickly strengthened by the four modern destroyers of SG10.

The *U-371* had earlier been strafed by a British aircraft and, with her skipper and others wounded, had aborted her patrol. In the course of returning, she was first to sight the convoy and succeeded in vectoring-in seven other boats. During the remaining daylight hours an aggressive defence kept these at a safe distance but, during the night of 8–9 October, two managed to find targets.

First casualty, in the small hours, was the Polish destroyer *Orkan*. Launched a year earlier as the *Myrmidon* for the Royal Navy, she had been Polish-manned from the outset and had changed her name. At the time, she had been engaged in a sweep with a sister ship, *Musketeer*, also of SG10. As earlier with the *Itchen*, a T5 from *U-378* detonated a magazine and the loss of life was heavy.

A second loss was the 5,600-ton American freighter *Yorkmar*, sunk by the *U-645*. With daylight returned solid air support, two B-24s of 86 Squadron accounting for *U-419* and *U-643* that were tailing the convoy and a third, *U-610*, falling to a Canadian-manned Sunderland, operating at extreme range. An innovation on the following night was to mount a patrol by a Leigh Light Wellington.

Group *Rossbach*'s losses had outweighed its successes but its skippers were able to report that escorts, chary of the T5, were not so keen to press home their attacks.

Determined to continue with a resurgent North Atlantic

campaign, Dönitz formed Group *Schlieffen* from thirteen fresh boats. Using new D/F equipment, *U-584* obtained a bearing on what was assumed to be slow convoy ONS.20. Similarly-equipped boats at either end of the search line were intended to detect any change of course on the part of the convoy. Late on 15 October, *U-844* made a visual contact but, as ON.206 was in the near vicinity, it is not certain on which. She was quickly obliged to fall back, but continued to report. Her group was widely scattered and an over-enthusiastic BdU ordered them to fight their way in on the surface, defying air patrols.

The escort to ON.206 was the British B-6 group, already reinforced by Peter Gretton's very experienced SG7. With ONS.20 was the British B-4 group, the first, entirely homogeneous six-ship formation composed of American-built DEs serving under the White Ensign.

From a combined total of 117 merchantmen, the enemy's sole success was a British vessel, straggling from ONS.20 and sunk by *U-426*. For this he paid handsomely.

The new *U-844*, which had opened proceedings, succeeded in shooting down a B-24, only to fall victim to another. Next for the indefatigable Liberators was *U-964*. A Canadian-crewed Sunderland badly damaged the *U-470* but, in the process, was severely hit by automatic fire and had to ditch with half its crew already dead. Two of 120 Squadron's B-24s responded to the Sunderland's distress call and finished off the tenaciously-defended *U-470*. To round off what had been a field day for the aircraft, two more B-24s attacked the *U-540* so accurately that their depth charges broke her in two. The instruction from BdU had proved suicidal.

The surface escorts, meanwhile, had not been idle, the *Byard* getting the DEs off the mark with the *U-841* and the veteran corvette *Sunflower* disposing of the *U-631*.

So scattered were the attackers that a change of course by the convoys caused them to lose contact, one of the D/F-equipped boats having been sunk.

Dönitz admitted to having received a 'setback' and again, that there was little future in remaining surfaced in the presence of air cover. Seven submarines had been converted to specialist 'flak' boats and he ordered that those remaining be brought back to their original configuration. His hopes again were placed in a future weapon, in this case the 37mm guns to be fitted throughout the U-boat fleet during November and December 1943.

Further experience with *Wanze* had not been encouraging and high hopes were thus placed in *Naxos*, supposedly due at any time. Dönitz stressed the importance of rescuing Allied aircrew, through whose interrogation could be learned the means by which U-boats were being located. He apparently had no knowledge that, where *Naxos* would work in the 8–12cm band, new Allied airborne radars were using a 3cm wavelength.

For the moment, there was little alternative to keeping submarines submerged by day and relying on existing firepower to deter less-precise nocturnal air attack. This procedure spelt slow progress, necessarily offset by hard driving when surfaced at night. In turn, of course, this was heavy on fuel and, with most of the U-tankers already destroyed, replenishment at sea was unlikely. The consequence was that operations in the western Atlantic would need to be abandoned for the time being. A limit was, therefore, established at meridian 35 degrees west, which was also the effective operating limit for the new Junkers Ju290, due to enter maritime support service by mid-November 1943.

Coastal Command and carrier-borne aircraft both deployed the SAP rocket to great effect. Its drawback lay in the requirement to aim the whole aircraft at the target, presenting the enemy gunners with a nil-deflection shot for several seconds. For this period the attacker was vulnerable to the four or more 20mm cannon carried by all U-boats. Aircraft such as the Beaufighter and Mosquito carried a centreline pack of cannon and machine guns and fired these in a continuous burst to knock out the target's topside personnel. A two-way tracer stream thus marked the attempt by each party to disrupt the aim of the other. As mentioned above, the less well-endowed Avenger was usually supported by Hellcats for flak suppression but for a Swordfish to attack singly would now be suicidal. Yet all still operated to excellent effect from CVEs and MACs.

The original 450-pound airborne depth charge had been superseded by the handier 250-pounder. Although carried by the Avenger, it was the primary weapon of the heavier aircraft, increasingly complemented by acoustic AS torpedoes ('Fido').

Extended range was a function of fuel capacity, bought at the expense of payload. Thus VLR B-24s could carry only a single stick of four or six depth charges, while standard B-24s, B-17s, Halifaxes and Sunderlands might load two sticks. It followed that the valuable VLR aircraft usually had a single chance of a kill, encouraging their pilots to take great risks to avoid error. Air Marshal Slessor's standing instruction was for B-24s to attack from between fifty and one hundred feet, aiming to centralize their stick about a surfaced enemy's conning tower. If the enemy gunners stood their ground to the end they thus had an even chance of taking their attacker with them.

Fido considerably improved the average aircrew's life expectancy. If the aircraft circled patiently at a safe range, a U-boat would inevitably seize the first likely juncture to dive. Even as the boat's forward end dipped (and a well-trained Type VIIC could disappear in less than twenty-five seconds) the aircraft would bore in and, from minimum height, release a torpedo at the head of the swirl that momentarily marked the spot. The tight circling was then resumed as all eyes watched for the usually unspectacular evidence of an explosion followed, hopefully, by debris and the slow spread of a diesel oil slick that flattened the surface chop.

Such moments were balanced by countless hours of noisy, cold, mind-numbing boredom. Full alertness for the duration of a long patrol was not possible, and pilots and observers needed reliefs. Yet, with a sighting, every second counted in what, very often, had to be a 'first-time' attack.

Rising sheer from an eastern spur of the Mid-Atlantic Ridge at about 38 degrees north are the islands of the Azores. They are Portuguese territory and, because of ancient ties with the British, the latter sought early leave to establish facilities there for convoy escorts and, later, for VLR aircraft. Negotiations began in the spring of 1941 but, at a time when the Allied cause was still hard-pressed, the Portuguese feared German retaliation. From the end of 1942, however, Axis military reverses pointed clearly to the eventual outcome of the war, and the Portuguese position softened. By a skilful exercise in political semantics it was agreed that the Anglo-Portuguese relationship pre-dated accepted neutrality laws and, therefore, was not bound by them. This tenuous argument could, of course, apply only to a British presence.

Early in October 1943 Prime Minister Churchill was able to announce that the Royal Air Force had permission to operate from the airfield at Lagens (Lajes) on the island of Terceira. By the end of the month, B-17s and Hudsons were already deployed, administratively part of Coastal Command's 19 Group. As the aircraft had been somewhat delayed by bad weather, it fell to the Fleet Air Arm to initiate the tenancy when, in a politically-important move, the CVE HMS *Fencer* landed her Swordfish to stand patrols from Day One.

As the existing runway at Lagens was too short to accommodate fully-loaded VLR aircraft the British, in a thinly-disguised subterfuge, contracted an American 'private concern' to extend and upgrade the facilities. American B-24s were eventually allowed to operate if carrying British markings, on the precedent that the same wing worked from south-west England under British operational control.

A second facility was commenced on Santa Maria, the most remote of the Azores, but would not be functioning for a further seven months.

During September and October 1943 alone, twenty-five U-boats had been destroyed in the North Atlantic, over half of them by shore-based aircraft in support of convoys. In that time, sixty-four convoys had crossed, losing only nine merchantmen of the 2,468 involved.

With the force of U-tankers virtually eliminated and the requirement to travel extensive distances submerged, the enemy had temporarily withdrawn from the Western Atlantic. Although now fighting on the back foot, the U-boat was, however, far from beaten. Hundreds of boats remained in the order of battle and, despite every Allied effort, delivery of new craft outstripped sinkings. Achievements per boat per patrol had certainly reached new low levels but, to Dönitz' personal credit, morale and fighting spirit remained high, buoyed by the perennial promise of new technology yet in the pipeline.

For some time, convoys between the United Kingdom, Gibraltar and Freetown (Sierra Leone) had enjoyed a comparatively trouble-free existence. Once heavily disputed, they now sailed under virtually continuous air cover. Because of the new requirement to fight closer to home, Dönitz considered the situation afresh. With the availability of the Ju290 there was the promise, at last, of reliable long-range aerial reconnaissance while his skippers' increasing familiarity with the T5 torpedo should make untenable the situation of the much-respected Allied support groups that patrolled north-west of Cape Finisterre.

The major shift to the east began on 7 November 1943, with thirty boats adopting the search strategy of dividing into ten groups of three, initially covering a swathe from Cape Farewell south-eastward to the latitude of Finisterre. A perceived advantage was that Allied intercepts would give little information on the composition and intentions of so attenuated a force, named Group *Eisenhart*. Its extent covered several major convoy routes so that, although there were inevitably large gaps between groups, the chances of sighting a convoy were good at a time when improved aerial reconnaissance had yet to become a reality.

Even as the sweep began, *B-dienst* decrypts indicated the presence of three convoys. All were travelling well to the south, BdU correctly attributing this to the fact that air cover was now available from the Azores. The search was, therefore, moved further to the south-east, but nothing except the sighting of the odd AS escort indicated anything of the five convoys which had, in fact, passed through.

Acknowledging that old-style convoy battles were now out of the question, Dönitz considered that the best chance of success lay in attack by a maximum of eight boats in the course of a single night.

Seven boats, coded Group *Schill*, were thus deployed between the Azores and Portugal, across the assumed track of the next northbound convoy. This was SL.138 from Freetown which, as was common, had joined with a convoy from the Mediterranean, in this case MKS.28. The combined sixty merchantmen were screened by the British escort group EG39 which, lacking an escort carrier, had been loaned the auxiliary anti-aircraft ship *Alynbank*.

Duly reported on 27 October by a patrolling Bv222, the

convoys were attacked by two U-boats on the night of 29–30 October. The sinking of a 3,000-ton Norwegian vessel was quickly offset by a pair of escorts locating and sinking *U-306*. It might be noted that the ships concerned were the *Whitehall* and *Geranium*, a destroyer dating from the earlier war and a Flower-class corvette. Now often castigated as obsolete or inadequate, these little ships were still performing nobly.

Still unhappy with air cooperation, BdU regrouped to intercept the next-in-line MKS.29. Helpfully, the Luftwaffe located this convoy on 7 November, only for their reported position to be so far in error that it passed without hindrance. In searching, the *U-707* ran foul of an Azores-based B-17 and was sunk by depth charge attack.

A fortnight later, the Luftwaffe assembled a force of twenty-five He177s to attack the combined MKS.30/SL.139 with glider bombs. Although only one small merchant ship was sunk and a second damaged, the raid was delivered at a range of 800 miles and, as a first attempt, was rated a success by BdU. Such assaults were potentially devastating in the absence of a fighter defence, but the simplest antidote was to route the convoys further to the west.

Beyond the fifty transferred to the British flag, many 'four-stacker' destroyers were still rendering valuable, second-line service to the US Navy. Narrow-gutted, lightly built and the youngest over twenty years of age, they were far from ideal for Atlantic service but, in a campaign where every ship still counted, they were run hard.

In Britain, manpower shortages were becoming apparent and a significant proportion of 'the fifty' were operating with Allied crews. Those ships in poor material condition were already being retired into support roles with reduced crews as skilled personnel were drafted to new frigates and DEs.

In common with all destroyers, the veterans were designed for speed rather than endurance. For the Atlantic struggle, however, these qualities were reversed in priority and it became common to convert one boiler room for extra accommodation and bunker capacity. As the power/speed relationship takes off steeply at the top end, the loss of half a ship's boiler capacity left her still with a more than adequate 25 knot speed. Those thus converted typically stowed an extra eighty tons of fuel, increasing endurance to about 3,500 miles at 10 knots.

In British service, all had their aftermost three funnels reduced in height, while long-range conversions had two removed. Varying numbers of guns and torpedo tubes were landed to further decrease topweight and to increase the margin available for depth charges.

For all elderly destroyers, convoy escort meant days and weeks of low-speed progression, neither beneficial to high-speed machinery nor economic in the use of fuel. Their frail hulls, wet and cramped, were subjected to every conceivable mode of stress by the tireless action of the ocean, and leaked copiously through every loosened, wasted rivet.

American-flagged four-stackers commonly escorted CVEs engaged on support duties. Provided 'special intelligence' and gaining quickly in experience, these little carriers were running up some impressive scores. By the end of 1943 the USS *Card* was claiming eleven U-boats sunk, the *Bogue* eight, the *Core* five, the *Santee* three and the *Block Island* one.

Each of the carriers usually had a screen of three or four of the old destroyers (alternatively labelled 'four-pipers', 'flush-deckers' or, more picturesquely, 'tin cans'). The *Card*'s escort comprised the USSs *Barry, Borie* and *Goff,* the group working the CVE's most productive zone, around the Azores, where they were also well placed to cover the passage of the American GUS convoys running between Casablanca and Hampton Roads. (The Royal Navy provided the escort for the Mediterranean-Gibraltar-Casablanca leg).

The fifty-two ship GUS.18 had begun its long passage at Alexandria on 9 October 1943 and, by the end of the month, the *Card* group had seen it safely on its way before returning to its operational box. During the afternoon of 31 October an excellent Huff-Duff fix was quickly followed up by Avengers, which found a pair of surfaced Type VIIs. The *U-91* was preparing to transfer fuel to the *U-584*, returning from the long haul to Florida. Slow to submerge, the latter fell victim to a pair of acoustic torpedoes.

The *U-91* made good her escape but, understandably, was reported by debriefed Avenger pilots as a Type XIV U-tanker. For so highly-regarded a target, the *Borie* was detached to locate and keep contact throughout the night. She arrived at the scene after dark and, in heavy seas, quickly obtained a radar contact. This quickly vanished as the craft submerged. The *Borie* released three patterns over the spot and optimistically reported the target, which was in fact the *U-256*, as sunk.

Then, in the small hours, came a second radar contact. Again, the target dived in good time and, with a good sonar response, the destroyer attacked again. A fault on her depth charge rails saw their complete contents released. Fairly blasted, the unfortunate *U-405* staggered to the surface, only to be caught in the glare of the *Borie*'s searchlight as the destroyer opened fire and turned to ram. Pitching heavily, the ship made no real contact, her bow riding over the U-boat's forward end. Here she lay, stranded, as both crews piled out to battle by hand.

For an estimated ten minutes it was battle by small arms as the two vessels ground together. The *Borie*'s thin skin came off decidedly the worse but, when the two finally came apart, the submarine could not dive for the injured, still topside, while the destroyer could not close again because of her far larger turning circle.

In the course of the ensuing dogfight, each tried unsuccessfully to torpedo the other while the *U-405* attempted a 'first' by ramming the destroyer. The latter finally managed to use her throwers to fire shallow-set depth charges, bringing her battered opponent to a standstill.

Half the submarine's crew abandoned ship but the destroyer's captain thought himself threatened by another and left the scene. None survived.

With her hull badly gashed, the *Borie* herself was foundering. She summoned assistance from her group but twenty-seven of her crew were lost in the course of abandonment. The ship was beyond salvage and, after the *Barry* failed to torpedo her, she was dispatched by an Avenger.

As winter gripped the North Atlantic, the weather again reminded the groups that U-boats were not the sole enemy. In comparison with fleet carriers, CVEs were short and, while weight distribution could influence their roll characteristics to a degree, pitch amplitudes and accelerations could be fierce.

Aircraft on deck could be lost overboard, those struck below damaged by bodily movement. Those landing on board, sometimes already damaged, had to contend with a small, violently oscillating deck, perhaps partly occupied by other aircraft.

A new British CVE, HMS *Tracker*, was allocated to 'Johnny' Walker's SG2 early in November 1943. On the 6th the group disposed of two more U-boats but then ran into such foul weather that Walker reported the little carrier to be a liability, unable to operate her aircraft yet still requiring to be protected. His own sloops were sound and weatherly, yet themselves were incurring damage sufficient to cause the whole group to seek shelter in Newfoundland.

With the course of the war turning inexorably in favour of the Allies, the situation was not lost on the government in Madrid. A benevolent neutral with respect to Germany, Spain had allowed her waters to be both highway and safe haven for U-boats seeking to avoid the attentions of Allied hunting groups. A greatly changed situation saw the Allies active in North Africa, Sicily and the Azores, compounded by the demoralizing defection of the Italians in September 1943. The Franco administration felt it time to distance itself somewhat from the Axis cause and damaged U-boats which, hitherto, would have sought sanctuary in Spanish waters, were now instructed to scuttle themselves. Their crews could thus be classed as 'survivors' and eligible for repatriation.

Even at this late stage, Anglo-American aerial cooperation was not entirely without scope for misunderstanding. The US Navy's Fleet Air Wing Seven had arrived in England in mid-August to relieve US Army squadrons in support of RAF Coastal Command's operations over the Bay of Biscay. So badly had Dönitz' U-boats been persecuted that they were operating increasingly from the protected facilities now completed in Norway. The Bay had consequently assumed an unnatural quietness and 19 Group (now commanded by Air Vice Marshal B.E. Baker), including its American component, made only sixteen attacks during the whole of September and October. These resulted in just one kill.

Admiral King arrived at the premature conclusion that the Bay was the scene of a problem solved and ordered one B-24 squadron to North Africa. Dönitz then changed his mode of operation and, yet again, Biscay came alive with transiting submarines.

Lacking sufficient aircraft, Baker requested American support directly, only to have it refused by the commodore commanding. As the request had been specifically linked to air cover for an SL/MKS convoy then under attack, the commodore construed the task as 'defensive' and, therefore, not within his remit.

Representations were made by Air Marshal Slessor to Admiral Stark (Commander, US Naval Forces Europe). Stark supported his commodore, the incident pointing up the potential advantage of unified command, attempts at the creation of which had been effectively abandoned.

Following the *Paukenschlag* campaign, the American Eastern Sea Frontier had also gone quiet, Dönitz shifting his focus elsewhere after July 1942. Not the least reason was that the defences were now up to what was required of them. Traffic was now well regulated, most of it moving in convoy but with the occasional single ship accompanied by a 'blimp', or non-rigid airship. Inevitably, as normality was established, Admiral Andrews' command began to be plundered of experienced units and personnel for transfer to hotspots elsewhere. By May 1943, all destroyers and DEs had been withdrawn, leaving again only small craft. Within the Canadian sector there fortunately remained about 100 AS aircraft, both American and Canadian.

Ever probing for weaknesses, Dönitz dispatched half-a-dozen Type IXs, four for the eastern seaboard, two for Brazil. Their fortunes varied considerably, with *U-129* faring best. South-east of Bermuda she sank the valuable 12,800-ton British refrigerated cargo liner *Melbourne Star*, which was proceeding independently. Within the month she had added the American Grace liner *Santa Catarina* and a Panamanian-flagged tanker.

Off the Canadian coast, meanwhile, *U-161* found aerial activity so daunting that she returned to France having sunk just one fishing boat. Her colleague, *U-174*, was sunk on 27 April by the depth charges of a Newfoundland-based US Navy Ventura aircraft.

Of the following trio, which arrived at the end of May, the

U-190 narrowly escaped sinking by a B-24 soon after arrival and spent the remainder of her patrol evading both action and retribution, finally returning empty-handed.

The *U-521* on 2 June, was attempting to attack a southbound convoy off the coast of Virginia when it was detected and sunk by the tiny *PC-565*, assisted by the USS *Brisk*. The latter was an interesting example of reverse lend-lease, being a Flower-class corvette built in Canada to British account as HMS *Flax* but transferred to the US Navy on completion to assist in meeting its then-chronic shortage of AS escorts. Because the term 'corvette' was not used in that service, she was reclassified a 'patrol gunboat' (PG), one of eight such.

Despite generally unencouraging results, a steady trickle of Type IXs continued to arrive in American waters. More fortunate than most, the *U-66* headed southward from her Cape Hatteras landfall and, on 10 June, encountered the Philadelphia-bound tanker *Esso Gettysburg* some 130 miles off the Georgia coast. One of 525 similar vessels eventually completed as part of the huge United States standard ship construction programme, she was a turbo-electric ship of a class known collectively as 'T2s'. Large and valuable, each was of 10,448 GRT and could load 16,613 deadweight tons. Capable of up to 16 knots, the T2s were intended to be fast enough to travel independently of convoy. Struck by two of *U-66*'s torpedoes, however, her fifteen-month career terminated in a fiery pyre reminiscent of the bad days of 1942.

Evading the ensuing hunt the *U-66*'s commander, Friedrich Markworth, decided to remain in the area and, on 1 July, was able to repeat the exercise on another T2, the empty *Bloody Marsh*. Both vessels had been well armed and carrying a party of the Naval Armed Guard. Each had been accompanied by a blimp but, in both cases, the aircraft was experiencing trouble with electrical storms.

Again Markworth survived the inevitable furore and, eventually, made for home. Outside the Bahamas he met with yet another T2, the empty *Cherry Valley*. He still appeared to have plenty of torpedoes, hitting the tanker with two from six. Empty tankers in the gas-free condition do not sink easily and the *U-66* attacked with the deck gun still carried by U-boats on distant patrols. The tanker's armed guard responded and the ship survived through out-pacing her assailant.

In this time of mediocre results, Markworth learned that he had been rewarded with a *Ritterkreuz* and, being short of fuel, his boat was ordered to rendezvous with the XB minelayer *U-117*. Their designated meeting point lay unfortunately close to the track of the UGS convoys and, proceeding there on the surface, the *U-66* was surprised on 3 August by an Avenger/Wildcat team from the expert *Card* support group. The submarine survived, but considerably damaged. Strafing had injured several crew members including the skipper, who sustained a stomach wound. Their suffering was protracted as it was a further four days before the two boats finally met. The *U-117* transferred her first officer to take temporary command as Markworth and his colleagues were treated by the larger boat's medical officer.

Engaged in this and the transfer of fuel, the pair were discovered by another *Card* Avenger. Its first target, the *U-66*, escaped by diving promptly while the better-armed *U-117* kept the aircraft at a safe distance. This, however, only delayed the inevitable for the Avenger's call for assistance quickly brought two more Avengers and two Wildcats to the scene, resulting in the minelayer's destruction.

To anticipate somewhat, the *U-66*'s penchant for high drama was to continue. Following repair, she was one of several boats sent to West African waters early in the following February. Under her new skipper, Gerhard Seehausen, she sank one French and three British ships, whose aggregate tonnage of 19,754 was a good result for this period. Again, however, *U-66* was short of fuel for her return passage and was ordered to rendezvous with *U-488*, one of the few remaining U-tankers, some 700 miles west of the Cape Verdes. Such was the Allied preponderance by this juncture that three American CVE-based support groups were active in the area. Following an Ultra lead, the *Croatan* group obtained an accurate D/F bearing on the *U-488*. Unusually, this was followed up by a 'plastering' from the whole escort force of five DEs.

The *U-66* was close enough to monitor proceedings on her passive sound equipment, a long series of explosions followed by the characteristic noises of the hull collapsing as it sank into the darkness where so many good merchant vessels had gone before.

Now critical on fuel, *U-66* was directed to meet with *U-188*, on passage from Penang with a cargo of raw rubber. Every attempt by the two boats to make radio contact was, however, D/F-ed and followed up aggressively by carrier aircraft, and the meeting proved impossible.

A night-flying Avenger pinpointed Seehausen in the darkness of 5–6 May and vectored in a DE from the screen of its carrier, *Block Island*. Probably already damaged, for she remained surfaced, the U-boat fired on her approaching nemesis, the USS *Buckley*. Although the latter possessed adequate firepower, her commanding officer again could not resist the temptation to ram. In a rerun of the *Borie*'s action, the two locked together.

Fearing that the Americans would board, Seehausen desperately tried to destroy classified material. He could not scuttle with so many still below so, to buy time, he ordered away a party to storm the *Buckley*. Hand-to-hand combat developed on the DE's forecastle but as the Americans mowed down enemy reinforcements emerging from the submarine, the boarding party was isolated. Five survived to surrender.

Not quite finished, Seehausen succeeded in breaking free but the DE, with her torn and buckled bows, followed on. In desperation, the German succeeded in ramming her opponent aft, causing severe damage to a shaft, but then, unable to resist further, Seehausen scuttled. Thirty-six of the U-boat men survived this extraordinary scrap. They included neither Seehausen nor his two British prisoners, the master and chief officer of the *Silvermaple*, sunk off the Ivory Coast.

Since to attack a convoy was now increasingly to invite the deadly and undivided attentions of a support group, Dönitz changed tactics on the eastern seaboard by embarking on a mining offensive. This was entirely logical since, almost from the juncture at which he had succeeded Raeder as head of the German Navy, he was aware that his enemies could more than make good any losses that he could inflict upon them. His policy now had to be to use his forces to cause maximum disruption, obliging the allies to devote the greatest number of resources in retaining control. Minelaying would never suit the temperament of the more offensively-minded U-boat skipper, but its clandestine nature reduced risks to individual boats.

Small clutches of mines, well separated, would each announce its presence through a single ship being sunk or damaged. The whole area would then need to be closed to traffic, with all the associated disruption, while mine clearance resources were committed to ensuring that it was thoroughly swept.

No longer was it sufficient to use pairs of 'traditional' minesweepers to steam back and forth to cut the cables of buoyant moored mines. Shallow coastal waters are ideally suited to ground-laid influence mines, magnetic or acoustic. Germany was also producing a pressure-activated ground mine but, for the moment, held back from deploying it, thus divulging its existence before its availability in large numbers could make the maximum impact. Influence mines were also being equipped with simple counters, enabling them to ignore a selected number of stimuli. Because of these, a single pass over an area was no longer sufficient to pronounce it mine-free.

The minelaying effort was, in no way, a 'blitz', involving just thirteen boats over the space of five months. Five of these craft were lost, either in American waters or in the more perilous Bay of Biscay whilst in transit. Nevertheless, the reappearance of U-boats close inshore caused great concern, for all personnel blooded in the *Paukenschlag* campaign had long been transferred, with their hard-won experience, to newly-active theatres elsewhere. Once again, although fortunately on a far smaller scale, German U-boat skippers were reporting on their 'rookie' opponents with a degree of derision. Admiral Andrews again moved from a situation where he was having to justify the resources that he controlled to one of rapid build-up.

Dönitz was certainly creating a nuisance but, together with the remainder of the German High Command, was all too aware that it *was* only a nuisance. Ten submarines dispatched to the Caribbean sank barely 16,000 GRT over the space of six weeks. Five boats were destroyed there and two more on the return trip.

A further force, mainly of the long-range Type IXD2s, conducted a sustained effort in the Indian Ocean. In all, it cost BdU twenty-two U-boats, but Dönitz was able to claim a total of fifty-seven merchantmen of 366,000 GRT destroyed.

Again, many of the enemy's losses occurred whilst boats were in transit in the Atlantic. The Admiral's account speaks disparingly of endless aerial intervention by VLR and carrier-borne aircraft, of the enforced abandonment of refuelling due to the ever-present risk of being surprised and the consequent shortening of patrols. Most importantly, as his forces probed constantly for soft spots in the Allies' distant shipping network, he knew that, in the background, the all-important North Atlantic convoys were shuttling constantly, almost unmolested, transforming the United Kingdom into a vast armed camp with the single, inevitable objective of reclaiming continental Europe.

The defence of the British home islands, so close to enemy-occupied Europe and, for so long, vulnerable to direct assault, had absorbed considerable resources in men and matériel. In the latter half of 1943, however, as Allied war-planning shifted into the offensive mode, this changed significantly.

To deter U-boats accessing the Atlantic northabout from German bases a huge Allied effort had been expended in re-creating a deep water mine barrier between the Faeroes and Iceland. Its maintenance required the services of a dedicated minelaying squadron. Only one U-boat is thought to have been destroyed in the barrier, and that not until August 1943, while several Allied vessels had come to grief on 'friendly' mines that had broken adrift from their deep moorings. Because of the poor material result, the enterprise is commonly dismissed as a failure, but it is impossible to compute the total effect that it exerted on the enemy's submarine movements. In September 1943 it was decided to maintain the barrier no longer and the squadron was disbanded to free the manpower.

A similar decision awaited the east coast mine barrier, planted to protect the seaward flank of the vulnerable but vital inshore convoy route. Its traffic had braved the shifting hazards of the swatchways, direct attack by E-boats and enemy aircraft, and mining by every agency that an ingenious and determined foe could muster. The length of the route from the Thames to the Forth and beyond was marked by the gaunt and rusting top hamper of the many wrecks that attested to the enemy's past success. Although powerful E-boat flotillas based in the Netherlands could still create a nuisance, things were now quieter along this, the far eastern extremity of the long North Atlantic convoy route.

As late as October 1943 a total of twenty-eight E-boats was assembled for an attack on an east coast convoy, in this case the joint FN.1160/FN.1164. A typically fast-moving action developed between the marauders and the escort, which comprised elderly second-line destroyers and the hard-hitting little Hunts, supported to seaward by an independent cover of light forces, mostly Motor Gun Boats (MGB). In contrast to the patient escort and defence of the deep water convoys this was the sort of bewildering, exhilarating, opportunistic encounter that marked inshore warfare. Short and brutal, individual actions could last seconds and require rapid reflex decision-making. It was very much the province of young men.

The ports, which had earlier suffered the attentions of large enemy bomber formations, were still targeted, but now sporadically and, as like as not, by groups of 'hit-and-run' fighter-bombers. Potentially, these could deliver a score of 250kg bombs with pinpoint accuracy from below radar cover and with minimal warning. In practice, the threat of retribution resulted in damage being fairly widely scattered. The civil population thus continued to suffer, but little lasting damage was inflicted on the nation's war potential, not least because vital inland transport links were never thoroughly targeted.

The Allied shift to the offensive at this time resulted also in the decommissioning of the remaining Armed Merchant Cruisers (AMC), their personnel being urgently required to man the growing numbers of escort carriers (CVE). As related in an earlier chapter, about fifty passenger liners had originally been converted for the task. With scant recognition, and always at risk of being savaged by a superior opponent, they had given convoys basic cover against surface attack, had again enforced a northern blockade and had cruised interminably in the search for the enemy's supply ships. In all these tasks they had substituted for regular cruisers, whose insufficient strength resulted from decades of political cheeseparing.

Hungry of manpower and with their functions now increasingly confined to the oceanic backwaters of the South Atlantic and Indian Ocean, they passed from the order of battle as un-obtrusively as they had joined, their contribution unsung and under-estimated.

It was the turn of Admiral Dönitz to demonstrate resilience and strength of character. By the end of 1943 he had been obliged to finally abandon his wolf-pack tactics, with U-boats having to operate singly or in small groups to avoid drawing attention to themselves. Allied shipping losses were, as a result, now well below an average of 100,000 GRT per month, a fraction of what was being built. The last four months of the year had seen the destruction of sixty-two of his submarines, one every other day. With no surface fleet to speak of, however, the Admiral knew well that the only means by which he could continue to contest the Allies' command of the sea was through his submarine service. New technologies and new boats were in the pipeline. He had to make them work and, from belief as much as from bravado, his end-of-year assessment to his leader reassured him that 'the submarine weapon has not been broken by the setback of 1943 . . . In 1944, which will be a successful but hard year, we shall smash Britain's supply (sic) with a new submarine weapon.'

Chapter Seven

Cleansing the Stable
(January 1944 – May 1945)

As the year of 1944 dawned, the war was a weary fifty-two months old. From above the fog of propaganda that sustained the will of ordinary Germans, their High Command clearly viewed a future fraught with difficulty. A patient progression of North Atlantic convoys and 'Winston's Specials', virtually unopposed, poured men and matériel into the United Kingdom. All evidence pointed to an Allied re-entry into continental Europe being imminent. With this, the opening of the so-called 'Second Front', Germany would slowly be crushed against the Soviet tide advancing from the east. For its very survival, Germany could not allow an invasion to succeed.

From Belgium to Brittany her military strength stood ready behind the optimistically-named Atlantic Wall. To German generals who, in 1940, had convincingly demonstrated the futility of massive fixed defences, the chances of a successful Allied invasion must have appeared good. The subsequent support of Allied armies in Europe would, however, demand ever more shipments. The convoys would have to keep rolling, but Dönitz' forces, revitalized by a steady stream of the new *Elektroboote*, would destroy them. Starved, throttled, the Allies' great gamble would stall, and the campaign lapse into stalemate, an end result which was by now the best outcome that the German High Command could anticipate. For both camps, a combination of technology and pre-fabrication, successfully applied, could be decisive.

*   *   *

178

American merchant shipbuilding had actually peaked during the 'crisis year' of 1943. Of ocean-going cargo ships, their shipyards had produced in 1941 a little over 1 million GRT. In 1942, 8 million. For 1943, a target of 16 million had been set, the industry responding with over 19 million.

The bulk of this tonnage was composed of the basic Liberty ship, the American derivative of the simple cargo carrier ordered by the British mission of December 1940. The entire programme had been kick-started by a British investment of 96 million dollars in the United States and Canada, the sum including funding for two specialized facilities. By 1943, these had been expanded and joined by sixteen others, all American funded.

With an eye to post-war interests, powerful American lobbies originally opposed the Liberty type, whose simplicity was held to fit the requirements of the British merchant marine rather than their own. To suit their own trading patterns, fewer ships of higher quality were demanded. These were eventually built in parallel, typified by the turbine-driven Victories and C3s.

In February 1941, six months before the launch of either the British prototype, *Empire Liberty*, or the American-built *Ocean Vanguard* (the first to British account), the President announced an order for 200 of an American-funded derivative, and a still-neutral United States began to invest in its own new shipbuilding facilities.

Dominating the American scene was the controversial figure of Henry J. Kaiser. He makes an interesting contrast with what might be termed his German 'opposite number', Otto Merker. Neither was a shipbuilding specialist. Kaiser was the lesser engineer but, where the self-effacing Merker employed order and method to achieve his objectives, the self-publicizing Kaiser brought a genius for organization on a scale that beggared the imagination. Kaiser was not the only star name in this great enterprise and, once started, they produced ships on an heroic scale. In September 1941, little over six months from signing of contracts, greenfield sites launched their first Liberty ships, the first of 2,710.

Further to the Oceans, for which they had paid, the British also manned and operated the near-identical Forts. These stemmed from Canadian yards, but were funded and owned by the Americans, who bareboat-chartered them to the British for a

179

nominal one dollar per ship per month. It will be noted that, while this assisted in the overall war effort, it did nothing to staunch the haemorrhage of loss to British-owned tonnage.

Fully mobilized, the United States was facing a manpower problem by 1943. Their merchant marine was particularly affected as its pre-war size was less than two-thirds that of the British (11.4 million v. 17.9 million GRT) and its pool of trained seamen was smaller. With scores of new vessels hoisting the Stars and Stripes, a manning crisis was inevitable. Each Liberty required a crew of fifty-two, together with a twenty-nine strong naval party to man the considerable armament.

In contrast, British ships were lost in large numbers but the greater part of their crews were being rescued so that, by 1943, there was a fully-trained surplus of 10,000 seamen. Through the offices of the exotically-named American-British Combined Shipping Adjustment Board, therefore, it was arranged to transfer to the British flag fifteen to twenty Liberty ships per month for a period of ten months.

Although the ships remained American property and the British had already created a precedent by freely transferring scarce Oceans to other Allied flags, American unions, politicians and sectors of the public press, with an eye to the post-war shipping scene, loudly denounced the scheme. Britain, having lost her assets, her shipping and her trade, faced an end-of-hostilities situation where markets would have to be re-established in the face of a glut of cheap American shipping whose operators had every intention of establishing what might be termed a 'new order'.

Where America and Britain had pulled together in the interests of the very survival of European democracy, disharmony began to be evident once the crisis was past, the issue no longer in doubt and post-war considerations assumed higher priority.

From July 1943 British crews took over Liberty ships to an eventual total of 182 (which neatly accounted for 10,000 seamen) but, because of political clangour, the Americans imposed more rigorous conditions on all charter-party agreements made with the British.

In general, Liberty ships were named after figures who had made significant contribution to American life. Those transferred to the British flag were managed by all the great, long-established companies, each of which had its own distinctive nomenclature. Despite this, they were renamed with synthetic words commencing with 'Sam', e.g. *Sambolt* and *Samlamu*. The reason remains unclear but it certainly served to remind their operators of the ships' American ownership.

With the decision by Dönitz, on 13 August 1943, that all future U-boat construction would be of Type XXI and Type XXIII *Elektroboote*, responsibility for the programme passed to Speer's Ministry for Armament and War Production. On 30 September existing contracts for over 400 Type VII and Type IX were cancelled. As current output was about twenty-five boats monthly, and each took about nine months to construct, the inertia of the programme would carry it through to April 1944. The very last Type VII was laid down in that January.

The new Type XXI would be assembled from eight fully fitted-out modules in facilities at Hamburg, Bremen and Danzig. Although weighing anything up to 165 tons, each section had to be built to a tolerance of better than 2.5mm to ensure alignment. Items so large could be transported only by water, on special barges that were tailored to the inland waterway system. It soon became apparent to Allied intelligence that the Dortmund-Ems canal, running north and south, and the Mittelland canal, running east and west, were of critical value to the enemy's interests. In total, they offered 200 miles of embankments, aquaducts and locks that were vulnerable to bombing attack which quickly acquired high priority.

Speer planned for each boat to absorb six months' building time, working up to an output of twenty-five Type XXI and twenty-one Type XXIII per month. As with American pre-fabrication methods, success depended on many people, each doing one task. All depended upon a regular flow of components of which some, such as periscopes, torpedo tubes and battery cells, had few, if any, alternative sources and were vulnerable to specific targeting.

It was also apparent that although matériel was sourced over a wide area, it became more concentrated as it moved through the assembly process. The hull assembly facilities were thus most critical, requiring the greatest protection.

Covered fitting-out berths were already built or were being planned at the major shipyards but huge new structures were now put in hand. That near Bremen was large enough to house modules and assembly lines for three Type XXIs simultaneously. This required an internal working space of about 1,400 × 185 feet. Even given every priority for labour and materials, however, such undertakings could not be complete before 1945 and, until then, construction berths were open to air attack. Every effort was thus made to improve Luftwaffe fighter defences, but events in Hamburg in the summer of 1943 showed that, however fiercely resisted, Allied bombing attacks were increasingly likely to be forced through with a strength and ruthlessness to cause significant disruption.

From its inception, Merker's programme was too tight. Heavily pressured suppliers forwarded sub-assemblies that were commonly either incomplete or outside tolerance. Relationships between managers along the line quickly soured and problems began in the supply of raw materials. Major setbacks began with Allied air raids in February 1944. Damage to the MAN diesel engine factory and Siemens-Schuckert's electric motor facility imposed the first forecast delays in submarine production. This, however, slid so rapidly adrift that the very first of class, *U-2501*, did not commission until the end of June, by which time the plan called for twenty-three to be in service.

Once fully accepted, the Hedgehog spigot mortar proved to have twice the success rate of standard depth charges. That its bombs did not explode unless they actually hit the target was, however, seen as a major drawback by the crews of the AS ships. The spectacular plumes of an exploding depth charge pattern were, psychologically, as encouraging to the hard-working deck teams as their nerve-splintering concussions were demoralizing to those targeted. Work thus continued on what, in 1938, had been conceived as the then-unfunded Fairlie Mortar, but which now emerged as the Squid.

This weapon was a true mortar, whose three barrels each hefted a bomb with a 200-pound charge of the new Minol II explosive. The bombs landed 300 yards ahead of the ship, falling as an equilateral triangle with 120-feet sides. Designed to sink rapidly, the projectiles could be fused to explode down to 900 feet, later increased by 50 per cent. The effect was essentially two-dimensional, so the weapon was deployed also as a 'Double Squid', where the two sets of three bombs were separated by about sixty feet in depth and whose double triangle formed, in plan, a hexagon.

Closely associated with the Squid was the new Type 147 Asdic set, which could track the target in three dimensions while giving the operator a continuous printout of the target's relative position in terms of bearing and depth.

So heavy and space-consuming was Squid that it proved impracticable to retro-fit it to existing classes of AS ship. This, unfortunately, included the excellent American-built DEs which were commissioning in the Royal Navy in powerful numbers (sixty-seven by the end of 1943, eleven more by February 1944).

Two new classes of British escort thus emerged. To continue full utilization of yards too small to build frigates, the Castle-class corvette was designed around a single Squid, located in a super-imposed position forward of the bridge. Handsome little ships, they were derived from the later Flower type but were fifty feet longer with generous sheer and flare. A long forecastle form permitted covered access to a point well aft. Forty-four Castles were built in British yards, with the first of class, *Hadleigh Castle*, commissioned in September 1943. Twelve were transferred to the Royal Canadian Navy and one to the Norwegian. Five more were fitted out specifically to act as convoy rescue ships.

The River-class frigates had a worthy successor in the Loch type, much of a size but proportionately beamier. A double Squid was located forward of the bridge and, despite the weapon's novelty, it was so highly rated that the ships' depth charge capacity was reduced to just fifteen, in comparison with the Rivers' 200. The first of class, *Loch Fada*, entered service just three months after the *Hadleigh Castle*.

With the Loch-class, the British also adopted prefabrication. Simplified design minimized the use of complex curvature and the whole structure was reduced to modules, mostly weighting under three tons. They could thus be easily transported by road having been built, for the most part, by firms unskilled in shipbuilding.

A dozen yards were involved in assembly, but fitting-out was restricted to only four.

By virtue of a different armament fit, the basic ship could be fitted out for the anti-aircraft role. Those so modified were intended primarily for service with the expanding Pacific Fleet. Thirty-six in number, they were known as the Bay class. A total of fifty-five further baseline hulls was ultimately cancelled.

At the end of 1943 the Allied leaders, including Stalin, conferred at length in Cairo and Teheran. The general mood was now optimistic, but Prime Minister Churchill was increasingly aware of the extent to which his debilitated and impoverished nation had shrunk in status to that of junior partner.

Affecting the Atlantic directly was the decision to invade Europe (Operation Overlord) in May or June 1944. Despite the defection of Italy in September 1943, German forces held firm there. From the Allied viewpoint this was an advantage in reducing their strength in France, but it meant that the Mediterranean remained strategically important.

The Allied build-up in the United Kingdom could still be interdicted by Dönitz' forces at sea. The command war diary at this time listed their strength at 168 operational boats, 181 under repair and eighty-seven working up and devoted to training. To keep Allied AS forces at full stretch, the Admiral decided to double U-boat strength in the Mediterranean, and to use his last two U-tankers to support distant operations in the Central and South Atlantic.

Hitler remained obsessed with the notion that the huge level of Allied activity in southern England could be a ruse to cover a major move against Norway. Bases here as well as in western France thus came under great pressure as the pens filled with U-boats, with more having to be berthed in the open. Urgent work continued to fit Snort gear, while Atlantic patrols continued to keep the increasing numbers of boats fully battle-trained.

Those U-boats involved in the North Atlantic adopted an increasingly defensive posture, however, proceeding no further than 35 degrees west. The promised reconnaissance support to this meridian proved, as ever, unreliable with the Luftwaffe being able to provide only eight of the new Junkers Ju 290s, due to 'higher priorities'. Two or three aircraft searched in vain for three specific eastbound convoys shortly before Christmas 1943. The waiting U-boat force, Group *Rügen*, was reorganized from three subgroups into six, each of three boats. This was the pattern adopted by the Americans in the Pacific but, here, the aim was to keep constantly on the move, to confuse the Allied perception of their true strength and disposition.

They were successful in locating three further convoys in the last days of the year but no group was able to mount an attack. On 7 January 1944, therefore, the sub-groups were dissolved as being useless in the absence of reliable air support. 'That the virtual discontinuance of pack attacks would further diminish our prospects of success had to be accepted and, henceforth, the individual U-boat would generally have to cope single-handed with the entire convoy escort and bear the brunt of its counter attack' reported the war diary.

Neither had the enemy's deception worked, for the U-boat Situation Report for the week ending 3 January, issued by the Submarine Tracking Room, refers specifically to 'six groups of three boats . . . scattered irregularly roughly on an arc of about 500 miles radius from North Channel. They remain submerged by day and have been ineffective against the convoys which have passed close amongst them.'

Dönitz made strong representations that he needed aircraft in order to evaluate joint air/sea operations in the face of powerful Allied defences. During January, therefore, he was successful in boosting support to eleven Ju290s, two Bv222s and four 'long-range' Ju88s. Nineteen FW200 Kondors were also available but these, even when serviceable, could not fly by night.

Those *Rügen* boats still on patrol were reorganized as Group *Stürmer* and placed squarely across the North-West Approaches awaiting a positive aircraft report. The first Ju290 dispatched had a radio failure and it was ten hours before a second reported an expected convoy. It was westbound, and the *Stürmer* line was already behind it. Those boats armed with 37mm guns were, therefore, ordered to surface and to make every effort to close the convoy by nightfall. The relief aircraft had to return with engine problems and, by dusk, no U-boat had made contact. During the small hours, a third aircraft located the convoy again but was unable to transmit homing signals. Fog on British airfields was robbing the convoy of its own air cover and it steamed on largely oblivious of the enemy's strenuous efforts to intercept it. The whole operation was abandoned in farce, when a separate enemy reconnaissance flight over the Bay of Biscay reported a Spanish fishing fleet as an Allied invasion force, initiating a short-lived emergency.

The absence of Allied aircraft should have been of great assistance, but Dönitz' disappointment was compounded by skippers' reports of the topside weight of a 37mm gun and additional armour threatening a boat's surfaced stability when driven hard. Severe rolling added to a crew's exhaustion and prevented the watch keeping a proper lookout. The gun itself proved to corrode rapidly. It needed frequent test-firing to keep the bore clean but could not be relied upon to operate first time.

Revived enemy activity in the North-West Approaches resulted in a rapid increase in Allied countermeasures. The area was 15 Group Coastal Command's responsibility but reinforcements arrived from neighbouring 19 Group. Airfields, particularly in Northern Ireland, were busy day and night in deployment of AS aircraft, with Beaufighter patrols to counter the enemy's reconnaissance aircraft. 'Johnny' Walker's 2EG again distinguished itself, working with two escort carriers to the west of Ireland.

On 31 January the sloop *Wild Goose* detected a submarine stalking the CVE *Nairana*, which was engaged in flying operations. Walker came to assist in the *Starling*, and one of his standard 'creeping' attacks accounted for the *U-592*. The boat was already returning home following damage incurred two days earlier through a B-24 depth charge attack.

A week later, 2EG joined the escort of the combined SL.147/MKS.38, which was in close proximity to two other convoys. Despite the efforts of the CVE's fighters, Luftwaffe reconnaissance was successfully tracking the convoys as Dönitz rushed in the twenty-two boats of Group *Igel* (Hedgehog). These were organized in two sections, one of which closed Walker's convoy.

Late on 8 February, the *Wild Goose* sighted a surfaced submarine. This promptly submerged but was held by Asdic as the *Woodpecker* quietly moved in. A rolling carpet of twenty depth charges then destroyed *U-762* from which, again, there were no survivors.

At first light on the 9th, the *Wild Goose* obtained a radar contact at nearly ten miles and, closing, found *U-734* by Asdic. A T5 torpedo was defeated by the sloop's low speed but the ship quickly accelerated, replying with depth charges. Arriving to assist, the *Starling* then tried an unsuccessful creeping barrage. This attracted two further T5s, also evaded. Walker patiently repeated the exercise, this time leaving the submarine's debris as evidence of a kill.

Two further sloops of the group, *Kite* and *Magpie* had, meanwhile, D/F-ed yet another enemy in an attacking position ahead of the convoy. *Kite* obtained fleeting radar and visual contact before the U-boat submerged. Expecting a T5 as a response, the sloop dropped a single depth charge. A second explosion showed the supposition to have been correct. For six hours the two ships played cat and mouse with no result. At this point, Walker joined with the *Starling* and *Wild Goose*. Even so, it took a further three hours and the expenditure of a record 266 depth charges to bring the wily *U-238* to the surface.

As *Starling* and *Kite* rendezvoused with a passing HX convoy to replenish depth charges, business proceeded as usual for the other three of the group. Steaming in line abreast early on the 11th, they were rewarded with another Asdic contact, again by the *Wild Goose* which, with the *Woodpecker*, disposed of the *U-424* after three passes.

Still on station on the 19th, 2EG was sweeping astern of the convoy ONS.29 when *Woodpecker*'s Asdic operator obtained a contact. It was then mid-morning but it was dark before she and the *Starling* forced the *U-264* to the surface. She had been the first Snort-equipped Type VII to make an operational patrol. Her crew was rescued, the first survivors from six U-boats destroyed by 2EG in a spell at sea that had lasted nearly a month.

On the same day, however, success was marred when the *Woodpecker*, following up a D/F contact, lost her after end to a T5 from the *U-764*. There were no fatal casualties but, following a seven-day fight to save her, she sank while under tow, in sight of the English coast.

During this busy period, twelve convoys had passed through

the North-West Approaches for the loss of just one straggler. Besides six U-boats sunk by Walker's group, five more had succumbed to air attack. Two Coastal Command aircraft had been lost but, from the enemy's meagre establishment of maritime aircraft, two Ju290s, one He177 and an FW200 had been destroyed. Three had been shot down by carrier-borne fighters (two at night) and one by the Royal Air Force. The enemy noted that his airborne radars were being jammed in the vicinity of convoys.

Late in 1943, *U-763* sailed with the first *Hohentwiel* air search radar, but her skipper refused to use it in the very areas for which it was intended, fearing that, as an active source, it would betray his location. It would not have been detectable at this time but its six or seven miles of effective range would have given only two minutes' warning.

Allied strategic bomber units continued to enjoy the highest priority for new radars of 3cm wavelength. Coastal Command's C.-in-C., Sir John Slessor, was well aware of the enemy's efforts to get *Naxos* into production, when it would detect existing radars. His pleas for some of the new sets were overridden, whereupon history repeated itself when, in February 1944, another wrecked bomber, in this case American, yielded a working 3cm set to grateful German scientists.

It was at a fortunate juncture for the enemy since Dönitz, dismayed at the record, so far, of his scientific services, had recently formed a Naval Headquarters Scientific Directorate whose appointed head, Professor Karl Küpfmüller, reported directly to him.

Küpfmüller turned out to be a 'hands-on' scientist, quickly improving the basic *Naxos* unit by focusing incoming signals to make it directional. This, in turn, required a rotating antenna but, to avoid delay, an *ad hoc* set, known as *Tunis*, entered service in May 1944 pending a final engineered version of *Naxos*, promised for the end of the year. *Tunis*, oddly enough, entered service before opposing aircraft acquired 3cm radar, but it was largely wasted as the U-boat crews, steeped in the 'Metox radiation' fable, rarely dared to use it.

Two further aids, code-named *Fliege* and *Mücke*, were also under urgent development, specifically to detect 3cm radar pulses at better than twenty-five miles' range.

A further Küpfmüller initiative was to fit out a U-boat for signals intelligence. In addition to monitoring equipment to observe and measure all incoming Allied signals the *U-406* carried three supernumerary electronics specialists. Her career was brutally short as the British frigate *Spey* caught her stalking the aforementioned convoy ONS.29. Together with a sister ship, *Lossie*, she depth charged the U-boat to the surface. All but four of her crew were taken prisoner, including the supernumeraries. The boat, already settling, was riskily boarded by the *Spey* but she foundered before anything of intelligence value could be recovered.

Until the end of 1941, U-boats could reach longitude 18 degrees west, the approximate outer limit of the busy North-West Approaches, in three to five days. Now, in early 1944, it took ten to twelve, and the war diary comments on the increased physical and mental strain thus endured by crews. The endless watch for Allied predators was engendering a defensive mentality in some crews causing, the diary notes, 'a bad effect on the readiness to attack'.

There were certainly signs of shaken morale in the U-boat service. Each month about 20 per cent of operational boats were lost. If the radar watch indicated that a boat was being illuminated by an enemy transmitter there was no means of telling whether its source was air-or-shipborne, or its range and, probably, bearing. An emergency crash dive was thus the usual response.

Fanciful tales of new Allied weapons and detection devices quickly gained wide currency. Foxer gear tow cables 'strummed' with a distinctive note which propagated well underwater. Sensitive to every noise, U-boat hydrophone operators decided that it was caused by a new type of sound-ranging equipment. Distant depth charge explosions were feared to be a means of echo ranging. Expended sonobuoys should have sunk automatically on exhaustion but, occasionally sighted still afloat, were thought to be noise transmitters, used to mimic the sound of escorts and Asdics, either to act as decoys for T5 torpedoes or to put further psychological pressure on a hunted submarine skipper.

It was discovered by *B-dienst* intercepts that regular U-boat radio transmissions were being D/F-ed by up to twenty Allied shore stations. Despite continued centralization of BdU control, skippers thus became reluctant to report in, some observing total radio silence. As the level of losses remained high, BdU was unable to account for many which, thus, simply 'disappeared'. This slowly rising tide of uncertainty also exerted an adverse effect on morale.

Of three Snort-equipped boats at sea the *U-164*, as we have seen, was destroyed on 19 February. Early on 13 March a Leigh Light Wellington supporting convoy ON.227 sighted a second, *U-575*. The aircraft attacked unsuccessfully and the boat remained surfaced. Her skipper, Wolfgang Böhmer, had sunk the corvette *Asphodel* with a T5 just four days previously and now used his 37mm gun to confidently fight off a B-17 that arrived in support of the Wellington. The gun jammed and Böhmer was fortunate to be able to submerge. Damage to the *U-575* left a thin oil trace, however, and this was hopefully, but again unsuccessfully, depth charged by a second B-17. This aircraft then circled the area as it vectored-in the experienced *Bogue* support group. The group had exchanged its venerable four-stackers for four new DEs, and two of these, supported by a Canadian frigate and *Bogue*'s Avengers, spent several hours in bringing the stubborn U-boat to the surface. Thirty-seven of her crew survived.

The sinking illustrated well the extensive resources that were often needed to carry a hunt through to its conclusion. Two or three years before, such resources simply were not available.

Interrogation of the *U-575*'s survivors painted a somewhat miserable picture of life aboard a 'Snort-boat'. To prevent water ingress, the top of the Snort mast was fitted with a fairly rudimentary flap valve. Even a moderate sea would immerse it regularly, causing it to close and the diesels to momentarily suck air from the boat's interior. This instantly created a partial vacuum, to the great distress of the crew. Their misery was compounded by fumes that leaked from the diesel exhaust trunk while snorting. Spending so long submerged, U-boats now depended to a greater extent on their passive hydrophone arrays to locate convoys. The racket of the diesels considerably degraded the performance of this gear while themselves providing a potent noise source for a quietly-listening frigate. The Snort was not greatly loved.

On 22 March 1944, a decisive date, Dönitz again admitted defeat in an Atlantic campaign. Since the beginning of the year, thirty-six boats had been lost in this theatre. Only seven had been sunk while in transit, demonstrating the value of the slow, submerged routines. The remaining losses, however, showed how dangerous it was to approach convoys singly. During this period, 105 convoys had passed, with 3,360 ships escorted for the loss of just three. Such an exchange rate was totally unsupportable.

Dönitz had, in any case, to reorganize his forces in order to meet the threat of the now-inevitable Allied invasion of Europe. This plan greatly affected the Allies themselves. Back in 1942, Torch had demanded the withdrawal of large numbers of escorts from convoy duty, affecting both convoy cycles and loss rates. The coming operation, Overlord, would require an even greater effort.

A first response was to reorganize Atlantic convoys under three speeds, 10, 9 and 8 knots, referred to as Fast, Medium and Slow respectively. A second was to slow the cycle a little but to run larger convoys. Confounding the opinions of Admiral King, these might include over 100 ships. It was now safe enough to detach faster ships near the end of the passage, to berth ahead of the mass and thus ease port congestion.

The dissolution on 22 March of the last group, *Preussen*, formed to oppose convoys, marked the beginning of a general re-disposition. From the summer of 1943, only 70 per cent of boats could be expected to return from patrol, many damaged and requiring lengthy periods in dockyard hands. A total of fifty-six Type VIIs had been transferred to Norway and the Mediterranean and numbers of operational boats in the Atlantic were actually falling. The group (*Landwirt*) now held in French bases specifically to oppose an invasion as yet numbered only fifteen boats, it being unclear how they would be expected to operate.

Only half a dozen U-boats were now in the North-West Approaches, their important function being the transmission of weather reports. Even though they moved on quickly following each report, two were still lost.

With an eye to gaining experience of operating in soundings, BdU dispatched five single boats to work the waters of south-west and north-west Iceland, the Minches and the Bristol Channel. Bound for south-west Iceland, *U-744* encountered the composite SL.149/MKS.40 convoy. Her skipper Heinz Blischke, succeeded in torpedoing an LST (Landing Ship, Tank) and, having tasted success, decided to remain on the major convoy track. He was rewarded on 5 March by the approach of the fast eastbound HX.280. Sweeping ahead of the convoy, however, was the Canadian C-2 group and Blischke, although his presence was unsuspected, rashly, and unsuccessfully, fired a T5. Acting in a support role, C-2 had the time, the inclination and the means to follow a hunt through to a conclusion. For over thirty hours, *U-744* was worried by depth charges, Hedgehog and the first operational use of Squid, courtesy of the new British corvette *Kenilworth Castle*. Finally blasted to the surface and abandoned, the U-boat sank so slowly that a party from the Canadian *Chilliwack* was able to board and even run up the White Ensign while three of their number 'persuaded' a German crewman to guide them below. As a great haul of classified material was assembled, unsuccessful attempts were made to take the submarine in tow but, still obstinately settling, she had to be finished off by torpedo.

Coastal operations by U-boat were largely unrewarding. Defences were both active and strong and, being obliged to remain submerged, boats encountering convoys were unable to gain attacking positions. Their sole success was the sinking of the veteran destroyer *Warwick* off the north Cornish coast.

In the French bases, boats newly fitted with Snort gear were being held back for 'the day', but were unable to exercise due to shallow inshore waters and a proliferation of mines. Venturing to deeper water invited air attack. Those boats so fitted in Germany were able to gain necessary experience by operating from the Norwegian base at Horten.

The enemy war diary noted that Coastal Command's 18 Group had stepped-up its operational tempo to counter greater U-boat activity in the North-West Approaches but also that 19 Group retained its grip on the Bay of Biscay. Individual boats now swapped scarce *Fliege* sets as they had once exchanged Metox. The equipment gave sufficient warning for targets to become scarce in deep water. Inshore, however, U-boats had to proceed surfaced, under escort and led by minesweepers. Because of the considerable combined firepower of these convoys they were best targeted by groups of Mosquito or Beaufighter aircraft. During March and April there were several fierce encounters between these and covering Ju88 fighters. Such scraps proved expensive in aircraft, although the 57mm Tsetses destroyed the *U-976* just outside St Nazaire and badly damaged the la Pallice-bound *U-960*.

In truth, the 'Bay offensive' was in its final stages, but 19 Group would see it through to the end. Its achievements and sacrifices had been considerable, with fifty U-boats destroyed and rather more than that sent back with action damage. Overall, however, seven aircraft had been lost for every submarine. A great, un-quantifiable success was that the seemingly universal presence of marauding aircraft caused U-boat crews to adopt a defensive mentality, reducing the aggressiveness necessary to take on a convoy escort.

Post-war analysis nonetheless proved unforgiving. Aircraft working in direct support of convoys accounted for fifty-eight U-boats and a further five shared with escorts. Thirty-nine more had been obliged to abort their patrols through action damage. In exchange, seventy aircraft were lost. The aircraft-to-U-boat loss ratio was, therefore, about one sixth that for 19 Group, while hours flown per U-boat loss were also considerably less. Final assessment also showed that only 1 per cent of all mercantile losses occurred in convoys protected by a combined air and sea escort.

In the Bay offensive more than half of the enemy's losses occurred during the period when Dönitz, acting on poor scien-tific advice, misjudged the efficiency of night-flying, radar-equipped aircraft and ordered boats to remain surfaced by day. Once this directive was rescinded, submarine losses reverted to their previously low level.

The inescapable conclusion is that aircraft, like AS surface ships, are more efficiently deployed in the vicinity of convoys than in the mounting of 'offensive' patrols. Without exception, every fleet, every air force encountering a submarine threat for the first time made the wrong assumption that convoy escort was 'defensive' and best left to 'defensive' forces. Even with the experience of others plain to see, this truth was still ignored.

Although Dönitz' 'conventional' U-boat force was clearly beaten, it was far from dead, and his policy of 'containment' rather than outright assault was still costing the Allies considerable loss and commitment of resources. The trend, however, was decidedly in the Allies' favour. Once again, statistics can tell us much about the course of the campaign, as evidenced by the table opposite:

Between March and May 1944, Dönitz noted, 80 per cent of U-boat successes had ben attained in 'distant areas', i.e. other than in North Atlantic or British waters. Meagre though these successes were, they were still some 30 per cent inflated by skippers' estimates, disguising further the decline in the force's fortunes.

A dozen Allied and neutral ships had been sunk off the United States eastern seaboard and in the Central Atlantic, an aggregate of 44,500 GRT. To achieve this result, seven Type IXs had been deployed, four of which were sunk. An attack on a convoy now meant swift retribution and the general picture is one of isolated boats taking hasty shots and immediately disengaging.

One of the casualties, *U-550*, was first employed on weather reporting, a duty whose regular transmissions invariably attracted attention. An Iceland-based Canadian PBY caused damage and casualties but, as instructed, the boat's skipper, Klaus Hänert, moved on to waters east of New York. Here, on 16 April, he found himself in the path of one of the American CU fast tanker convoys that ran from the Caribbean to the United Kingdom via New York. With his only opportunity, Hänert hit and destroyed the *Pan Pennsylvania*, fully laden with 15,000 tons of petrol and a deck cargo of seven aircraft. Her escort closed to assist, leaving only one DE to keep Hänert at a distance. Thinking she was alone the German, slightly damaged, surfaced to fight it out. The three other DEs promptly took her under fire, causing her to be scuttled. There were only twelve survivors.

Dönitz had stationed his last U-tanker, *U-488*, west of the Cape

	Total Tonnage Lost*	North Atlantic	South Atlantic	Mediterranean	Indian Ocean	Percentage sunk by submarine
Jan–Jun 1940	1,580	31.2	0.4	3.0	0.9	45.3
Jul–Dec 1940	2,412	54.4	2.0	0.7	6.5	60.9
Jan–Jun 1941	2,884	62.4	3.5	13.6	2.1	50.3
Jul–Dec 1941	1,445	43.1	2.1	7.4	0.7	49.8
Jan–Jun 1942	4,147	68.2	2.3	3.3	10.1	74.2
Jul–Dec 1942	3,641	72.5	10.0	6.2	8.4	87.4
Jan–Jun 1943	2,125	63.7	7.4	12.1	10.2	88.3
Jul–Dec 1943	1,095	27.8	9.1	34.0	24.5	64.6
Jan–end May 1944	515	23.1	7.0	29.7	38.0	80.5

* x 1,000 GRT

All figures other than those in the first column are percentages, relating to six-monthly periods. Several interesting conclusions may be deduced:

1. The extreme right-hand column shows that the U-boat was the most prolific destroyer of mercantile tonnage, latterly by a very considerable margin.

2. The six-monthly totals of tonnage lost began to decline from mid-1942, not after the 'critical' convoy actions of mid-1943. As an increasing number of U-boats were operational, sinkings per patrol were deteriorating sharply.

3. From the outset of the decline in tonnage sunk, the percentage sunk by U-boat increased significantly. This points to decreasing effectiveness of alternative agencies, e.g. surface raiders, mines, aircraft, etc., Dönitz was, therefore, correct in his assertion that the U-boat arm, being the most potent, should be accorded the highest priorities for manpower and materials.

4. Compared with losses sustained in the North Atlantic, those in other theatres were relatively low until 1943, when the U-boat was decisively defeated on the North Atlantic convoy routes. As the percentage of the total sunk in the North Atlantic thereafter declined, those in other theatres increased significantly as BdU dispatched U-boats to previously peripheral areas in order to keep the force gainfully employed. Although these percentages increased considerably, however, they were percentages of a declining total and represented no more than nuisance value to the Allies.

Verdes. Her first customer, *U-801*, was bound for the Indian Ocean but never made the rendezvous, having run foul of the *Block Island* support group. Five refuellings were, however, conducted during April, all on boats bound to and from remote areas. The tanker then shifted position and, as related earlier, *U-66* was ordered to meet up with her. This signal was decrypted and the data transmitted to the *Croatan* support group, which arrived first. The *U-66* was actually close enough to hear the destruction of *U-488* on her sound gear.

U-boat operations in the Indian Ocean were now accounting for a third of all sinkings but, the area being so remote, depended upon Japanese cooperation in the use of the port of Penang. Two supply ships also cruised the area with fuel, lubricating oil, spare parts, provisions and medical facilities. Operations in this theatre are peripheral to the subject of this narrative but, suffice to say, the British used Ultra information not only to dispose of the two supply ships but also to use Ceylon-based submarines to make Penang a dangerous landfall for U-boats.

So successful were the American CVE-based support groups (although the *Block Island* and one of her DEs would be sunk on 29 May in hunting the *U-549* to destruction) that Admiral Cunningham, the British First Sea Lord, requested of Admiral King that they ease off, particularly at ocean rendezvous points, for fear that the enemy would conclude that his Enigma keys were compromised. King refused in a typically tart rejoinder, reminding Cunningham that the Royal Navy had recently run a similar risk in destroying the Indian Ocean supply ships.

The American CNO now spoke from a position of strength for, where the British were experiencing problems building and maintaining the so-called 'four-rotor bombes', necessary to deal with later Enigma traffic, the Americans had built nearly 100. Operated by the US Navy, these were delivering about 1,400 decrypts per month, many of them to purely British tasking.

This huge flow of information enabled the Allies to second-guess many of the enemy's intentions and it was too much to hope that things would continue indefinitely without problems. Such a problem became apparent in March 1944 when, faced with an imminent invasion of Europe, the enemy extended the use of a new complication which he had been trialling on specific networks. This, a so-called 'internal reflector', enabled an individual operator to create his own rotor wiring sequence. With considerable advance warning, the Americans pre-empted the situation by building a vast and frighteningly expensive machine, developed from the four-rotor bombe but employing far more computing power.

As it turned out, the enemy was overtaken by events. Following the invasion, U-boat bases on the French Atlantic coast were soon isolated, communications being necessary via a radio link rather than secure land line. This, together with the greater volume of traffic generated by an increased number of U-boats at sea, produced adequate numbers of procedural glitches, or 'cribs', so essential as starting points for the codebreakers. In addition, the general outlook for the enemy, post-Overlord, was changed so fundamentally that the planned complexities appear never to have been introduced.

In June, a major Enigma blunder was narrowly averted when the *Guadalcanal* support group intercepted the *U-505* near the Cape Verdes. Heavy automatic fire persuaded her crew to surrender and the Americans were not only able to plunder her for intelligence material but also prevent her from sinking. Flushed with success, the *Guadalcanal*'s captain, Daniel V. Gallery, took the U-boat in tow and, rather like Peter and his wolf, headed in triumphant procession towards Dakar in Senegal. He had made a valuable haul but, unforgivably for one so senior, had failed to appreciate the paramount importance in keeping it secret. King and Cunningham were both horrified and furious. At no cost should the enemy ever suspect that any U-boat had been boarded, let alone captured. Gallery was ordered to put about and make the long haul to the British dockyard at Bermuda, a reasonably isolated location where *U-505* was docked by night and under maximum security. During the tow, Overlord had preoccupied the enemy to the extent that the precise fate of *U-505* attracted no particular notice. To intense Allied relief, no changes were made to German naval codes.

Gallery's haul of material weighed, literally, half a ton and, besides current Enigma settings, gave those due to replace them. Without the need to derive solutions from 'cribs', all American bombe capacity could, at least for the time being, be devoted to breaking coded material from other sources.

The *U-505* also yielded confirmation of a new burst transmission system, *Kurier*, not yet in service. A message fed into this system would be transmitted in a very short space of time, and at one of a number of frequencies. Such a procedure would simply be too rapid for Allied D/F procedures to cope with, the consequences being potentially very serious. The warning was timely for, although *Kurier* never reached production stage, American laboratories had time to progress the difficult task of providing an antidote.

Also good reading was the operator's manual for an air and sea navigational system called *Sonne*. Intense Allied air activity over the Bay of Biscay had long resulted in the monitoring of specific enemy transmissions on regular frequencies. Rather like the British 'Gee' system, employed by Bomber Command for blind targeting, several stations were involved, transmitting dots and dashes to provide a 'fix'. Transmitters were located in Norway, the Netherlands, Brittany and neutral Spain. Recognizing something useful, British aircraft did not target the stations but, instead, plotted the signal pattern which, printed as an overlay to standard charts, served Coastal Command well under the name 'Consol'.

But what of the enemy's new *Elektroboote*? Propaganda endlessly alluded to their imminent appearance and it was with very real concern that Allied intelligence sought clues regarding the actual state of the programme.

As conventional submarine construction was on open slips, regular aerial reconnaissance could give accurate numbers and rates of construction. It was noted that, between the summer of 1943 and the spring of 1944, numbers had decreased steadily from about 270 to nearer 160. The reason, of course, was that the Type VII and Type IX programmes were being wound down as new production procedures were being put in place for the Types XXI and XXIII. As the giant new facilities were yet incomplete, the first *Elektroboote* would also need to be assembled on existing slipways.

Thus it was that regular photographic coverage of Danzig

showed that, between the first week of March and the middle of April, a submarine had been assembled and launched. Laying alongside was the first photographed Type XXI, *U-3501*, which had occupied the slip for just thirty-one days. Photographic interpreters also identified other prefabricated sections awaiting location on the slip. What they could not see was that Allied bombing had so badly delayed vital components that *U-3501* had had to be launched as a propaganda exercise, being very far from complete.

For Coastal Command the Bay of Biscay had become something of a backwater. Of the fifteen U-boats sunk in January 1944, three had been lost in the Bay. In February there was none and only one in each of the three following months. Except against Arctic convoys, where pack attack could still be expected, U-boats now operated largely alone, their skippers reconciled to spending a considerable time in transit across the Bay in order to avoid drawing attention to themselves.

At the beginning of the year, responsibility for Coastal Command had passed from Sir John Slessor to Air Chief Marshal Sir Sholto Douglas, whose superior rank reflected the size and importance that the Command had attained. With Overlord just months away, planners were awake to the fact that U-boats based in Brest were located on the flank of heavy mercantile traffic that would be entering the English Channel from the South-West Approaches. They would also be uncomfortably close to the invasion beaches themselves. It was decided that Coastal Command would be reinforced to operate a round-the-clock 'swamp' operation, creating a barrier from the southern Irish coast to St Nazaire. Except for its easternmost fringe, the zone was the responsibility of Air Vice Marshal Brian Bromet's 19 Group which, for the duration, would be boosted to a strength of twenty-five squadrons and extra Royal Air Force strike squadrons drafted in.

The objective was to cover all points on the barrier by radar at least once every thirty minutes. To achieve this, the zone was parceled up into a dozen rectangular boxes, some of which abutted, rather riskily, on the enemy-held French coast. Thirty aircraft would be airborne at all times, patrolling the peripheries of the boxes. As the intention was to effectively block the Channel, the flights were termed 'Cork' patrols.

In a full-scale exercise, a British submarine simulated a U-boat. The interesting result was that the boat was sighted by only two of the nineteen aircraft whose boxes she had crossed, but she had been obliged to dive so frequently to avoid detection that she arrived in no condition to conduct operations, her batteries being virtually flat. It was known, however, that many of the enemy's Biscay force were Snort-equipped, with a performance that remained something of an unknown quantity.

Any U-boat that successfully evaded the Cork patrols and random destroyer sweeps would then meet the flanking defences of what was termed the 'Spout'. From a point south-east of the Isle of Wight to a line a long gunshot from the sandy beaches of the Bay of the Seine would be created a cordon sanitaire, an invisible highway of maritime superiority along whose parallel swept channels the necessary huge numbers of ships and craft would shuttle without let or hindrance.

It had long been decided that the Battle of the Atlantic proper had to be won before Overlord could be considered. During March 1944 the First Lord of the Admiralty was able to inform Parliament: 'In 1941 one ship was lost out of every 181 which sailed; in 1942 one out of every 233; in 1943 one out of every 344. The losses in these [i.e. North Atlantic and Coastal] convoys during the second half of last year were less than one in every thousand.' While his figures might have benefited from a little qualification, their message was unmistakable.

The potential for enemy mischief was considerable as, from the Scillies to the Downs, convoys followed the English coast to access the Spout. This coastal route offered an enterprising enemy over 300 miles of opportunity and, with their North Atlantic burden lightened, it was the task of Admiral Horton's support groups to deny him that opportunity. Intensive retraining was required for, where ocean warfare had covered a broad canvas of inter-service cooperation, based largely upon intelligence input, this was a new picture of constricted and shallow waters, where threats might be unpredictable and develop quickly. It was not appreciated that Snort boats used their equipment for only two or three hours daily and, by remaining submerged, were fortunate to make good sixty miles in twenty-four hours. It was, however, anticipated that Asdic conditions, unpredictable enough in the open sea, would be very difficult in the Channel, with its irregular, rocky bottoms and villainous tidal flows.

Horton withdrew escort and support groups wholesale from the Atlantic and drilled them without respite. As Overlord neared, he was able to signal his command that, 'to his great satis-faction', 286 out of 295 vessels that had passed through this particular mill were 'at this moment fully fit for sea service'.

Operation Neptune, the naval component of Overlord, involved no less than eighty fleet destroyers, twenty-five Hunts, sixty-three frigates and DEs, and seventy-one corvettes. Although this huge force took Dönitz' Snort boats very seriously, the Germans recognized that they and the pathetically few remaining surface warships left in French waters were unlikely to defeat the invasion in its critical phase. The problem was compounded by uncertainty regarding the likely location of the landings and the fact that the Luftwaffe had virtually been beaten from the skies over western France. Like the Japanese in the Pacific, the Germans accepted that their enemy would get ashore in strength. It would be the task of the army's mobile reserve to contain and to defeat the beachhead. The submarine arm would need to do its best to hinder a rapid buildup. Both forces, however, had been greatly hampered by a sustained Allied air campaign, designed to knock out key points on the French road and rail network. Not only was the mobile reserve thus hobbled but the delivery of vital kits of Snort gear prevented. As these lay useless in obscure sidings, many U-boats had been robbed of the opportunity to regain their one great asset, their invisibility.

A total of seventy-nine U-boats were variously deployed to meet the invasion threat. Twenty-two of them, none Snort-equipped, were based in Norway as the Führer maintained the fiction that the Allied preparations could be no more than a feint to disguise a major move in the north. To prevent these boats from moving south to the western Channel, six Allied support groups with three CVEs lay astride their likely tracks.

To meet the heavy traffic expected to come from the United

States, twenty boats (seven with Snort) had been dispatched to the Atlantic. Thirty-seven boats, codenamed Group *Landwirt* (Farmer), therefore, remained in the Biscay bases. Only nine were fitted with Snort. Cautious deployments into the western English Channel had proved that boats could operate submerged for a month or even more, but the effect on crews can only be imagined.

These patrols established that the head of a Snort mast could be detected by Allied 3cm radars in calm conditions. They also generated a characteristic plume and a haze of exhaust gas which could be spotted by alert lookouts but, in the short, breaking sea characteristic of the English Channel, both eyeball and radar could be defeated.

It was with a heavy heart that Dönitz ordered his few boats against the concentrated might of the Allies. In directing them to take every risk to destroy men and matériel short of the beach, he knew that he was sending many of his loyal crews to their destruction. He had known personal loss, and all too recently. A year before, his younger son, Peter, had died with the crew of *U-954* and then, in May 1944, his elder brother Klaus had been killed. The latter death had been unnecessary as, training to be a naval doctor, Klaus had taken an unofficial trip with E-boats operating from Cherbourg. A fierce exchange of gunfire with two British frigates off the Sussex coast caused the loss of Dönitz' craft and he was not among the survivors.

Early on the morning of 6 June 1944, Group *Landwirt* was stood-to and, at 09.50, ordered to direct its thirty-six operational boats to an area about thirty-five miles north of Cherbourg. Each skipper had been exhorted by BdU: 'Men of the U-boat arm! On you too, now more than any other time, the future of our German people depends. I therefore require of you the most unstinting action, and no consideration for otherwise valid precautionary measures'.

Despite the urgency, progress was slow and, by noon on 10 June, Cork patrols had demolished five non-Snort boats still to the west of Ushant. Bordering the French coast, this particular box was the parish of Mosquitoes, able to look after themselves as well as strafe a surfaced submarine to destruction. Within forty-eight hours of setting out, five more non-Snorts had been damaged by aircraft to the point where they had to return. This rate of attrition was so high that the remaining eighteen non-Snort boats were ordered to retire, to form a line to defend the approaches to the Biscay bases. Even here they were harried by Coastal Command to the extent that they could not recharge their batteries and, on 13 June, all were recalled to base for fitting of such Snort outfits as might become available.

In all, fourteen Snort-equipped boats became involved. Their reports speak of insuperable odds, a matter of survival. Caution superseded boldness and their successes were slight. Harassed beyond endurance by air patrols, several put in to the Channel Islands or returned to Brest with 'mechanical problems'. Some pressed on.

Near Ushant, the *U-953* encountered the four Canadian destroyers of EG12. For sixteen hours the group grappled with the problems posed by shallow water and shoals of herring to nail their elusive and dangerous quarry. Asdic and Hedgehogs appeared equally ineffective while the U-boat's skipper, Karl-Heinz Marbach, fired in all a total of eight torpedoes, mostly T5s. All missed, the latter seduced successfully by the destroyer's towed Foxers (known to the Canadians as CAT gear). Evading his pursuers, Marbach returned to Brest for minor repairs. Claiming three destroyers sunk his 'achievement' was rewarded with a *Ritterkreuz*. He finally reached the invasion area a month late, sinking a single ship, the Leith coaster *Glendinning*.

For their part, the Canadians had not been aware that two submarines had been involved. The *U-984* also returned to Brest for repair. Sailing again on 12 June her skipper, Heinz Sieder, was obliged to enter St Peter Port in order to recharge batteries, so heavy was the air cover. Trying again, he ran into an escort group some forty miles off Start Point and, with a T5, Sieder blew the after end off the British DE *Goodson*. She remained afloat but, like most escorts damaged at this time, was written off rather than repaired.

Traffic in the Spout was dominated by nine convoys daily from either side, all of which were timed to arrive in daylight hours. On 29 June, Sieder finally succeeded in arriving as one of these convoys swept by. He fired a full bow salvo but didn't dally to check the result. From the resulting detonations he claimed two ships sunk and one damaged and, returning safely, he too received his award.

Sieder had in fact been more successful than he had claimed, having hit four vessels, all Liberty ships. Surprisingly, for these vulnerable 12-knotters, it was common American practice to carry up to 600 troops in the tween decks, and three of those hit were carrying a total of nearly 1,500, of whom over 100 died. Salvage facilities were readily available and all four ships were brought safely to anchorages, but three were declared constructive total losses.

Thus the U-boats and their diminutive cousins, the Minor Battle Units, pecked at the periphery of the Allied armada, but to no significant effect. At no stage was the flow seriously incommoded and the build-up proceeded steadily despite the far greater opposition from the weather.

In its appreciation for the week preceding D-Day, the Admiralty's Submarine Tracking Room noted 'the complete inactivity of the U-boats in the Bay of Biscay ports and the extent to which boats are now being transferred from South Norway to the Atlantic'. It remarked also on 'a remarkable exodus of boats from the Baltic', thirty-three in May being twice the average number.

Because of the presence of friendly submarines, Norwegian waters were largely out of bounds to Coastal Command. During May, however, Allied boats had been withdrawn to give 18 and 15 Groups free reign. Where the enemy had been able to undergo training and Snort familiarization without constantly watching for aircraft, the RAF's sudden onslaught came as an unpleasant shock, sinking seven boats and damaging five more within the space of five weeks.

Allied AS forces were thus more than ready to make life difficult for any U-boats seeking to access the English Channel from the North. Of eleven Snort boats that attempted the passage, just four arrived. One casualty, *U-971*, survived separate attacks by two Sunderlands, a Leigh Light Wellington, a Halifax and a B-24 before being dispatched by two destroyers. Unusually, all but one crewman survived. That they were still dangerous was evidenced by the frigate *Mourne*'s destruction by a T5 prior to the culprit, *U-767*, being sunk by the experienced SG14.

The four Snort boats that reached the English Channel accomplished nothing there. Their sole 'success' had been the destruction of a 200-ton fishing boat in the Minches by the *U-247*. Having expended three torpedoes to no effect, the boat surfaced and riddled the fishing craft with her anti-aircraft cannon. Only two men, badly wounded, survived.

The official British assessment of U-boat reaction to Overlord was 'prompt, energetic but remarkably confused'. Following deliberate Allied targeting of enemy communications, BdU had to use less secure means of liaising with Captain, U-boats West. What was said was intercepted. As so little experience had been gained in shallow water Snort Operations, BdU could give only the most basic of operational guidelines. As few boats reported in, news of their progress was sparse. It was thought that 'one or more' U-boats had reached the Spout area by 11 June, but nothing more was known. Until now, British aircraft had not attacked St Peter Port harbour but it was noted that every U-boat that sought sanctuary there now attracted fighter-bomber strikes, indicating efficient intelligence.

An American appreciation of 18 June stated that, in the preceding eleven days, there had been sixty-one sightings of U-boats in the western Channel, resulting in twenty-two contacts, forty-six attacks and six kills.

Early in August 1944 the Allies broke out of the Normandy enclave and, from this point, the future of the U-boats' Biscay facilities was limited. On 27 August BdU admitted defeat in what was termed unofficially the Battle of the Spout and ordered all remaining boats in the area to leave for Norway.

On the following day Rodger Winn, now a Captain but still the guiding force behind the Submarine Tracking Room, assessed the results since D-Day to be as follows: The total number of U-boats involved was forty-four, of which twenty-five (possibly twenty-eight) had been destroyed. Ten merchantmen had been sunk and seven damaged. Four AS escorts and three other warships had been destroyed and six more damaged. Thirteen U-boats had been sunk by surface ships, eleven by aircraft, and one shared. The increased proportion credited to surface forces would now be a trend, reflecting the heightened invisibility of a snorting U-boat.

During July 1944, with minimal opposition from the

Luftwaffe, Allied surface groups operated ever further down the Biscay coast, sufficiently close inshore to deny transiting U-boats their customary escort and to interfere with regular minesweeping.

Once Allied military forces had made their August breakout, the enemy bases at Lorient and St Nazaire looked vulnerable although Brest, on its peninsula, was something of a fortress. Sixteen U-boats were sent south to Bordeaux and la Pallice as German shore staff struggled to complete repairs and refits on those remaining. Four boats, beyond repair in the time available, were scuttled. Retreating, demoralized troops completed the picture by seeking to use the huge bunkers as shelter.

There came a succession of heavy bombing raids, the Bordeaux shelter receiving no less than twenty-six hits from 12,000-pound bombs. Its roof now comprised a twenty-feet layer of reinforced concrete, overlaid with a small gap and an upper 11.5-feet 'burster' layer of concrete. No bombs had penetrated although surrounding installations had been laid waste.

As, by the end of August, relentless Allied surface sweeps had effectively eliminated enemy shipping, U-boats slipped unobtrusively away, twenty-two from Biscay ports and nine from the western Channel, all bound for Norway. To disguise the exodus, other boats were dispatched to English coastal waters to create a nuisance.

Effectively neutralized, the Biscay bases were left isolated and contained by Allied forces. Only Brest was taken, for its value as a port. For four years, the enemy's main effort in the Battle of the Atlantic had stemmed from the French Atlantic coast and now, with that threat at least lifted, shipping could again be routed through the South-West Approaches.

In view of the total failure of the U-boat arm to influence Overlord, it was something of an irony that the first of the revolutionary *Elektroboote* commissioned within days of the landings. She was, however, a Type XXIII coastal boat, the first Type XXI not hoisting her pennant until the end of the month. Neither was she yet fit for deployment as much evaluation was still required to be carried out in parallel with the breakneck production schedule.

The programme called for 144 Type XXIs and eighty-seven Type XXIIIs by the end of 1944 and, although a now-imploding Third Reich was beset by a growing number of woes, it is to the credit of Speer and Merker that sixty-seven and thirty-one respectively did commission.

The predicted high-speed performance of the Type XXI was not met. A hoped-for submerged sprint of 18 knots for 100 minutes proved in reality to be a still formidable 16.5 to 17.3 knots for sixty to eighty minutes. Trials showed expectations at lower speed to be met more closely.

To compensate for the weight and size of the battery installation, diesel engines of compact and lightweight design were adopted. Totally untried, they required to be powerfully turbocharged to achieve their required output. They proved to be unreliable, needing to be run at much reduced power. This was a significant drawback, for the huge battery required three hours' snorting each day to remain charged.

Although German scientists had demonstrated only limited expertise in the field of seaborne radar and countermeasures, the same was not true for torpedoes once the early problems were solved. As we have seen, looping and zigzagging types had proved effective against convoys, as had T5 *Zaunkönig* against escorts. With improvements in electronics, greater sophistication was evident in other types which, fortunately, never entered regular service. Unlike the T5, T11 would have ignored Foxers by virtue of incorporating hydrophones with an acoustic 'dead spot'.

Two advanced concepts, still in use today, were the wire-guided *Lerche* (Lark) and the wake-homing *Ibex*, which used two sets of hydrophones to zigzag along a target's wake in the direction of greatest disturbance.

On 9 July 1944, with the Normandy beachhead still being consolidated, Captain 'Johnny' Walker died suddenly from a stroke, attributed to strain and overwork. He had typified the many officers who had not thrived greatly in the 'spit and polish' of the peacetime service but who discovered their true potential in the challenge of crisis and action. Most men of his experience would long have been drafted ashore to train a new generation. Had Walker done so, it might well have saved him; it would certainly have saved many U-boats. He had remained, however, where he was happiest, directing his sloops from the open bridge of the *Starling*.

The loss of the Biscay bases caused BdU immense problems. At the centre of Atlantic operations, they had always enjoyed priority at the expense of facilities in Norway, which became the new focus. Only one-third of boats retreating from France could be accommodated in Norwegian bases, where many had to lay unprotected, and even those in bunkers had considerably less concrete over their heads. Many boats had thus to work out of Baltic bases, whose location added between 600 and 1,000 miles of passage length to their operational areas.

A new factor now emerged as boats working the North-West Approaches reported considerably reduced Allied activity. It required little intelligence to discover that convoys were now sailing directly to French and south coast English ports via the South-West Approaches. Submerged almost constantly, Snort-equipped Type VIIs needed up to twenty-five days to travel each way and, consequently, could remain only ten days or so in the western English Channel. As there were no longer any U-tankers to support distant operations, larger Type IXs could now rarely be deployed further than Canadian waters.

Very heavy air raids were now directed against the Norwegian bases, where several boats were destroyed. With the Dover Strait effectively blocked, boats required to pass through one of the several gaps between Iceland, the Faeroes, the Shetlands, the Orkneys and northern Scotland. These were all within the parish of 18 Group Coastal Command and their cooperative neighbours, 15 Group.

The latter's responsibilities extended down to the west coast of Ireland where they abutted 19 Group's territory. With the fall-off in business further south, many of 19 Group's experienced assets had also been transferred north.

The shallow waters of the Baltic, where U-boats were increasingly obliged to work-up and exercise, were well suited to mining. After August 1944, in operations that the Royal Air Force whimsically referred to as 'gardening', activity increased, with over 7,000 mines being air-dropped during the year. Losses to neither side could be termed excessive but disruption to the enemy's training was considerable.

Deep minefields were also added on convoy routes around British coasts. They presented no hazard to surface shipping but, so ran the theory, any U-boat in a position to attack an oncoming convoy would need first to go deep to avoid its escort.

With Snorting now customary, aerial success against U-boats continued at a lower tempo, with surface forces returning the best results. Again, it was escorts acting in the direct defence of convoys that were most successful, more so than the free-ranging support groups. Even 'successful' U-boat skippers now rarely sank more than a single ship. Those with a greater score usually finished by paying the supreme penalty.

Late in August 1944, for instance, *U-482* discovered the fast tanker convoy CU.36 in the North Channel and succeeded in destroying the 10,450 GRT American tanker *Jacksonville*. On 1 September she hit the British corvette *Hurst Castle* with a T5. Like their Flower-class antecedents, the Castles were built to mercantile standards and were not large enough to normally survive a torpedo. The *Hurst Castle* sank in six minutes.

Gaining confidence, the *U-482*'s skipper, *Graf* von Matushka, then picked off the 4,500-ton Norwegian tanker *Fjordheim* from the slow convoy ONS.251. Again moving on quickly, he was rewarded by sighting the fast inbound convoy HX.305. Prominent in this was the old whale factory ship *Tafelberg*, of 15,700 tons. Renamed *Empire Heritage*, she was doing duty as a tanker but, due to her unusual layout, quickly capsized on being torpedoed. Her survivors were immediately assisted by the convoy rescue ship *Pinto*, late of MacAndrew's Iberian fruit trade. Hove-to, she was an easy shot for von Matuschka, how-ever, sinking rapidly with 113 crew and rescued seamen.

Surviving this successful trip, the Count returned to the same waters in November. It was to be the new year before he was able to break his duck, sinking the 7,430 GRT Westfal-Larsen tanker *Spinanger* on 15 January. Almost immediately, at the entrance to the Firth of Clyde, he also hit the CVE *Thane*. She survived, but was never repaired.

The *U-482* became, inevitably, the subject of a concentrated hunt. Ironically, 'Johnny' Walker's old ship *Starling*, now led three other sloops and the Squid-equipped frigate *Loch Craggie* in a new support group, SG22. They plastered a suspected contact on 16 January with no evidence of a kill, but the *U-482* was never heard of again.

Casualty rates for these solitary U-boat forays were now running at one in three, but there were still unpleasant surprises, as when *U-486* sank the 11,500-ton Belgian troopship *Leopoldville* outside Cherbourg on 24 December with the loss of over 800, mainly American, troops. Shortly after, the same boat was discovered by the British EG1 but neatly turned the tables with a pair of T5s. One sank the DE *Capel*, the other wrecking her sister ship *Affleck*.

At the outset of October 1944 there were over 400 U-boats in existence. Barely one-third of them, however, could be termed 'operational' and, of these, only one in four, just thirty-six boats, were actually at sea.

Operating close inshore, the boats' Snort heads were given anti-reflection coatings of dubious worth. They also carried detectors which, at last, could reliably respond to Allied 3cm radar emissions. A stalemate developed with skippers rarely attacking for fear of overwhelming retaliation yet causing sufficient nuisance to warrant continuing full attention.

Shallow waters affected a submarine's listening gear and an escort's Asdic alike. Aircraft now rarely sighted a U-boat and even more rarely attacked one. Now well aware of how precisely the Allies D/F-ed their transmissions, U-boat skippers reported rarely, if at all. This, in turn, greatly affected the flow of intelligence to the Admiralty's Submarine Tracking Room, a situation acceptable only because of the low level of mercantile loss. Captain Rodger Winn had, indeed, to remind the First Sea Lord, Admiral of the Fleet Sir Andrew Cunningham, that the danger was far from past and that there was no room for complacency.

From Cunningham's viewpoint, however, with Allied supremacy now firmly assured, the convoy war had assumed trifling proportions. During October 1944, no ships were lost in either Atlantic or European waters. Huge convoys of 150 or more ships were crossing with minimal escort. Six U-boats were lost at sea from various causes but, for the first time in the war, heavy strategic bombing was destroying boats in yards now in-adequately defended by the Luftwaffe.

To reinforce the crumbling Western front, the Germans began to strip Norway of its garrison and resources. A considerable volume of ship movement was thus generated and, to draw attention elsewhere, there was an upturn in U-boat activity toward the end of the year. The enemy claimed the ruse to have been a success and, certainly, over the last two months, eleven merchantmen and two escorts were lost against five U-boats. For Coastal Command it was very frustrating, while ahead loomed the apparently imminent threat of the *Elektroboote*.

During January 1945 advancing Russian forces obliged the U-boat headquarters staff to move to Wilhelmshaven. Still quartered in Berlin, Grand Admiral Dönitz had, at last, to relinquish his direction of the submarine war.

His assurance to his Führer, that considerable numbers of the new boats would be thrown into the fray by December 1944, had been reassessed to just a handful of the hoped-for forty by February 1945, with larger numbers by the April. He had, however, badly underestimated the technical shortcomings of complex designs rushed into production without thorough prototype testing. In parallel, Allied bombing was now having a serious effect on production.

Allied leaders met in Malta and Yalta during January and February. The British pushed to transfer large numbers of flotilla vessels to the Far East for politically-important participation in the closing stages of the war against Japan. Intelligence indicated, however, that nearly ninety Type XXI and over forty Type XXIII were now complete, with fifty and twenty respectively under construction. In the face of this threat, nothing could be sent east.

Among much else the leaders agreed, therefore, to step up the bombing campaign, to be directed at submarine assembly areas, yet incomplete and still much in the open. Where in February the combined Anglo-American effort had amounted to about 230 sorties, delivering about 650 tons of bombs, March saw a massive increase to over 2,800 sorties and 8,350 tons. Yet more 'gardening' operations were undertaken in the eastern Baltic to force U-boats to work-up and to exercise farther west, to where

Coastal Command, increased by a further half-dozen squadrons, held sway.

By February 1945, Germany was beaten, its mighty war machine ceasing to function. The *Elektroboote* programme was just one more that could no longer pretend to be running as planned. Building at Danzig ceased with the approach of the Russians, while the yards at Bremen and Hamburg, besides suffering badly from bombing, were receiving even basic commodities only intermittently. Hull modules were subject to continual delays as the banks of major inland waterways were breached by bombing. At least nine Type XXI tail cone modules were captured by Allied forces far up the Rhine, near Strasbourg.

Only on 18 March did the very first Type XXI, the *U-2511*, leave Kiel for Norway. She was skippered by one of the very few surviving early 'aces', Adalbert Schnee. Deep diving trials caused mechanical damage and it was 30 April before she departed on her first operational cruise. On this ill-starred day, Dönitz was nominated Führer following Hitler's suicide.

On 4 May he ordered U-boat command, now quartered in Flensburg, to instruct all boats to cease hostilities and return to base. Schnee claimed that, en route, he easily manoeuvred to an attack position within the screen of a British cruiser, disengaging from his dummy attack without being suspected.

Four of the small Type XXIII had already made war patrols, two of them on two occasions. First away was *U-2324*, which sailed from Kristiansand on 31 January. She quickly demonstrated the craft's limitation of carrying only two torpedo tubes, with no space for reloads. Encountering a coastal convoy, she missed with both and had to return. The first kill to a Type XXIII was thus to *U-2322*, which sank a 1,310-ton DFDS 'bacon-boat' sailing under British control.

Although tiny, the Type XXIII proved itself able to stay at sea for anything up to thirty-three days. In a total of eight sorties, Type XXIIIs sank six ships for no losses. That, at the end of the U-boat war, was no mean achievement.

During the closing weeks of the war, many operational U-boats, and others from training units, were ordered from the Baltic to Norway, probably to act as a bargaining chip should capitulation be other than non-conditional. The route north through the Belts was infested with mines; swept channels were both narrow and shallow. Compelled to travel some stretches on the surface and without air cover, they were massacred. In a final Happy Time of their own, aircraft from B-24s to Typhoon fighter-bombers ranged the skies in numbers that saw single U-boats attacked by a score or more aircraft. Between 1 April and the enemy surrender some five weeks later twenty-seven submarines were sunk, seven of them Type XXIs. A further eighteen were destroyed in their bases.

Honour demanded that Dönitz order his skippers to scuttle their boats rather than surrender them. This intention, Operation *Regenbogen* (Rainbow), had been already communicated and, despite the Allied requirement for surrender without conditions, many carried it out. In all, 218 boats, including eighty-two Type XXIs and twenty-nine XXIIIs, went to the bottom, mostly in the Baltic.

The forty-three boats at sea were ordered to proceed on the surface, flying a large black flag, to designated ports where their future would be decided.

The last ships known to have been sunk by submarine torpedo were the 1,790-ton Norwegian vessel *Sneland I* and the British *Avondale Park*, of 2,880 tons. Both were sunk by the Type XXIII *U-2336* off the Firth of Forth on 7 May 1945.

On 12 April President Roosevelt died. More than anybody he had engineered victory, providing, through a blend of far-sightedness and skilful politics, the tools with which brave and determined men 'finished the job'.

Chapter Eight

Retribution

The *Regenbogen* directive resulted in half of Germany's U-boat force being scuttled, mostly in deep water. Like the immolation of the High Seas Fleet at Scapa some twenty-six years earlier, the action was intended both as a snub to the victor and as a symbol of 'death before dishonour'. In both cases, however, events suited the British very well.

In 1919, squabbling between the victorious powers regarding the post-war division of the ex-enemy fleet was neatly quashed by that fleet's sudden destruction. Neither Great Britain nor the United States had any use for ex-German warships, but neither had they wished to see modern vessels upsetting the established balance of naval power by mass transfer to lesser fleets.

Stalin's thwarted wish to create a blue-water Soviet fleet had resulted in his unsuccessfully demanding a large share of the Italian fleet surrendered in September 1943. Fobbed off at the time with a handful of over-age Allied warships, he now laid powerful claim to a major portion of the German tonnage.

Except for investigative purposes, the Americans and British again had no wish to acquire ex-enemy warships. Indeed, the British desired the total eradication of the U-boat force. Following their depredations of the First World War, their total prohibition had been sought at the various inter-war disarmament conferences, but without success. History had now repeated itself. By the Royal Navy, the U-boat was loathed, and there was a fierce determination that it should not survive in any form.

Somewhat optimistically, the British had begun planning for the post-war demilitarization of Germany as early as June 1942,

214

with a tri-service military sub-committee reporting to the so-called Ministerial Committee on Reconstruction Problems. By mid-1943 the smaller group was subsumed into a Post-Hostilities Planning Sub-Committee. As the war progressed, the intended control and disarmament of post-war Germany became an Allied concern with the project name of Talisman. Within this highly-detailed plan the size and role of the participating Royal Navy contingent was defined. The Navy's mission statement was unequivocal and encapsulated the feelings of the time. In its 'Outline Plan for the Control, Disarmament and Disbandment of the German Navy', dated August 1944, one reads: 'We this time intend that no vestige of the Germany Navy either in respect of its personnel, its material, its dockyards, its manufacturing, its establishments, its schools, its depots, its barracks, or anything which might assist in keeping alive any form of German naval *esprit de corps* ... or permit the revival of the German Navy, shall remain.' In 1918, the Royal Navy's attitude had been correct but chivalrous, as towards a beaten but honourable foe. Second time around, things had changed. The pronouncement was almost biblical in its intensity and its objectives were to be pursued by the Navy with great diligence.

At the post-war Potsdam conference, the British made concessions regarding the Soviet acquisition of ex-enemy surface ships in return for the desired elimination of the surviving U-boat force. Except for thirty boats, to be divided among the Allies for experimental purposes, the entire force would be destroyed.

This was not completely straightforward. Beyond those units scuttled on receipt of the *Regenbogen* order, 174 had been surrendered. The bulk were in German and Norwegian ports but some had been brought directly to the United Kingdom or the United States. Others were scattered as far distant as the Argentine or Japan.

In an operation called, appropriately, Deadlight, U-boats were gradually concentrated at two British reception points, Loch Ryan and Lisahally near Londonderry. From November 1945 the final act was carried out in deep water north of Malin Head. Adjacent to the North-West Approaches, the scene of so much wanton destruction, the perpetrators were taken out in groups and destroyed unceremoniously by depth charge, gunfire or

215

aircraft attack. There was no interest in their salvage value, only their destruction. The operation, which involved 110 boats, was completed by 14 January 1946.

The whole of the German minesweeping organization was retained, its flotillas working under Royal Navy direction on the immense task of clearance. In parallel, however, the British proceeded with the elimination of the *Kriegsmarine*'s infrastructure.

One protracted and hazardous task was to dispose of the 85,000 tons of naval munitions discovered at scattered locations. These included 8,500 torpedoes, 5,900 warheads and 26,000 mines, many of the latter configured for submarine laying. Most were disposed of at sea, either by direct dumping or in obsolete merchantmen. Some were retained by smaller Allied navies but what remained was used mainly in demolition.

Royal Navy parties toured installations and compiled lists for the military. Of high priority were the massive submarine shelters. Most, however, were adjacent to built-up areas and the required quantity of explosive for their destruction would have caused an unacceptable level of collateral damage. The majority, therefore, remain today, their ugly presence an enduring reminder of the perils of laissez-faire.

Germany, war-ravaged and awash with refugees, had a desperate need for temporary accommodation but, in the face of considerable protest and criticism, the British blew up naval barracks and even naval hospitals. It took a year of hard work to demolish coastal defences, while dockyards were stripped of useful equipment and demilitarized.

Most spectacular was the 'Big Bang' operation on Heligoland. As the island's installations had proved remarkably resistant to months of Royal Air Force bombing practice, they were wired to 6,700 tons of explosive. Staged as a public event, the Navy touched-off its largest-ever explosion on 18 April 1946.

Shipyards were reduced in capacity to prevent their building ships of more than minor tonnage. The Navy even intended to destroy the huge monument at Kiel-Laboe, dedicated to the U-boat dead of the earlier war. The indictment was that 'any Memorial to a branch of the Navy that so flagrantly disobeyed the rules of warfare is distasteful'. Due to the anticipated reaction of the local population, however, the order was rescinded, the parties contenting themselves with the removal of a swastika symbol, a later addition that adorned the top.

The process of methodical and selective destruction occupied two years and, for the Royal Navy, was very much a process of catharsis.

In contrast, the Navy's senior figures were not in favour of trying Dönitz and Raeder as war criminals, considering that the *Kriegsmarine* had fought 'a pretty clean war'. They understood well that it was the task of armed forces to take the fight to the enemy, and they recognized that the submarine forces of both Great Britain and the United States had operated, themselves, on a largely unrestricted basis. Politically, however, it was unacceptable that the deaths of so many seamen, the loss of so many ships, could go unremarked. Dönitz, also, had briefly acted as Germany's last Führer but, until the resignation of Raeder, he had only carried out his instructions. After 30 January 1943, however, Dönitz was fully responsible for all activities of the *Kriegsmarine*. Both men were therefore arraigned before the Allied Military Tribunal at Nuremberg, in company with the remaining top figures of the late administration.

Charged with the prosecution of both, the British encountered difficulty in mounting a convincing case, particularly against Dönitz. Each was eventually charged with conspiring to commit crimes against peace and humanity, of planning and initiating wars of aggression in violation of international treaties, and authorization, direction and participation in war crimes. In Dönitz' case, the last-named was 'particularly the crimes against persons and property on the high seas'.

On the first count, Dönitz was not guilty as, being still a comparatively junior captain, he did not formulate general policy. With respect to count two, a military court recognized that it was the duty of a responsible officer to conduct an aggressive war as instructed by his superiors. Only when such orders ran counter to internationally-accepted standards of civilized behaviour could an officer refuse to carry them out and, in Hitler's Germany, that would have required a brave man indeed. It proved difficult to argue convincingly that Dönitz accepted orders that *were* criminal but he was judged guilty of conducting the U-boat war contrary to the Submarine Protocol of 1936.

Contravention of the Protocol was the basis of the third count on which Dönitz was charged. The main plank of the prosecutor's argument was the so-called 'Laconia Order' of September 1942. This, it will be recalled, arose from the Allied bombing of Axis submarines engaged in an advertized mercy operation. It was alleged that, implicit in the order not to assist the survivors, was the requirement to kill them. Superficial reading suggests that such is not the case but at least the commanding officer of one training flotilla on the Baltic thought that it was, and so implied to skippers under instruction. The commander, Karl-Heinz Möhle, agreed to testify against Dönitz. Another junior officer, Peter Heisig, also agreed to appear as a prosecution witness. He had been involved in the serious case of the *Peleus*, a Greek vessel whose helpless survivors were machine-gunned by order of the skipper of *U-852* in March 1944.

The *Peleus* incident was an isolated case and, although skippers followed Dönitz' injunction to 'be harsh', they acted in general within the law. It was not difficult for the defence to demonstrate that both witnesses were acting from self-interest. Dönitz' case was greatly assisted by affidavits from large numbers of his late skippers that they did *not* understand the Laconia Order to mean that survivors should be shot, and neither did they do so. Of powerful assistance to Dönitz was a written contribution from American Fleet Admiral Nimitz, who pointed out that the US Navy had conducted a similar submarine war, in which survivors were rarely assisted. Many senior Americans disagreed with Dönitz being charged at all, although this was illogical inasmuch as instructions had been issued to shoot specific groups of survivors including Allied aircrew in the Bay of Biscay, ships' crews in American waters and Allied special forces.

Despite a broad agreement that all these activities conformed to accepted standards of war, where people inevitably became casualties in the destruction of property, and where mistakes and violations occurred in contravention of orders, both the British and Soviet authorities were determined that both Dönitz and Raeder should pay for the destruction for which they were held responsible. Dönitz was handed down a ten-year sentence, which he served in full. Raeder, as his earlier senior, was involved in pre-war policy making, and received a life sentence. Because of ill health and advanced age, he served only nine years.

Following the success of *guerre de course* during the First World War, the Germans made a great effort to repeat it in the Second. Overtaken by events, they started badly, with only fifty-seven U-boats in commission. A further 1,113 were added, however, of which about 200 were completed too late to see action. In spite of these numbers, the maximum strength at any one time was about 460, of which only one half were operational.

In all, U-boats undertook about 3,200 war patrols, in the course of which they sank about 2,600 of the 2,830 Allied and neutral merchantmen destroyed by all Axis submarines, an aggregate of about 14 million GRT. Of these, about 2,450 ships of 12.8 million GRT were sunk in the Atlantic. To this appalling total should be added 175 Allied warships and naval auxiliaries.

Dönitz' own yardstick for U-boat efficiency was his 'Ship Sinking Rate', expressed as gross registered tons (GRT) destroyed per U-boat day at sea. To put matters in perspective, this figure needed to be compared with the rate of U-boat loss (expressed as the percentage of U-boats lost at sea over the same period). From these were deduced the 'Exchange Rate', of ships sunk per U-boat lost. The results may be tabulated as an index of U-boat effectiveness (see page 220).

Column (1) shows well the heady days up to mid-1941. During this period the interlocking convoy system was still being evolved, and far too many 'independents' were still being sailed. There were insufficient escorts and few aircraft, all with crews of little experience. While there were few U-boats, all were skippered by men with years of pre-war training. Their relatively high loss rate (2) reflects the small number actually at sea rather than the efficiency of the defence.

The latter half of 1941 shows a sharply reduced success rate as the defences tightened up and the original band of 'ace' skippers was whittled down. (It should be remembered that the twenty top-scoring skippers accounted between them for about one quarter of all losses to submarines.)

That the situation was temporarily reversed from January 1942 was due entirely to the unnecessary slaughter of the *Paukenschlag* campaign, when success was cheap and retribution unlikely. The

	Ship Sinking Rate (1)	U-boat Loss Rate (2)	Exchange Rate (3)
Sep–Dec 1939	276	16	10
Jan–Dec 1940	550	13	23
Jan–Jun 1941	484	11	24
Jul–Dec 1941	119	8	8
Jan–Jun 1942	284	4	40
Jul–Dec 1942	170	9	11
Jan–Jun 1943	78	15	3
Jul–Dec 1943	39	25	0.9
Jan–Jun 1944	27	24	0.6
Jul–Dec 1944	34	19	1
Jan–Apr 1945	41	33	0.7

U-boat loss rate, (2), was low over the whole North Atlantic theatre, reflecting the rapidly rising number of boats at sea.

From the beginning of 1943, once the Americans had taken the necessary remedial action in organizing an efficient integrated convoy system, the enemy's success rate resumed the downward trend first evident in the latter half of 1941. The all-important Ship Sinking Rate (1) slumped alarmingly as an increasing percentage of inexperienced U-boat skippers had to tackle overwhelming defences. Although many more boats were at sea, the percentage sunk (2) began to soar as escorts and aircraft took their toll, while the exchange rate (3) hit new lows.

Dönitz developed the U-boat arm and its methods to defeat the convoy system, but events showed that the convoy system evolved to be the nemesis of the U-boat.

For too long, it proved difficult to convince many that, in an ocean context, a convoy was nearly as difficult to locate as a single ship. Surprisingly, it then proved equally difficult to explain that a large convoy was negligibly more conspicuous than a small one. It was explained earlier how doubling the number of ships in a convoy would double its area but increase its periphery by a smaller factor, and peripheral length determined the density and effectiveness of its escort.

The Admiralty rule-of-thumb for the required number of escorts was a minimum of $(3+N/10)$, where N was the number of ships being convoyed. A twenty-ship convoy thus needed $(3+20/10)$, or five, escorts. It followed that three twenty-ship convoys would require fifteen escorts yet, if combined would need only $(3+60/10)$, or nine, escorts. Larger convoys would clearly effect economies in escort numbers while reducing the number of convoys to be protected at any one time.

In any one attack, a U-boat could launch only a single spread of torpedoes and was unable to damage a large convoy any more than a small one, while the chance of any one particular ship being hit was decreased. To exploit this, it was important that an attacking submarine be prevented from doing an 'end-around' and making a further attack. Aggressive defence was an answer but so, too, was the speed of the convoy itself. Experience showed that, all else being equal, a 9-knot convoy suffered only half the loss rate of a 7-knot convoy.

Once air cover became generally available, it was also soon apparent that aircraft accompaniment for just eight hours in twenty-four reduced losses by a further two-thirds.

Atlantic, i.e. ocean, convoys were thus vulnerable to submarine attack only as long as their defence was deficient. The fact that the correct type of defence was initially unavailable was due to a lack of naval foresight as much as political parsimony.

By the final year of the war a U-boat attack on a defended convoy verged on suicide. A skipper setting out on a war patrol had a near 40 per cent chance of being destroyed but only a one in eight chance of receiving damage sufficient to justify the sortie being aborted. Worse, he had only a one in ten chance of sinking even a single ship.

Dönitz, his objectives now far beyond reach, still had to keep his crews battle-trained pending the entry into service of the new super-boats. The result was that one in three U-boats was sunk on its very first patrol. There were rarely any survivors. In fact, of the 648 boats listed as destroyed on operational patrols, 429 yielded no survivors. Of about 40,000 men in the German submarine service, 28,000 died in action. This was only a little short of the 30,000 British seamen whom they killed.

Long after their cause became totally hopeless, German submariners retained their dedication and morale, for which much credit has to go to Admiral Dönitz himself. The pity was that such qualities were devoted to so vile a regime.

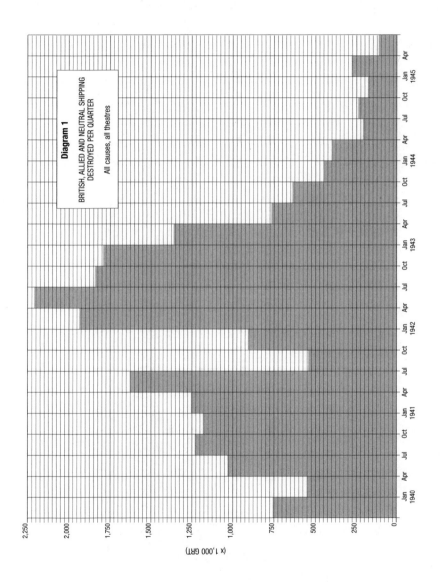

Diagram 1

BRITISH, ALLIED AND NEUTRAL SHIPPING
DESTROYED PER QUARTER

All causes, all theatres

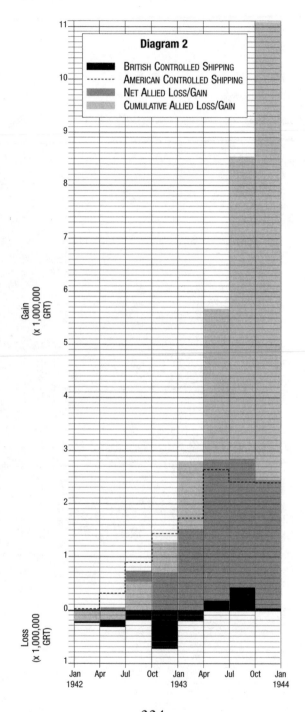

Diagram 2

BRITISH CONTROLLED SHIPPING
AMERICAN CONTROLLED SHIPPING
NET ALLIED LOSS/GAIN
CUMULATIVE ALLIED LOSS/GAIN

Gain
(x 1,000,000 GRT)

Loss
(x 1,000,000 GRT)

Jan Apr Jul Oct Jan Apr Jul Oct Jan
1942 1943 1944

224

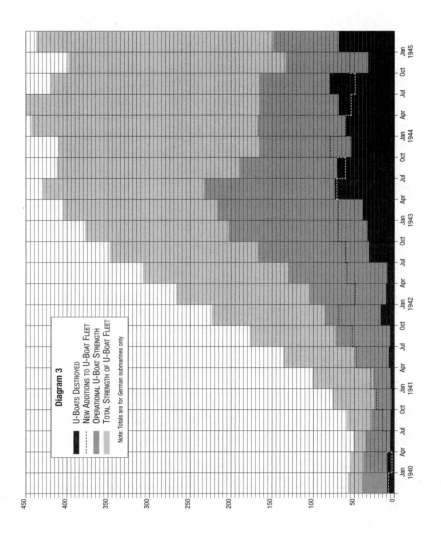

Diagram 3

U-Boats Destroyed
New Additions to U-Boat Fleet
Operational U-Boat Strength
Total Strength of U-Boat Fleet

Note: Totals are for German submarines only

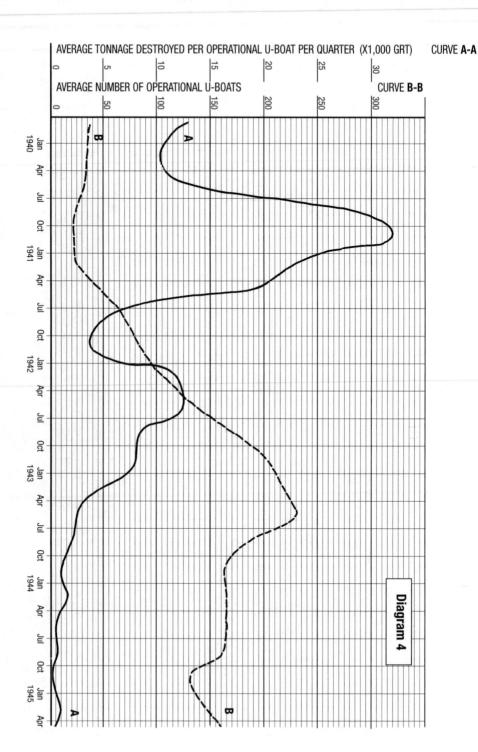

AVERAGE TONNAGE DESTROYED PER OPERATIONAL U-BOAT PER QUARTER (X1,000 GRT)   CURVE **A-A**

AVERAGE NUMBER OF OPERATIONAL U-BOATS   CURVE **B-B**

Diagram 4

Index

228